INSTITUTIONAL BYPASSES

Institutional bypass is a reform strategy that creates alternative institutional regimes to give citizens a choice of service provider and create a form of competition between the dominant institution and the institutional bypass. Although novel in the academic literature, the concept captures practices already being used in developing countries. In this illuminating book, Mariana Mota Prado and Michael J. Trebilcock explore the strengths and limits of this strategy with detailed case studies, showing how citizen preferences provide a benchmark against which future reform initiatives can be evaluated, and in this way change the dynamics of the reform process. While not a "silver bullet" to the challenge of institutional reform, institutional bypasses add to the portfolio of strategies to promote development. This work should be read by development researchers, scholars, policy makers, and anyone else seeking options on how to promote change and implement reforms in developing countries around the world.

Mariana Mota Prado has published extensively on law and development, including two co-authored books with Michael J. Trebilcock: *What Makes Poor Countries Poor? Institutional Determinants of Development* (2011) and *Advanced Introduction to Law and Development* (2014). She has taught at the Centre for Transnational Legal Studies in London, the Getulio Vargas Foundation (FGV) Law School in Brazil, ITAM Law School in Mexico, Los Andes Law School in Colombia, and University of Puerto Rico School of Law.

Michael J. Trebilcock has published on many subjects related to institutional reforms and development and has won multiple awards for his work, including the Owen Prize for *The Common Law of Restraint of Trade*. He has also authored *The Limits of Freedom of Contract* and *Dealing with Losers: The Political Economy of Policy Transitions* (winner of the Donner Prize, 2014) and co-authored *Rule of Law Reform and Development: Charting the Fragile Path of Progress* (2008).

Institutional Bypasses

A STRATEGY TO PROMOTE REFORMS
FOR DEVELOPMENT

MARIANA MOTA PRADO

University of Toronto Faculty of Law

MICHAEL J. TREBILCOCK

University of Toronto Faculty of Law

CAMBRIDGE
UNIVERSITY PRESS

University Printing House, Cambridge CB2 8BS, United Kingdom

One Liberty Plaza, 20th Floor, New York, NY 10006, USA

477 Williamstown Road, Port Melbourne, VIC 3207, Australia

314–321, 3rd Floor, Plot 3, Splendor Forum, Jasola District Centre, New Delhi – 110025, India

79 Anson Road, #06-04/06, Singapore 079906

Cambridge University Press is part of the University of Cambridge.

It furthers the University's mission by disseminating knowledge in the pursuit of education, learning, and research at the highest international levels of excellence.

www.cambridge.org
Information on this title: www.cambridge.org/9781108473811
DOI: 10.1017/9781108563116

First published 2019

Printed and bound in Great Britain by Clays Ltd, Elcograph S.p.A.

A catalogue record for this publication is available from the British Library.

ISBN 978-1-108-47381-1 Hardback
ISBN 978-1-108-46258-7 Paperback

Contents

Figures

Figures

Preface

Over the past three decades, a substantial consensus has emerged among development scholars and development agencies that the quality of a country's institutions – political, bureaucratic, and legal – is an important determinant, perhaps the most important determinant, of its development trajectory. However, over the same period, a much less settled consensus has emerged as to how to reform dysfunctional institutions, reflected in the recognition that most reform efforts – often promoted by external agencies – have yielded mixed to weak results. This has in turn led to a growing sense of modesty, even humility, about the robustness of our knowledge base as to what reform strategies are likely to be effective in various contexts. There is now a growing recognition that the particularities of a country's history, politics, culture, economic, and social structure often create a form of path dependence that renders institutional reform a speculative and indeed daunting enterprise.

Against this backdrop, we explore an institutional reform strategy that may be particularly useful for developing countries: the institutional bypass. An institutional bypass seeks to create alternative institutional regimes that provide citizens with a choice of service provider, potentially creating a form of competition between the dominant institution and the institutional bypass. Revealed citizen preferences then provide a benchmark against which future reform initiatives can be evaluated. The bypass may change the political dynamics of the reform process by attracting a constituency that has come to appreciate from lived experience that the previous status quo is not inevitable, eternal, or preordained.

We discuss the strengths and limits of a bypass strategy through a series of case studies. Their success or failure should be judged on the ground and analyzed in the context in which they are operating and not on whether they conform to some predetermined blueprint or best-practice manual. We do not claim that the concept of an institutional bypass is a new "silver bullet" to the challenge of institutional reform, but rather an enlargement of the portfolio of reform strategies for development.

Acknowledgments

This book has been in the making for much longer than it should. A preliminary version of the concept of institutional bypass was made available on Social Science and Research Network (SSRN) in 2011, under the title "Institutional Bypass: An Alternative for Development Reform," and it has been referred to in a previous co-authored book, *Advanced Introduction to Law and Development* (2014).[1] Since then, we have benefited from numerous conversations and collaborations that have not only helped us refine the concept but also have made this book possible.

We are very grateful to our collaborators and previous co-authors, with whom we have explored a number of the case studies discussed here. Ana Carolina Chasin was the co-author of an earlier study of the Poupatempo, entitled "How Innovative Was the Poupatempo Experience in Brazil? Institutional Bypass as a New Form of Institutional Change" (2011) 5:1 *Brazilian Political Science Review* 11. Graham Denyer Willis was the co-author of a previous analysis of the police reform in Brazil (UPP), entitled "Process and Pattern in Institutional Reforms: A Case Study of the Police Pacifying Units (UPPs) in Brazil" (2014) 64 *World Development* 232. The analysis of the labour union reforms builds on joint work with Ana Virginia Gomes, which is still in progress, and is currently entitled "Institutional Bypasses in Brazil's New Unionism Movement: Central Unions and Workers' Committees." The analysis of low-cost schools in India was co-authored with Lindsey Carson and Joanna Vieira Noronha, and published as "Held Back: Explaining the Sluggish Pace of Improvement to Basic Education in Developing Democracies: The Cases of India and Brazil" (2015) 6:2 *Journal of Poverty Alleviation and Development* 1. The emergency care units (UPAs) became a case study thanks to the suggestion of Viviane

[1]   Cheltenham, UK: Edward Elgar.

Albuquerque, who originally articulated this as an example of institutional bypass in a response paper for a course in which one of us was an instructor. Viviane not only authorized us to use the example but has also joined our team of talented research assistants to help us develop the analysis. The conclusion incorporates some of the ideas articulated in joint work with Kevin Davis, published as "Law, Regulation, and Development," in Bruce Currie-Alder et al., eds., *International Development: Ideas, Experience, and Prospects* (2014). Some of the reflections presented here have been articulated in a book chapter entitled "Institutional Bypasses in Brazil: Overcoming Ex-Ante Resistance to Institutional Reforms," in Pedro Rubim Fortes et al., eds., *Law and Policy in Latin America: Transforming Courts, Institutions, and Rights* (2017).

This book would not have been possible without our team of dedicated research assistants, who diligently helped us conduct all the research and develop the analysis in the book. The team, in chronological order, was comprised of Farah Sidi and Jisu Min, then law students (JD) at our faculty; Patricia Galvão Ferreira, then a doctoral student pursuing a joint PhD/SJD in law and global affairs at the University of Toronto; Kristen Pue, a PhD candidate in the Political Sciences department at the University of Toronto; and Sindura Dar, Viviane Albuquerque, Stephane Serafin, and Kanksha Mahadevia Ghimire, all master students (LLM) in our faculty.

We are also very grateful for the numerous opportunities to discuss this work with colleagues and scholars in a number of conferences and workshops. Miguel de Figueiredo and the late Betty Ho provided insightful comments during a presentation of the concept at Tsinghua University in Beijing in May 2009. Susan Rose-Ackerman, Katharina Pistor, Bruce Ackerman, Henry Hansmann, and other participants in the Comparative Law and Economics Forum at Yale Law School provided insightful feedback to a very early draft in June 2010. An earlier version of this work also benefited immensely from comments and suggestions from Anupam Chander, Lawrence Friedman, Gillian Hadfield, Mario Schapiro, and other participants in the Harvard–Stanford Junior Faculty Workshop in October 2010. Ben Ross Schneider and Kathleen Thelen were very generous with their time in reading and discussing very early drafts of this project during a research visit by one of the authors at the MIT Political Science Department in 2012–13. We are also grateful for the suggestions of Aldo Mussachio, who served as commentator to the paper in a workshop at the David Rockefeller Center for Latin American Studies at Harvard University in March 2013. We are especially grateful to our colleagues at the University of Toronto Faculty of Law for comments provided in draft chapters and for a group discussion of an earlier version of this manuscript in a faculty workshop in April 2016. We also benefited immensely from the conceptual discussions for a parallel project on international institutional bypasses, which held workshops in São Paulo in August 2016 and in Ottawa in May 2017 and has now been partly published at the online version of the American Journal of Comparative Law (AJIL

Unbound). Special thanks to Athanasios (Akis) Psygkas, whose suggestions vastly improved the last version of the manuscript.

We are also deeply grateful to the attendees of a book workshop held in Toronto in March 2016, who agreed to spend an entire day discussing institutional bypasses: Susan Rose-Ackerman, Thana Campos, Kevin Davis, Marc Gallanter, John Greiss, Ron Levy, Rohinton Medhora, Mariana Pargendler, Wilson Prichard, Kerry Rittich, David Schneiderman, Frank Upham, and Joseph Wong. The workshop was co-sponsored by the Faculty of Law through the Scotia Bank fund and the Munk School of Global Affairs, and was enormously helpful in guiding us through the necessary revisions.

Last but not least, we are also grateful to many classes of students in our Law, Institutions and Development course at the University of Toronto, at the Center for Transnational Legal Studies in London, at the Getulio Vargas Foundation Law School in Rio de Janeiro, and at Los Andes Law School in Bogotá for stimulating discussions over the past few years of many of the issues addressed in this book.

In keeping with the social sciences tradition of spending "much of our time explaining events that have not finished happening,"[2] we should alert the reader that our case studies were last updated in the fall of 2017. All remaining errors are entirely ours.

---

[2] Barbara Gueddes, "Challenging the Conventional Wisdom" (1994) 5:4 *J Democracy* 104 at 117.

1

Why Do We Need Institutional Bypasses?

In 1997, the government of the state of São Paulo, Brazil, implemented what became one of the most successful bureaucratic reforms in the country. The *Poupatempo* ("Time Saver"), an initiative that has often received international praise, created a one-stop shop for Brazilian citizens who need documents and other governmental services. Before *Poupatempo* was created, citizens had to migrate through multiple offices scattered throughout the city, often encountering long waiting lines and a severe lack of information about requirements to obtain a wide range of services, such as identity cards, drivers' licenses, and criminal records. *Poupatempo* changed this by placing offices of the federal, state, and, in some cases, local administration in one location that was easily accessible to the general public (normally in the vicinity of subway and bus stations). This not only reduced the citizen's burden of commuting from one place to the next but also improved the speed and efficiency with which these services are provided by facilitating communication between the various federal, state, and local offices involved.

Poupatempo had a fast and impressive uptake. What started as a pilot project in 1997, with one unit in the capital of São Paulo, became the prevailing mode of delivery of governmental services to citizens in the state of São Paulo. There were a total of eighty-five units in the state by 2017, when *Poupatempo* was providing services to an average of 190,485 people a day.[1] The overall impact of the project was also significant: the total number of people who benefited from services provided by *Poupatempo* from 1997 to 2017 was approximately 530 million.[2] The project has been replicated in most Brazilian states, and it has also been exported to other countries, although its continuous expansion has raised questions about the diminishing returns of new units and raised challenges regarding its sustainability on its present scale.

---

[1] Portal Poupatempo, "Histórico de Atendimentos desde 1997: Dados Estatísticos," online: www .poupatempo.sp.gov.br

[2] Ibid.

Poupatempo could be interpreted and analyzed simply as a case of public management and public administration reform. Indeed, one-stop shops for bureaucratic services have enjoyed a significant boom in the last decade around the world, and these projects could serve as interesting case studies of successful attempts to promote bureaucratic modernization by tailoring private-sector management techniques to the public sector, a strategy known as the New Public Management. The idea was largely influenced by the business strategies of shopping centres and supermarkets and contrasts with previous attempts at reforms in Brazil, which had focused on traditional public-sector management principles, such as hierarchical structures, anonymity of public servants, and input- and output-centred program management. By contrast, the *Poupatempo* project centred on the customer, de-emphasized hierarchy, and focused on outcomes. This shift in the focus and approach of bureaucratic reforms could serve as a potential explanation for *Poupatempo*'s success, but it is also possible that the positive results were associated with the recruitment of motivated civil servants who were granted a great deal of autonomy to improve users' experience.[3]

Regardless of the most compelling explanation for its success, we believe that *Poupatempo* can also offer broader insights about institutional reforms, which are relevant, but not confined, to the bureaucratic sphere. Specifically, *Poupatempo* may provide an effective strategy to overcome obstacles to institutional reforms and institutional change. Indeed, we argue that this project characterizes a type of reform that we call an "institutional bypass." Like coronary bypass surgery, in which transplanted blood vessels are needed to create a new circulatory pathway around clogged or blocked arteries, an institutional bypass creates new pathways around clogged or blocked institutions. Following this strategy, *Poupatempo* did not try to modify or reform the existing offices of the state bureaucracy. Instead, it created a parallel institution performing the same services and functions. Citizens were then offered an option: they could seek services in the pre-existing bureaucracy or in the offices of *Poupatempo*. The latter institution was vastly preferred because it offered numerous benefits over the pre-existing bureaucracy, such as shorter waiting times, convenient locations, and an efficient system of disseminating information about requirements, processing times, and fees. With increased demand for its services, the project gathered enough public support to allow for a significant expansion over a short period.

Poupatempo amounts to just one particular illustration of the many examples of institutional bypasses that one can find around the world, especially in developing countries. The concept of an institutional bypass is useful to describe a structural

---

[3] For a description of New Public Management, as well as Judith Tendler's conception of civil servants as communitarians, presented in her widely cited book, *Good Government in the Tropics* (Baltimore: Johns Hopkins University Press, 1997), see Michael J. Trebilcock & Mariana Mota Prado, *Advanced Introduction to Law and Development* (Cheltenham, UK: Edward Elgar, 2014).

commonality across reforms in a multitude of sectors. Bureaucratic reforms, police reforms, and education reforms are often perceived and treated as separate silos, where specialists tend to talk to each other but rarely see any value in reaching out to those working in other areas. The concept of an institutional bypass allows us to explore common elements of reforms in these different sectors, potentially creating a constructive dialogue among disciplines and areas of expertise that rarely interact with each other.

The purpose of this book is to analyze the concept of an institutional bypass, mapping its main characteristics, identifying its different configurations, and discussing its potential policy implications. From an academic perspective, the concept of a bypass may offer a descriptive tool to compare and contrast institutional reforms in different sectors. From a policy perspective, if used with full awareness of its limitations and shortcomings, an institutional bypass may prove to be a useful strategy for policymakers around the world.

1.1. INSTITUTIONS MATTER BUT ARE DIFFICULT TO REFORM

Over the past two decades or so, a consensus has emerged among development scholars and policy makers that the quality of a country's institutions (political, bureaucratic, and legal) is an important, and perhaps the major, determinant of its development trajectory.[4] Indeed, common understandings of "failed states" focus on extreme forms of institutional dysfunction.[5] While some scholars argue that, as a matter of historical record, economic growth has often preceded the emergence of strong institutions,[6] it seems likely that causation runs in both directions in a virtuous feedback loop.[7] Other scholars argue that while the quality of a country's institutions may be a proximate determinant of its development trajectory, more distal factors, including its history, geography, political economy, or culture, are important determinants of the nature and quality of a country's institutions; although it is likely again that, with respect to the latter two factors, causation runs in both directions.[8] While they may not be the sole variable in determining development

---

[4] Trebilcock & Prado, *supra* note 3 at ch. 3.
[5] Paul Collier, *The Bottom Billion: Why the Poorest Countries Are Failing and What Can Be Done about It* (New York: Oxford University Press, 2008).
[6] Edward Glaeser, Rafael La Porta, Florencio de Silane, & Andrei Shleifer , "Do Institutions Cause Growth?" (2004) 9:3 *J Econ Growth* 271; Dani Rodrik, "Institutions for High-Quality Growth: What They Are and How to Acquire Them" (2000) 35:3 *Stud in Comp Int'l Dev* 3.
[7] See Daniel Kaufmann, "Governance Redux: The Empirical Challenge" in Xavier Sala-i-Martin, ed., *The Global Competitiveness Report 2003–2004* (New York: Oxford University Press, 2004).
[8] Amir Licht, Chana Goldschmidt, & Shalom Schwartz, "Culture Rules: The Foundations of the Rule of Law and Other Norms of Governance" (2007) 35:4 *J Comp Econ* at 659; Daron Acemoglu & James Robinson, *Why Nations Fail: The Origins of Power, Prosperity, and Poverty* (New York: Crown Publishing, 2012); Daron Acemoglu, Simon Johnson, & James Robinson, "The Colonial Origins of Comparative Development: An Empirical Investigation" (2001) 91:5 *Am Econ Rev* 1369–1401; Daron Acemoglu, Simon Johnson, & James Robinson, "An African Success Story: Botswana" in

outcomes, there is strong evidence to support the idea that institutions do influence a country's development trajectory.[9] Even if one is skeptical of causal connections between institutional arrangements and development outcomes, one may embrace the idea that institutions matter for development because they are an end in and of themselves, as many proponents of the rule of law and democracy would argue.[10] Subject to these caveats, our starting assumption is that "institutions matter" – or "governance matters" – for development.

While adopting this starting assumption, we acknowledge that over the past two decades the record of mostly external donor-promoted institutional reforms in developing countries has been mixed to weak. Despite initial euphoria about the importance of institutions for development and the investment of billions of dollars in institutional reforms, cases of successful institutional change have been more the exception than the rule. Whether one focuses on attempts to promote democracy, a more robust commitment to the rule of law, or a more competent and less corrupt public administration, the mixed record of successes and failures yields a sober assessment of the challenges of institutional reform.[11] Indeed, state capability appears to have declined in many developing countries in recent years.[12]

Part of the challenge in reforming dysfunctional institutions is the lack of a "one-size fits all" formula. While blueprints for institutional design have been a common practice in the development field, a consensus is now emerging among development scholars (and to a lesser extent official development agencies) that contextual factors are of overriding importance in defining both the appropriate ends of development and feasible strategies for attaining them. In particular, it has come to be widely recognized that the specificities of a given country's history, culture, geography, political evolution, economic structure, ethnic, religious, and demographic

Dani Rodrik, ed., *In Search of Prosperity: Analytic Narratives on Economic Growth* (Princeton, NJ: Princeton University Press, 2003); John Gallop, Jeffrey Sachs, & Andrew Mellinger, "Geography and Development" (1999) 22:2 *Int'l Regional Sci Rev* 179; Daron Acemoglu, James Robinson, & Simon Johnson, "Reversal of Fortune: Geography and Institutions in the Making of Modern Income Distribution" (2002) 117:4 *QJ Econ* 1231–1294; Alberto Alesina & Paolo Giuliano, "Culture and Institutions" (2015) 53 *J Econ Lit* 898.

9 Dani Rodrik, Arvind Subramanian, & Francesco Trebbi, "Institutions Rule: The Primacy of Institutions Over Geography and Integration in Economic Development" (2004) 9:2 *J Econ Growth* 131–165; Edinaldo Tebaldi & Ramesh Mohan, "Institutions and Poverty" (2010) 46:6 *J Dev Stud* 1047–1066; Janet Aron, "Growth and Institutions: A Review of the Evidence" (2000) 15:1 *World Bank Research Observer* 99; World Bank, *World Development Report 2017: Governance and the Law* (Washington, DC: World Bank Group, 2017).

10 Indeed, this point is at the core of Sen's argument to conceptualize development as freedom rather than economic growth; see Amartya Sen, *Development as Freedom* (New York: Anchor Books, 2000).

11 Michael J. Trebilcock & Ronald Daniels, *Rule of Law Reform and Development: Charting the Fragile Path of Progress* (Cheltenham, UK: Edward Elgar, 2008); Matt Andrews, *The Limits of Institutional Reform in Development* (New York: Cambridge University Press, 2013).

12 See Matt Andrews, Lant Pritchett, & Michael Woolcock, *Building State Capability: Evidence, Analysis, Action* (Oxford, UK: Oxford University Press, 2017); World Development Report 2017, *supra* note 9 at ch. 1.

makeup, as well as a host of other country-specific features, will, to a large degree, shape what is both desirable and feasible as a set of development strategies for that particular country.[13]

An overarching theme running through much of this recent scholarship is that path dependence is a major constraint, both on the desirable ends of development and the feasible means of achieving them.[14] This concept helps to explain how institutions (or networks of institutions) take shape through self-reinforcing mechanisms and why – as a consequence – they are difficult to change. The key insight associated with path dependence is that, under certain conditions, economic and other activities may be subject to increasing returns, whereby the benefits of engaging in them increase rather than decrease over time. As more and more people invest in a given way of doing things, these investments – of time, money, skills, and expectations – cumulate and, as a consequence, the relative cost of exploring alternatives steadily rises. A simple model of path dependence would therefore emphasize three features of an arrangement: (1) an initial set of choices or random events that determine the starting position, (2) the subsequent reinforcement of those choices or events through "feedback effects," and (3) the degree to which switching costs may preclude good alternatives from being explored in the long run.

Self-reinforcement mechanisms increase switching costs, locking in certain legal, political, and institutional arrangements. In addition, mutually reinforcing mechanisms suggest that institutional interdependencies that are the historical legacy of myriad past events may undermine the success of nodal institutional reforms, implying that we cannot easily modify any of these institutions in isolation. However, path dependence is not entirely deterministic, in that it recognizes the notion of "critical junctures" – interaction effects between distinct causal sequences that conjoin at particular points in time – that place institutional arrangements on particular paths or trajectories. The literature recognizes that critical junctures may be either

---

[13] See e.g. Dani Rodrik, *One Economics, Many Recipes: Globalization, Institutions, and Economic Growth* (Princeton, NJ: Princeton University Press, 2007); Lindsey Carson & Ronald J. Daniels, "The Persistent Dilemmas of Development: The Next Fifty Years" (2010) 60:2 *UTLJ Law* 491; Andrews, *supra* note 11; Thomas Carothers & Diane de Gramont, *Development Aid Confronts Politics: The Almost Revolution* (Washington, DC: Carnegie Endowment for International Peace, 2013); William Easterly, *The Tyranny of Experts: Economists, Dictators, and the Forgotten Rights of the Poor* (New York: Basic Books, 2013); Ben Ramalingam, *Aid on the Edge of Chaos: Rethinking International Cooperation in a Complex World* (Oxford, UK: Oxford University Press, 2013); Brian Levy, *Working with the Grain: Integrating Governance and Growth in Development Strategies* (New York: Oxford University Press, 2014); Andrews, Pritchett, & Woolcock, *supra* note 12; World Development Report 2017, *supra* note 9.

[14] See Douglass North, *Institutions, Institutional Change, and Economic Performance* (Cambridge, UK: Cambridge University Press, 1990); Douglass North, *Understanding the Process of Economic Change* (Princeton, NJ: Princeton University Press, 2005); Paul Pierson, "Increasing Returns, Path Dependence and the Study of Politics" (2000) 94:2 *Am Political Sci Rev* 251; Mariana Mota Prado & Michael J. Trebilcock, "Path Dependence, Development, and the Dynamics of Institutional Reform" (2009) 59:3 *UTLJ* 341.

cathartic events in a country's history or minor perturbations that precipitate cumulative effects that place a country on a new or modified trajectory. Unfortunately, "critical junctures" are difficult to define prospectively, or even to identify with high levels of confidence while they are happening, without the benefit of hindsight in terms of the feedback effects that they trigger.

In contrast to this pessimistic view of the stability of institutions – even dysfunctional institutions – and their impermeability to change, a strand of literature emphasizes the incremental nature of policy reform and institutional change. In a book entitled *Explaining Institutional Change: Ambiguity, Agency and Power*,[15] James Mahoney and Kathleen Thelen argue that incremental institutional change is often endogenous, in contrast to the exogenous shocks seemingly required to disrupt institutional stability (punctuated equilibria) in more austere versions of path dependence. They argue in their introductory essay that changing coalitions of interests and dynamics of political mobilization may make one or more of these strategies feasible where wholesale reform may not be. This argument has challenged or at least heavily qualified the more pessimistic view of institutional change reflected in the concept of path dependence.

The assumption that gradual institutional change can produce significant transformations over time informs a vast body of literature, which includes areas as diverse as public policy,[16] development,[17] public administration,[18] and state/urban planning.[19]

1.2. INSTITUTIONAL BYPASSES: EMBRACING INCREMENTALISM

Institutional bypasses, which are the central focus of this book, fit comfortably within this view of incremental institutional change. As described earlier, an institutional bypass does not try to modify, change, or reform existing institutions – at least in the first instance – and hence has a more incremental character than "root and branch," top-down institutional reforms that more squarely challenge the status quo. These more traditional reforms are likely to confront the dual problems

---

[15] James Mahoney & Kathleen Thelen, eds., *Explaining Institutional Change: Ambiguity, Agency, and Power* (Cambridge, UK: Cambridge University Press, 2010); Kathleen Thelen, *How Institutions Evolve: The Political Economy of Skills in Germany, Britain, the United States and Japan* (New York: Cambridge University Press, 2004).

[16] Michael J. Trebilcock, *Dealing with Losers: The Political Economy of Policy Transitions* (New York: Oxford University Press, 2014).

[17] See e.g. Levy, *supra* note 13; William Easterly, *The White Man's Burden* (New York: Penguin Books, 2006).

[18] See e.g. Charles Lindblom, "The Science of 'Muddling Through'" (1959) 19:2 *Pub Admin Rev* 79.

[19] James Scott, *Seeing Like a State: How Certain Schemes to Improve the Human Condition Have Failed* (New Haven, CT: Yale University Press, 1998); Donald A. Schon, *The Reflective Practitioner: How Professionals Think in Action* (London, UK: Temple Smith, 1983); Bishwapriya Sanyal, Lawrence J. Vale, & Christina D. Rosan, eds., *Planning Ideas That Matter: Livability, Territoriality, Governance, and Reflective Practice* (Cambridge, MA: MIT Press, 2012).

of opposition from entrenched interests and genuine uncertainty about the likely impact of drastic reforms. In contrast, a bypass seeks to create a new pathway around existing institutions in an incremental, trial-and-error fashion in which functionality can be enhanced.

By creating a separate institution that operates in parallel with the dysfunctional institution, bypasses create a very different political dynamic compared to reforms implemented within existing institutions. While reforms of an existing institution would require reformers to engage in a negotiation process with those resisting changes to the status quo, the bypass allows them mostly to avoid engaging directly in such a negotiation process. This happens because the bypass does not modify the existing institutions. If the reforms were focused on the existing institution, in contrast, certain actors would have significantly greater ability and incentives to resist change.

Due to their design, institutional bypasses may be an especially effective mechanism to overcome self-interested resistance to reforms. People may resist modifications to existing institutions if these are likely to force them to internalize the costs of changing existing practices or attitudes. Another type of resistance is related to reforms that will impair rent-seeking activities. For instance, people who pay or receive bribes may actively resist anticorruption reforms that may deprive them of the rents associated with bribery.

Both kinds of resistance can be observed in the *Poupatempo* case. For some of the services, some civil servants resisted the creation of *Poupatempo* due to rent seeking, that is, when they stood to lose some benefit (financial or otherwise) from having services transferred to *Poupatempo*. Indeed, the creation of the project triggered resistance from corrupt bureaucrats who either received bribes to expedite the process of issuing documents, or were making money by selling falsified documents. In addition to the pre-existing bureaucracy, the government faced resistance from other interest groups. In particular, there was significant resistance from business professionals who offered services connected with bureaucratic services. For instance, doctors who provided medical examinations for drivers' licenses lobbied against offering them at the *Poupatempo* units because that would imply that civil servant doctors, working for the Brazilian public health system, would perform the examination *in loco* (expediting the services and reducing the time required for citizens to get their licenses issued). Another example is the middlemen with personal networks in the bureaucracy that offered expedited services for a fee (*despachantes*), often sharing a percentage of the fee paid with the bureaucrat who processed the paperwork. Users who were able to pay this fee would have their application processed faster through the back door. These groups strongly lobbied against *Poupatempo* issuing drivers' licenses, as it could potentially terminate their main (and perhaps only) source of income. Despite this resistance, the service was implemented in all *Poupatempo* units. Although this is counterfactual, our hypothesis is that these kinds of resistance could have been fiercer if reforms were implemented internally, rather than through a bypass.

That being said, institutional bypasses are not the only strategy to overcome these types of resistance to reforms. Another strategy is to strengthen interest groups that will benefit from the reforms, making them better able to press for change.[20] If this strategy is successful, it may be possible to implement internal reforms, and an institutional bypass will not be necessary. However, there is no assurance that those promoting change will not be overwhelmed by those resisting it. One possible obstacle to empowering beneficiaries to overcome rent seekers' resistance is a basic collective action problem. For example, imagine a country where citizens could benefit from faster and better bureaucratic services. At the same time, actors within a bureaucracy may not see changes to the current institutional arrangement as beneficial to them. Bureaucrats may earn additional income from discretionary schemes that allow for corruption and may resist any reform effort that could deprive them of these rents. Additionally, these bureaucrats may not want to employ greater effort and increase their workload if a reform increases the pace of processing requests for services.

This example illustrates that the dynamic of resistance to reforms may be hard to overcome, as often there are two very distinct interest groups. On one hand, there is a scattered, unorganized mass of citizens who could largely benefit from reforms. This group faces high transaction costs to organize and demand changes, and hence faces major collective action problems. On the other hand, there will be a small group of civil servants concentrated in one place or agency. Members of this group can effectively organize against the reform and strongly promote their preferences at much lower cost. The difference in costs makes it much easier for those resisting reforms to succeed. The prediction is that institutional reforms will only happen if the group demanding reforms has more power and influence or if there is a critical juncture (i.e., an external event that destabilizes the current arrangement, such as a war or a major political crisis). In most contexts, empowering the group that desires reforms and weakening the group that does not can be a formidable challenge.

Thus, one of the advantages of bypasses is that they do not change existing institutions, and therefore maintain the status quo from the point of view of those who benefit from it (e.g., the bureaucrats and private parties with corrupt relationships with them). To be sure, some level of cooperation by those inside the pre-existing institution in the design and implementation of bypasses may often be necessary. If nothing else, reformers will at least need information about internal processes and mechanisms that will help them identify problems and try to design solutions to fix them. This can be provided by a small group of people, or even one individual in some cases. This level of cooperation is much less than would be required if one attempted to reform the existing institution, where those opposing the reform could stall or boycott the design and/or implementation of reforms. As a consequence, bypasses face lower risks of being affected by the kind of strong reaction that is often

---

[20] Trebilcock & Daniels, *supra* note 11 at 354.

elicited by reforms that will directly and immediately affect existing institutions and those connected to (and benefiting from) them.

While maintaining the status quo from the point of view of self-interested groups, an institutional bypass will create choices from the point of view of the users. Once the bypass is created, those who are unhappy with the existing provision of public services can opt out of the existing system at any time. There is no collective action problem, as the decision is individualized. Those who want to continue using the old system retain the option to do so.

1.3. INSTITUTIONAL BYPASSES: CREATING ROOM FOR EXPERIMENTATION

Another advantage of institutional bypasses is that they create room for experimentation. Currently, there are few tools that can help reformers understand and predict, let alone control, all dimensions of institutional change. As a consequence, outcomes of reforms are often highly uncertain. Could we address these problems stemming from the uncertainty and risk related to the outcome of reforms by producing more information about outcomes? There is a great deal of uncertainty as to whether or not we can ever capture and systematize this knowledge in a way that allows us to predict with a high level of certainty the outcomes of reforms. Many scholars have supported the idea that academic studies need to acknowledge the complexity of exogenous and endogenous determinants of institutions and develop effective methods to investigate them.[21] The question is whether it is possible to ever perform this investigation with a level of certainty that would increase the chances of reforms succeeding.

At least part of this uncertainty comes from the fact that formal institutions – where most reform efforts are focused – are influenced by a set of social, cultural, and historical factors. These factors are sometimes referred to as informal institutions,[22] and they present a unique set of challenges to reformers, as it is hard to predict how they will interact with formal changes and the outcome of the resulting dynamic. Thus, these informal rules and norms have been called "the black box" of institutional change.[23] While it is almost intuitive to say that these informal institutions, such as cultural norms and values, play a role in influencing human behaviour, until recently very little attention had been paid to their actual role in institutional change.[24] The recognition of the importance of informal institutions may incentivize

---

[21] See e.g. Daron Acemoglu & Simon Johnson, "Unbundling Institutions" (2005) 113:5 *J Political Econ* 949.

[22] North, Process of Economic Change, *supra* note 14.

[23] Licht, Goldschmidt, & Schwartz, *supra* note 8.

[24] Amartya Sen, "How Does Culture Matter?" in Vijayendra Rao & Michael Walton, eds., *Culture and Public Action* (Stanford, CA: Stanford University Press, 2004). But see Alesina & Giuliano, *supra* note 8.

more rigorous attempts to systematize and generate knowledge about the complex interaction between formal and informal institutions. Nevertheless, they may still be plagued with uncertainties, as complex social determinants of institutional arrangements are rarely amenable to a few simplified algorithms.[25]

Many scholars argue that the solution to this conundrum is experimentation, that is, the only way to determine whether or not a reform will work is by testing it empirically.[26] Experimentation offers the possibility of generating information that is helpful to reformers and could potentially dispel resistance from fear of uncertainties related to the possible outcomes. Uncertain as to whether they will be among the winners or the losers, or uncertain as to whether the overall society will benefit from reforms, some interest groups may adopt a risk-averse position, resisting change. More than that, experimentation with positive results can actually generate political support from those who are assured that the benefits of reforms will outweigh their costs. In other words, experimentation creates demonstration effects. Those who are afraid of change can observe concrete results before deciding whether or not to support full-scale reforms. This is often touted as one of the advantages of pilot projects, and is also a feature of institutional bypasses. In both cases, undoing or abandoning the pilot project or the bypass will not generate significant disruption because the original institution has been left untouched. This makes these strategies highly reversible. Because it does not change the pre-existing institution, an institutional bypass can be structured such that it can be quickly abandoned if unsuccessful without having much impact on the status quo.

An institutional bypass allows for direct experimentation because it offers the same services to the same users that use the dysfunctional institution. Thus, the experiment is based on the actual conditions under which a reformed institution would operate. This is an important contrast with an experiment that is conducted in a lab or located in a distinct geographic location (another city, institution, or country), as such experiments do not guarantee that the same results will be achieved once transplanted elsewhere. Some scholars, including ourselves, have argued that countries should explore institutional reforms in locations with similar socio-cultural-historical circumstances to those where the reform is being implemented.[27] This approach

---

[25] See Eric Helland & Jonathan Klick, "Legal Origins and Empirical Credibility" in Michael Faure & Jan Smits, eds., *Does Law Matter? On Law and Economic Growth* (Antwerp, Belgium: Intersentia, 2011) at 99 for a criticism of the legal origins literature and other attempts to capture these dynamics through quantitative analyses.

[26] Michael C. Dorf & Charles Sabel, "A Constitution of Democratic Experimentalism" (1998) 98:2 *Colum L Rev* 267; Charles Sabel, "Dewey, Democracy and Democratic Experimentalism" (2012) 9:2 *Contemp Pragmatism* 35; Abhijit Banerjee & Esther Duflo, *Poor Economics: A Radical Rethinking of the Way to Fight Global Poverty* (New York: Public Affairs, 2011); Andrews, *supra* note 11; Gráinne De Búrca, Robert O. Keohane, & Charles Sabel, "Global Experimentalist Governance" (2014) 44:3 *Br J Polit Sci* 477; Deval Desai & Michael Woolcock, "Experimental Justice Reform: Lessons from the World Bank and Beyond" (2015) 11:1 *Ann Rev L & Soc Sci* 155; Andrews, Pritchett, & Woolcock, *supra* note 12.

[27] Michael J. Trebilcock & Mariana Mota Prado, *What Makes Poor Countries Poor?* (Cheltenham, UK: Edward Elgar, 2011).

may reduce some of the uncertainty, but is still not as secure (from an informational perspective) as "testing" the new institution under the actual conditions in which it will operate, as the institutional bypass does. Banerjee and Duflo argue that randomized controlled trials (RCTs) provide a scientific way of conducting such tests.[28] While RCTs may be useful and informative in certain circumstances, they present significant financial, logistical, ethical, and political obstacles in many circumstances.[29] In such cases, an institutional bypass or pilot project may be a preferable strategy. An institutional bypass may start as a pilot project and evolve into a full-blown institution without initially requiring any changes in the existing arrangements.

Poupatempo strongly exemplifies these experimental (along with incremental) features. It started as a small pilot project that did not require a significant initial investment. Indeed, the initial budget for the first unit of the *Poupatempo* project was approximately R$10 million (US$2 million in 2016 dollars).[30] In 2012, its annual budget had increased thirty times (R$357 million, roughly US$71.4 million in 2016 dollars). In large part, the budget increase was a result of the success of the pilot project, illustrated by the increasing demand for its services. Soon after its inauguration in 1997, the number of people seeking *Poupatempo* services quickly became larger than the existing unit's capacity. As the project began displaying positive results and gained popular support, it was easier to convince the office of the governor that it was a good investment, making it attractive to use part of the budget to expand it. Popular demand also made *Poupatempo* an attractive project for electoral purposes. Voters were the ones benefiting from its services, and politicians began to see *Poupatempo* as a very attractive "campaign card." After the initial success of the first unit, a series of units were opened in the capital and in other cities by the end of 1998, many shortly before state elections.

1.4. POTENTIAL LONG-TERM IMPACT OF INSTITUTIONAL BYPASSES[31]

Once an institutional bypass is implemented, its objective of being more effective than the pre-existing institution means that it can be considered a potential competitor, expanding the offer of a certain type of service and trying to attract users of that service. This offer may be attractive to users for a variety of reasons. In some cases,

---

[28] Banerjee & Duflo, *supra* note 26.

[29] William Easterly & Jessica Cohen, *What Works in Development? Thinking Big and Thinking Small* (Washington, DC: Brookings Institution Press, 2009); Kevin Davis & Mariana Mota Prado, "Law, Regulation, and Development" in Bruce Currie-Alder, Ravi Kanbur, David Malone, & Rohinton Medhora, eds., *International Development: Ideas, Experience, and Prospects* (Oxford, UK: Oxford University Press, 2014).

[30] This is an estimate, as this data is not available. The estimate is based on the cost to build a brand-new unit (R$6.5 million), plus costs in the implementation of the program (building up the team, diagnosing problems in the offices of the pre-existing bureaucracies, etc.).

[31] This section is largely drawn from Mariana Mota Prado, "Institutional Bypass: an Alternative for Development Reform" (2011) *SSRN*, online: http://papers.ssrn.com/sol3/papers.cfm?abstract_id= 1815442

services will be cheaper. In others, they will be more expensive, but faster. There may still be cases in which the price does not change, but users will prefer the bypass because of its quality, efficiency, or some other value that they find important. In sum, the pre-existing institution and the institutional bypass may be competing over price or other qualities that are relevant for users.

If an institutional bypass is attracting a significant number of users of governmental services, threatening the functioning (and perhaps the existence) of the pre-existing institution, it can generate three possible reactions: the pre-existing institution may decide to fight back and boycott the bypass; it may decide to shape up, and compete with the bypass; or it might do nothing. Each of these reactions may, in turn, generate more permanent institutional changes over the long term. More specifically, one could think of three different sets of stable outcomes: displacement (either the bypass disappears and the pre-existing institution remains in place or vice versa), merger (the bypass and the pre-existing institution become a single entity), or coexistence (both continue to exist but divide their tasks so as to avoid overlap and competition). While these results are more likely to appear in the long term, they are directly related to the immediate reaction that the pre-existing institution may have to the bypass, as follows:

(a) the pre-existing institution fights back and attempts to boycott or undermine the bypass, and if successful it may eliminate the bypass;
(b) the pre-existing institution simply does not react to the bypass and degenerates further as users exit, progressively losing more and more users until it fades away and is dismantled;
(c) the pre-existing institution may shape up in the face of competition, and this may generate at least two possible outcomes: a merger or a division of labour where one may assume responsibility for the most easily dealt with tasks (cream skimming), while offloading the rest onto the other.

We explore each of these hypotheses and their consequences next.

1.4.1. *Fighting Back*

Fighting back occurs when the pre-existing institution resists the implementation or operation of a bypass. This can take place either before the bypass is created or subsequently. Fighting back before the bypass is established would aim at stalling or preventing the project's approval or implementation. This can be accomplished by lobbying against its creation or, once approved, through efforts to block allocations of human capital and resources to the bypass, or to withhold critical information or other necessary forms of cooperation. However, this type of *ex-ante* resistance would require a significant amount of foresight and organization by existing interest groups, especially if the bypass is initially implemented as a modest pilot project.

In the situation in which the pre-existing institution was not successful in blocking the creation or implementation of a bypass, once the bypass becomes operational, the pre-existing institution may try to sabotage the ability of the bypass to provide services efficiently by employing tactics analogous to anticompetitive practices. A possible motivation for the pre-existing institution to try to fight and/or boycott the bypass is the perception of the bypass as a threat to its ongoing viability. It may fear being replaced or losing its political power, its social influence, or its status as the monopoly service provider.

There are a series of strategies that the pre-existing institution can use to boy-cott the bypass project. To the extent that the pre-existing institution is expected to contribute to or compete for resources (expertise, information, financial or human capital), it can create barriers and obstacles to the bypass obtaining these resources. For instance, the pre-existing institution could do so by lobbying to block adequate budgetary allocations to the bypass or refuse to cooperate in pro-viding necessary information to the bypass. Another strategy is to argue that the government is wasting resources by duplicating services and institutions within the public system. The redundancy argument can potentially create public resist-ance toward the bypass, but it can also backfire against the pre-existing institution. Thus, this could be a risky strategy. Moreover, the pre-existing institution can use negative publicity and spread misleading information, making users hesitant to use the bypass alternative.

What are the possible outcomes if the pre-existing institution decides to boycott the bypass? It may increase the costs to implement the bypass. By creating obstacles to the operation of a bypass, the pre-existing institution could make it more costly to pursue the project. This could make the reforms more burdensome and raise legitimate questions about the amount of resources that should be employed in promoting such reforms. If the boycott is effective, it can destroy a potentially suc-cessful bypass by depriving it of resources, or by exploiting information asymmetries that make individuals apprehensive about using it. The outcome would be that the least functional institution prevails by using anticompetitive tactics if the bypass is completely abandoned as a result of the boycott.

1.4.2. *Not Reacting and Disappearing*

Given that a bypass is replicating a function that is already performed in the sys-tem, one can imagine that a successful bypass will grow by progressively absorbing the demand for services previously provided (less effectively) by the pre-existing institution. For this to happen, certain circumstances must be present. Users need to use the option effectively by extensively switching to a service provider that bet-ter suits their needs than the pre-existing institution. Also, the bypass needs to be large enough to absorb this demand, which is not likely to be the case if it is imple-mented only as a pilot project. Consequently, this process assumes a progressive increase in the capacity and amount of resources allocated to the bypass as users continue to switch providers. If there is no effective boycott of the bypass, an increasing amount of government resources may become available to the bypass. With additional resources, the institutional bypass is likely to expand, and if it successfully employs these additional resources to fulfil the increasing demand for the bypass services, it is likely to grow from a pilot project into an established service provider that attends to the needs of an ever-greater number of users. If a critical number of people switch to the bypass, this may render the pre-existing institution obsolete.

This process will take place if the attempted boycott of the bypass fails or if the pre-existing institution does not react to it. The lack of reaction is likely to happen when the pre-existing institution either does not perceive the bypass as a threat or is not able to organize itself in a timely fashion to eliminate such a threat (i.e., it is unable to orchestrate a boycott or it fails to shape up in the face of competition). The inability to react in a timely fashion can happen because of a lack of foresight or because of collective action problems: the pre-existing institution may identify the threat but may be unable to organize its constituents to react in an effective way. In other words, collective action problems may prevent an effective response from the pre-existing institution.

If the bypass is controlled and/or funded by the government, the loss of a critical number of users per se does not render the pre-existing institution obsolete. Instead, a person or an institution needs to take the active step of proposing to eliminate what is now a redundant institution from the system. Governmental institutions do not simply disappear organically. Thus, even after the loss of a critical number of users, a governmental institution will only become obsolete due to a political decision. This political decision is the decisive step in this process. It may occur after the loss of a critical number of users, but it may also happen earlier or never. Considering the political nature of the decision, institutional obsolescence in these cases may be subject to various factors that influence this political calculus.

While there is no guarantee that this process will take place in any particular situation, the possibility that the pre-existing institution might become redundant and shut down highlights the ultimate appeal of bypasses in reducing obstacles to institutional reforms for development. Whereas the pre-existing and dysfunctional institution may be a strong and powerful entity before the creation of a bypass, it may turn into a less relevant institution over time. As a result, it may become incapable of resisting reforms once the bypass has evolved successfully to take over the "market" for certain public services. However, this scenario is unlikely to materialize if there is no political will to eliminate the pre-existing institution. In this case, the bypass will actually generate a vestigial body simply wasting public resources. Strong incentives to eliminate that vestigial body from the public system only exist in certain contexts, for example, where there is significant pressure to free up valuable resources and there is budgetary transparency. In these cases, there should be little resistance to its elimination. Indeed, in a context of scarcity, politicians and voters will often be motivated to eliminate redundancy.

In the long term, this may be a positive outcome as it resolves redundancy concerns and leads to fundamental changes within the government. There is, however, a risk that the bypass, after becoming the only provider, will begin to develop the same dysfunctionalities that plagued the old institution.

1.4.3. *Shaping Up*

The success and popularity of a bypass program might force the pre-existing institution to mimic the bypass or to seek other improvements to its own processes. This can happen because the current institution is inspired by the success and efficiency of the bypass, or it simply fears becoming obsolete, or some combination of the two. In these circumstances, shaping up can be a natural outcome of a competitive process, in which the pre-existing institution perceives the bypass as a threat but reacts to it by offering a service of higher quality. Here, a major strategic dilemma must be confronted: to incentivize pre-existing institutions to shape up in the face of lost user patronage, there must be consequences for its failure to do so (e.g., loss of budget, personnel, wage, and compensation reductions). However, these same consequences, at least if announced at the initiation of the bypass strategy, may instead intensify opposition to the bypass (fighting back), rather than encouraging shaping up. This suggests that the introduction of these consequences should only occur after a political constituency for the bypass has developed and solidified.

There are different strategies that a pre-existing institution might adopt in order to shape up. In some circumstances, the pre-existing institution may shape up simply by mimicking the bypass in terms of the way it provides services and by modelling its own processes on those of the bypass (in some cases, a form of duopolistic competition). This is a relatively cheap alternative, but it may not be possible in cases where the bypass offers a unique configuration of services that the pre-existing institution cannot easily replicate.

Even in cases in which the pre-existing institution could perfectly mimic the bypass and include all the advantages offered by it, this would only allow it, at best, to match what is offered by the bypass. This might prevent further decline in demand, but is unlikely to attract new consumers. If the pre-existing institution decides merely to "catch up" to the bypass, the government would likely face pressures to eliminate redundancies in the system, especially if the bypassed and the bypassing institutions are controlled and funded by the government. In this case, a possible outcome is that both the bypass and the pre-existing institution would be good candidates for a merger into a single entity.

Alternatively, instead of mimicking the bypass, the pre-existing institution might decide to innovate in an attempt to surpass the bypass. The question would then become how long the two institutions (the bypassed and the bypassing) would be able to sustain the competition before their ultimate fate is resolved. Multiple forms of equilibria can be imagined. They include (1) a stalemate in which the two institutions become merger candidates; (2) specialization, whereby both institutions divide responsibility over the services they both previously provided; and (3) one eventually loses its ability to compete successfully, becomes redundant, and is a target for elimination.

Any of these scenarios may or may not be preceded by significant and fruitful institutional innovations on both sides. The institution that remains at the end of the competitive process could potentially use such innovations. Thus, competition has the potential to generate fruitful outcomes. The risk is that before one of these equilibria develops, there may be a long period in which policymakers are confronted with a redundancy problem, and where users have two service providers, and one or both providers may consume significant fiscal resources. The lengthy coexistence of two institutions could lead to a waste of time, money, and human resources if both institutions together have the capacity to serve more users than the demand for their services.

There are other risks as well. If, for example, the government divides the allocation of fiscal resources between the two institutions, it could hinder the optimal development of each institution. In other words, it might be the case that each institution could improve even more if it had additional resources. There is yet another risk: because the state is making allocation decisions, it may try to pick the winner or favour one institution over the other. This might lead the state to invest more resources in one institution or the other, regardless of its capacity to offer more promising or self-sustaining innovations. This risk could be reduced if consumer fees or other types of demand-side subventions, such as vouchers, finance the service provision. Yet there are some governmental services where such arrangements are not possible (e.g., policing).

1.4.3.1. Merging

In the case of a merger, the bypass and the pre-existing institution become a single entity, which then assumes a monopoly over the provision of services. One of the rationales for a merger, as discussed earlier, is the possibility that the pre-existing institution might incorporate the innovations embodied in the bypass and begin to provide services with the same quality and expedition. In such a case, the government may have a strong incentive to promote a merger: to eliminate redundancy in public service provision.

A merger can also be seen as a strategy that a pre-existing institution can use to guarantee its survival. Thus, the merger may be conceived as a solution of last resort for an institution that foresees its own termination and is incapable of either generating a successful boycott of the bypass or shaping up in response to the competition. In these cases, the outcome of the merger is unclear. As is the case with an efficient corporate merger, it is possible that the less efficient entity will become more efficient as it is incorporated by the bypass and is forced to adopt its more efficient modus operandi. However, there is also a risk that the pre-existing institution will simply drag the bypass down. This will largely depend on the terms of the merger and which personnel, procedures, methods, and modus operandi will prevail: those adopted by the bypass, those used by the pre-existing institution, or a combination of both.

A merger can be conceived of as a potentially positive solution to the redundancy problem in cases in which the pre-existing institution's relevance has faded but there are still significant obstacles to expurgating it from the system. There are two important risks. The first is that the government, pressed to solve the redundancy problem, rushes into a merger. This may result in a bad outcome wherein the merger simply drags the bypass down. The other risk is that the merger can lead to an initially positive outcome but may progressively become less effective with the disappearance of incentives to improve in the absence of institutional competition. As noted earlier, this is not an exclusive risk of a merger but may also happen if the bypass begins operating alone after the pre-existing institution fades and disappears.

1.4.3.2. Dividing Tasks and Cream Skimming

The last hypothesis we analyze is the possibility that the pre-existing institution will preserve its existence by retaining an exclusive set of services while downloading others to the bypass. In this scenario, the division of tasks is structured in such a way that services do not overlap. The bypass would therefore no longer be a bypass. Instead, each institution would have a monopoly on the provision of a subset of services.

This might happen as a result of a strategic decision on the part of the pre-existing institution to use the bypass to its own benefit, transferring a block of services that it does not want to perform to the bypass, while continuing to function by providing other services. This would require significant political power, foresight, and strategic thinking by interest groups within the pre-existing institution. In this case, the division of labour would be combined with cream skimming, in the sense that the pre-existing institution may offload functions that are regarded as unimportant, more demanding, or nonfinancially rewarding. This division of labour might be proposed either at the time of the creation of the bypass or once the bypass has shown signs of success and is identified as a threat. If the balance of power is more favourable to the bypass than to the pre-existing institution, the off-loading of undesirable tasks could operate in the opposite direction.

This division of labour can also be temporary, being used as a strategic move by a government facing mounting resistance from the pre-existing institution towards the bypass (such as boycotts, for instance). If the government is unable to face this resistance down and fears that the resistance may kill the bypass, it may use the division of labour to help offset some of this negative reaction. If the government cream skims the services in favour of the bypass while keeping unimportant or less popular services with the pre-existing institution, the pre-existing institution may react negatively. If the division of labour does not generate a negative reaction, this strategy might facilitate the fading away of the pre-existing institution, while at the same time muting opposition that could potentially harm or even kill the bypass.

1.5. THE LIMITATIONS OF INSTITUTIONAL BYPASSES

Institutional bypasses are not a panacea for development reforms. On the contrary, there are some conditions under which they may be more desirable than others, and there are also important limitations as to how much institutional change can be achieved through bypasses. Without seeking to be exhaustive, this section identifies some dangers associated with this strategy.

Institutional bypasses can be used for questionable political reasons. The *Poupatempo* example illustrates how an effective bypass circumvented corrupt or incompetent bureaucrats resisting reforms that would otherwise benefit users seeking basic government services, such as drivers' licenses. However, sometimes resistance to reform can be led by legitimate veto players, that is, those who oppose the reforms for informed and principled reasons. These are veto players who use their power to protect the public interest. Indeed, many of the governance structures of modern societies revolve around the idea that veto power should be given to actors that are able and willing to exercise this authority in a way that is informed by or fosters the public interest. Constitutional protection of minority rights that could be easily overruled by democratic majorities is one example. Similarly, in implementing institutional reforms, it is possible to imagine groups of users, employees, or other interest groups resisting change due to broader concerns with its impact on overall societal welfare.

In the same way that institutional bypasses may offer a way around undesirable forms of resistance, they may also allow badly conceived or illegitimate reforms to overcome principled and legitimate sources of resistance. Such a use of institutional bypasses would be socially undesirable and points to dangers in their indiscriminate use as a means of instituting reforms. It is therefore important to differentiate between desirable and undesirable bypasses, and acknowledge that bypasses may also be used (or abused) to overcome legitimate mechanisms of checks and balances, thus presenting a significant danger to well-structured polities.

Governments in many developing countries are either autocratic or, at best, nominal democracies characterized by alternating predatory political elites, long-term single-party dominance, or autocratic traits masked under the formal rubric of liberal constitutional orders.[32] These countries face few incentives to be responsive to broadly

---

[32] Thomas Carothers, "The End of the Transition Paradigm" (2002) 13:1 *J Democracy* 5; Kim Lane Scheppele, "Worst Practices and the Transnational Legal Order (or How to Build a Constitutional

based citizen concerns about the availability and adequacy of government-provided services. These problems are often exacerbated in the case of many developing countries where large segments of the population are poorly educated, even illiterate, and widely dispersed through large rural areas distant from centres of government.

These features of the political environment in many developing countries raise a central dilemma. Namely, why would political elites in these countries be more incentivized to expand the range of choices available to citizens than they are to reform pre-existing institutions in the first place? Indeed, the perquisites of power are likely to be enhanced by maintaining strict public monopolies over a broad range of goods and services, where rents and bribes associated with the provision of these goods and services can be deployed to maintain politically salient patronage networks. This is, indeed, a discouraging scenario, where few (if any) public accountability mechanisms in the provision of a wide range of public goods and services are effective.

A more promising scenario is one where the political leadership is generally well intentioned and is concerned, at least to a significant extent, with the welfare of the citizenry at large. However, in responding to their concerns, this leadership faces opposition from entrenched interests in dysfunctional pre-existing institutions charged with responsibility for delivering public goods or services. This political environment, in our view, is the most hospitable to the creation of institutional bypasses in the provision of basic goods and services hitherto provided by public and often dysfunctional monopolies. However, even in this environment, not all institutional bypasses are created equal, and some are likely to have much more attractive properties and consequences than others.

In some cases, reformers know what the preferred alternative is, and the only question is how to design an effective transition strategy to move from the status quo to the desired arrangement. In *Dealing with Losers*,[33] one of us suggests that designing mechanisms to mitigate transition costs may be an effective, if not the only, way to make such transitions feasible. An institutional bypass could potentially be another strategy to deal with such transitions, especially in cases in which no form of compensation may be available to mitigate the losses of certain interest groups, or where engaging with any kind of mitigation strategy would be either illegal or undesirable. For instance, in an attempt to curb corruption in the delivery of bureaucratic services, such as drivers' licenses, the state is forced to deprive those benefiting from such corruption schemes from highly coveted rents. Offering some kind of compensation for the rents lost in this case does not seem prudent from a political, moral, or legal perspective. In such cases, an institutional bypass may offer a promising strategy to overcome the resistance to reform offered by corrupt public

'Democratorship' in Plain Sight)" (Nov 2, 2016) Wright Memorial Lecture 2016–2017, online: www .law.utoronto.ca/utfl_file/count/documents/events/wright-scheppele2016.pdf

[33] Trebilcock, *supra* note 16 at 3.

officials, while creating an opportunity to garner political support for the alternative mode of delivery of public services. This is effectively what *Poupatempo* did in an attempt to dismantle a mafia that sold false documents in Brazil. In other words, an institutional bypass may be especially useful when other transition strategies are not available or desirable.

There are other cases, however, where there is some consensus that reform is needed (i.e., the status quo is not desirable) but there is no certainty about what a socially beneficial alternative would look like. In such cases, the challenge is not to design a transition strategy to move from the status quo to an ideal arrangement, but instead it is to design a strategy to move away from the status quo while exploring potential alternatives. There is a vast literature advocating this as the most effective, if not the only, way of promoting reforms. In a famous paper "The Science of 'Muddling Through,'"[34] Charles E. Lindblom suggests that it is rare for reformers to have a pre-designed plan that simply requires an implementation strategy. Instead, the implementation of the reform is, in itself, the search for a plan. Along the same lines, the literature on urban planning has shown how the process of promoting reforms generates useful information that should be constantly fed back into the planning process in a virtuous cycle of reflexivity that requires reforms to move forward while constantly re-examining the right way forward and adjusting course as needed. This principle is most clearly embodied in the widely cited book by James C. Scott, *Seeing Like a State*,[35] which illustrates through a series of case studies the follies of central planning and the virtues of open-endedness. More recently, this principle seems to be the foundation of development strategies such as the "problem-driven iterative adaptation" (PDIA), more informally described as "purposive muddling."[36]

An institutional bypass is also designed to enable this constant search for answers (or quest for reflexivity). This is what the creators of *Poupatempo* did: there were constant adjustments and improvements largely based on user surveys and external evaluations. This created a self-reinforcing system of changes and constant improvements, modifying not only the culture of the service providers themselves but also the culture of the people using the services. The idea of asking for user feedback helps create a culture in which users feel entitled to demand better services and to request changes that improve the service. It is important, however, for such experimentation to be grounded on reliable data and impartial evaluation of the results. One could imagine, for instance, a trial-and-error process where self-interested

---

[34] Lindblom, *supra* note 18.
[35] Scott, *supra* note 19.
[36] Andrews, *supra* note 11; Robert Klitgaard, "Book Review: Matt Andrews (2013). The Limits of Institutional Reform in Development: Changing Rules for Realistic Solutions" (2013) 33:5 *Pub Admin Dev* 408; Andrews, Pritchett, & Woolcock, *supra* note 12; World Development Report 2017, *supra* note 9.

groups manipulate the results to convince stakeholders to adopt an institutional solution that generates rents to this group but is less beneficial to the public.

The question that these scenarios raise, however, is determining what is socially desirable – both as an end goal and as a principle to inform a reflexive trial-and-error reform process. This is a question that is hard to answer. Academics, policymakers, and citizens will often differ on what is desirable and what is not. Everything else being equal, it is certainly preferable to obtain required governmental documents (identity cards, drivers' licenses, etc.) in a shorter period of time. But it is less clear if reducing the waiting time is a preferred arrangement if it implies a significant increase in the costs of providing such documents (whether in the form of fiscal costs for the state, fees paid by the consumer, or higher error costs). Resolving these competing and often incommensurable criteria of what is desirable or not is frequently at the core of any reform strategy. Are parents better served by high-quality education, despite it being offered at a significant distance from their homes? Or are they better served having nearby schools that, despite offering lower-quality education, do not require one of the parents to quit their jobs in order to transport children safely back and forth from school on a daily basis?

Our discussion of the institutional bypass brackets these and other important questions by assuming that there is some method of assessing the social utility of the services being delivered by such bypasses. In many cases, the fact that bypasses offer a choice to users allows us to assume that the option selected by users maximizes their utility while avoiding the imposition of negative externalities on nonusers. In other cases, however, such choices do not provide reliable information. For instance, institutional bypasses that are only available to those who are willing to pay a premium may exclude a group of users who do not have the resources to exercise such choice. Along the same lines, cases in which choices may be driven by short-term goals (parents deciding to send their children to nearby schools so as to continue working) may reflect the challenge many citizens face in rationally comparing short- and long-term benefits (such as investing in a better education that may take more than a decade to generate benefits for the family).[37] Moreover, bypasses may be simply mitigating a symptom of a larger and more structural problem, potentially reducing the chances that citizens will press for more radical changes. *Poupatempo*, for instance, may make it easier to get government-issued documents, and may reduce some of the burdens associated with notarization, but it does not deal with the fundamental problem of excessive documentary requirements that characterizes Brazil and other countries with inefficient bureaucracies. Thus, while the exercise of choice may offer some information about superiority of certain options over others, such information needs to be used with caution.

---

[37] Ellen B. Goldring & Charles S. Hausman, "Reasons for Parental Choice of Urban Schools" (1999) 14:5 *J Educ Pol'y* 469 at 472.

It is also important to acknowledge that institutional bypasses are not immune to path dependence. As discussed earlier, institutional bypasses have the advantage of allowing for incrementalism and experimentation, and thus may increase the chances of overcoming obstacles to reform and promoting institutional change. However, it is difficult to predict the result of such changes. As the previous section indicated, many possible outcomes may be generated from the institutional competition produced by institutional bypasses. When the project is in its initial stages, an institutional bypass may be very easy to reverse, allowing policy makers to quickly revert to the previous status quo. However, the longer a bypass exists or the larger it gets, the harder it may be to dismantle, even if unsuccessful, as self-reinforcing mechanisms become established, strengthened, and consolidated.

Another risk of incrementalism is the fact that positive outcomes from initial pilots may not persist on a larger scale. As is often the case with pilot projects, these may be initially infused with significant resources and highly enthusiastic people. In the process of scaling up the project, it may become difficult to sustain similar levels of financing and/or enthusiasm. One of the reasons for this difficulty is economies of scale. For instance, *Poupatempo* has opened units in smaller cities in the state of São Paulo, where the fixed costs of the unit are similar to the ones in a larger city but the demand for services is lower. As a consequence, the budget has increased 709 percent from 2002 to 2012, but the number of people using the service has increased only 85 percent. This has increased the price of the service per capita from R\$2.77 to R\$12.10, raising questions about the need to limit *Poupatempo*'s further expansion.[38]

Similarly, the *Poupatempo* example reveals a particular difficulty that arises when such pilot projects are run as institutional bypasses of the pre-existing bureaucracy. In these cases, the existence of the pilot projects largely duplicates a series of services by offering them both through the pre-existing bureaucracy and through the institutional bypass. This entails start-up costs (building the unit, buying new equipment, furniture, hiring new personnel, etc.), and the total budget allocated for the delivery of a particular service needs to increase as a result. This initial investment occurs only once, and permanent costs will be only those for maintenance and salaries, which need to be considered in light of the increased capacity in service provision and circumvention of inefficiencies in the pre-existing bureaucracy. Nonetheless, reducing expenditures may require that the provision of certain services be made exclusive to the bypass over time, as the pilot project turns into a more established institutional framework. This occurred with the exclusive issuance of identification cards by the *Poupatempo*. Even then, however, it is difficult to determine whether the costs for the state were actually reduced in this case. Because the identification

---

[38] Renan Truffi, "Poupatempo Fica 700% Mais Caro em 10 Anos, Mas Atendimentos só Crescem 85%" (Sept 9, 2013) online: Último Segundo http://ultimosegundo.ig.com.br/brasil/sp/2013-09-09/poupatempo-fica-700-mais-caro-em-10-anos-mas-atendimentos-so-crescem-85.html

cards were originally issued in police stations, the costs to maintain the stations and its personnel remain, which may indicate that the overall cost for the government may be significantly higher now than it was before.

To overcome these limitations, it is preferable to adopt bypasses that are able to change rapidly enough to adapt to new circumstances and not become obsolete. Those that fail to adapt, like other institutions, are likely to become redundant or dysfunctional. However, the failure to adapt to changing circumstances should not be a reason to ignore the fact that these bypasses have been effective in performing their functions for a certain period. This was the case of *Poupatempo*. The units were highly functional in their initial years, and the quality of service provided, albeit declining in recent years, is still superior to that which users previously received in the offices of the old bureaucracy. Thus, despite its imperfections, *Poupatempo* opened the possibility for institutional change, especially in a context in which change would have otherwise been difficult, if not impossible.

Once the bypass itself is unable to adapt to changing circumstances and becomes dysfunctional, the solution may be to promote another institutional reform. In some cases, the bypass may have sufficient malleability to be reformed from the inside. If not, an institutional bypass of the bypass may be necessary. Thus, the success of a bypass does not lie in its longevity or in its flawless operation, but in its ability to promote change. An institutional bypass is a means to an end, not the end in itself.

In sum, an institutional bypass may offer an improvement in some relevant dimensions in the provision of services, as measured by the fact that users are opting for the bypass rather than the pre-existing institution. This is a relevant piece of information in assessing what may or may not be desirable in service provision, but it should not be analyzed without consideration of the broader context in which such choices are being made, or the competing goals that may be at stake in determining how users make such choices. Moreover, a bypass should not be perceived as a permanent or definitive arrangement. Similar to other institutions, bypasses need to adapt to changing circumstances and may themselves become dysfunctional if they are unable to do so. Thus, it is not inconceivable that institutional bypasses will themselves need to be bypassed.

1.6. CONCLUSION

Institutional bypasses offer a reform strategy that may help overcome resistance to reforms, while at the same time allowing for incrementalism, reflexivity, and experimentation in resolving genuine outcome uncertainties. These features make them extremely attractive in contexts where internal reforms are unlikely to be feasible.

Despite these advantages, we do not regard institutional bypasses as a panacea for all institutional failures confronted by developing countries, as the discussion in this chapter makes clear. Bypasses can also be used to overcome legitimate political resistance, becoming a tool to implement undesirable reforms. Even in the case of desirable reforms, the long-term consequences of institutional competition are speculative, with multiple equilibria possible. And, of course, because of their incremental nature, bypasses may be ill suited to effectuate major structural changes in the existing configurations of institutions and their roles.

Despite these reservations, this book is premised on the view that institutional bypasses are an insufficiently explored option for institutional reform, especially in developing countries. The conditions under which an institutional bypass may be an attractive option for reformers, and when it is more likely to succeed, are some of the central issues we will explore in the following chapters.

The book is structured as follows. After this introduction, Chapter 2 attempts to define the notion of institutional bypass by setting out its essential characteristics. These will first be outlined through an analogy with a highway bypass, before returning to the *Poupatempo* example as a more complete illustration of the concept. Chapter 3 then proceeds to further narrow the scope of the institutional bypass concept by comparing and contrasting it with a number of related notions in the institutional reform literature. Specific distinctions are drawn between the institutional bypass, on the one hand, and institutional layering, regulatory dualism, exit-voice, and institutional multiplicity, on the other. As we will argue in that chapter, the concept of institutional bypass can be distinguished from most of these concepts, although there may be overlap among some of them. Accordingly, some bypasses may coincide with or result from instances of layering and multiplicity, for example, but there is no perfect correlation between them.

Chapters 4 and 5 recognize a distinction between intentional and spontaneous bypasses. Intentional bypasses are conscious, pre-planned, and centralized attempts to fix what are perceived as dysfunctionalities in a system. In analyzing three case studies of intentional bypasses in Brazil in Chapter 4, a new police unit in the state of Rio de Janeiro (*Unidade de Polícia Pacificadora*), new health care units (*Unidade de Pronto Atendimento*), and a new labour law structure (*Central Única dos Trabalhadores*) – we show that one single actor designed and often implemented these reforms in an attempt to offer an improved option to users. The actor spearheading the bypass in the first two cases is a governmental actor, while in the third case it is a civil society organization. By contrast, spontaneous bypasses are scattered and uncoordinated solutions that emerge independently of each other, but collectively amount to an arrangement that offers an alternative institutional pathway to the dominant system. These are illustrated by three case studies in Chapter 5: private security services in Latin America; low-cost private schools in India; and *Lok Adalat*, an informal adjudication system, also in India.

As we show in these two chapters, institutional bypasses can be initiated under very different circumstances (intentionally or spontaneously), and the strategies adopted during their implementation and consolidation can vary significantly (such as being more or less experimental or reflexive, for instance). Yet the conditions under which bypasses are likely to arise seem to follow some clear patterns: intentional bypasses are often preceded by crises that create windows of opportunity for reforms, combined with insurmountable obstacles to promoting changes in existing institutions; in contrast, spontaneous bypasses often lack a clear leading actor or strategic plan, but exhibit more organic bottom-up characteristics.

In the final chapter, we conclude by acknowledging that this book is simply the first step in a much larger project of identifying, mapping, and analyzing institutional bypasses. Thus, we contextualize the contributions of this book within the current development literature and offer a nonexhaustive map of questions yet to be explored by those interested in strategies to promote development. We hope this book will encourage other researchers and policy makers to take up our invitation to further investigate the potential and limits of this concept.

2

What Is an Institutional Bypass?

Achieving a common understanding of the key characteristics of institutional bypasses poses some significant, and often subtle, conceptual and definitional challenges. It is important to address these squarely and explicitly before we proceed to review the literature on related reform strategies in the next chapter and our case studies of intentional and spontaneous bypasses in Chapters 4 and 5. We begin this conceptual and definitional task by drawing on some useful analogies.

The word bypass is used in multiple contexts, such as coronary bypass surgery in medicine and bypass routes in traffic engineering. The coronary bypass analogy suggests that the bypass does not try to fix the dysfunctional institution (the clogged artery), instead going around it to perform the same function (e.g., provide regular blood flow in the heart) in a more effective manner. The bypass route analogy, by contrast, presents the concept as a particular route that operates alongside, and can be distinguished from, two other road types. These are, respectively, the main route and an alternative route. Figure 2.1 captures the broad differences between each of these three road types.

As this image suggests, the *main route* provides one way to get to a destination, which we will call City A. While driving towards City A on the main road, one is forced to comply with much lower speed limits when the road is going through an urban area, as occurs, for example, while going through City B (an urban area represented

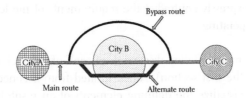

FIGURE 2.1. Bypass route

by the larger circle). True to its name, the *alternate route* also allows one to reach City A. However, similarly to the main route, the alternate route also imposes lower speed limits within the urban area that comprises the territorial limits of City B. Assuming that reaching City A faster is what drivers want, this alternate route is not a bypass route. By contrast, the *bypass route* offers an alternative to reach City A that avoids the urban zone of City B, and thus does not require reduced speed limits. If drivers are looking for a way to reach their destination faster, this route properly qualifies as a bypass.

In other words, both the bypass route and the alternate route keep the main and dominant route in place and offer an option to reach the same destination (City A). The difference is that the bypass route offers a feature that is not available on the main or alternate route: higher speed limits than the ones imposed in urban zones. Assuming drivers want to reduce travel time, this difference could make this option a bypass, rather than simply another alternate route.

This example captures three defining features of an institutional bypass:

1. it keeps the dominant institution in place;
2. it creates an alternative institutional pathway through which to discharge functions performed by the dominant institution; and
3. it has at least one distinctive feature that aims at addressing perceived dysfunctionalities or limitations in the dominant institution.

Each of these characteristics raises important questions that will be addressed in this chapter. Before addressing these questions, however, it is important to acknowledge that institutional bypasses perform functions that often involve the enforcement and application of rules and norms. As a result, some of its constitutive elements are not immediately evident in the road example. Considering this institutional/legal dimension, the definition of an institutional bypass needs to take into account some additional elements, as follows:

4. it is separated from the dominant institution, from a governance perspective;
5. it has effects in the same jurisdiction as the dominant institution; and
6. it does not expressly contradict the requirements of the legal system within which it is operating.

We will develop a more detailed discussion of each of these characteristics, using the road analogy (the first section). Albeit limited from a conceptual standpoint, the analogy helps visualize the defining elements of an institutional bypass, providing an accessible way of understanding what each element entails. Following this discussion, we will return to the *Poupatempo* example discussed in Chapter 1, providing further details that allow us to conceive it as a more complete illustration of the concept (the second section). This will lead us to conclude that the label of institutional bypass is designed to describe a very specific set of institutional arrangements, and thus should be used with care.

2.1. INSTITUTIONAL BYPASSES: DEFINING CHARACTERISTICS

2.1.1. *The Bypass Keeps the Dominant Institution in Place*

As we have suggested in previous joint work,[1] the term institution, as used in both the theoretical and empirical literature on institutional theories of development, exhibits significant ambiguity. For example, Douglass North defines institutions as follows: "Institutions are the rules of the game of a society, or, more formally, the humanly devised constraints that structure human interactions. They are composed of formal rules (statute law, common law, regulation), informal constraints (conventions, norms of behaviour, and self-imposed codes of conduct), and the enforcement characteristics of both."[2]

At least from a lawyer's perspective, this is an odd definition of institutions. Beyond a country's constitution, lawyers do not think of institutions as the rules of the game. For example, the legally prescribed speed limit on a given highway is not considered an institution but rather a legal rule promulgated by one set of institutions, enforced by another, and in the event of disputes, adjudicated by yet another. Moreover, by including informal constraints (cultural conventions, norms of behaviour, and self-imposed codes of conduct) in this definition of institutions, the concept of institutions becomes so all-encompassing that it includes almost any conceivable factor that may influence human behaviour and hence risks losing any operational content.

Considering these limitation, we will adopt an alternative definition of institutions that may be more attractive to lawyers, proposed in a previous co-authored book: "those organizations (formal and informal) that are charged or entrusted by a society with making, administering, enforcing or adjudicating its laws or policies."[3]

What is a dominant institution? For many governmental services, there is an assumption that the state has a monopoly in their provision. Policing is perhaps the clearest example, along with provision of government-issued documents, such as drivers' licenses and criminal records. While it is possible for the state to contract out the actual execution of such services, it is uncommon to find arrangements in which citizens are offered a choice between a private or a public provider. Similarly, many governmental services and functions are provided in a manner that leaves

---

[1]   Michael J. Trebilcock & Mariana Mota Prado, *Advanced Introduction to Law and Development* (Cheltenham, UK: Edward Elgar, 2014) ch. 3.

[2]   Douglass North, *Institutions, Institutional Change, and Economic Performance* (Cambridge, UK: Cambridge University Press, 1990).

[3]   Michael J. Trebilcock & Mariana Mota Prado, *What Makes Poor Countries Poor? Institutional Determinants of Development* (Cheltenham, UK: Edward Elgar, 2011) at 27–8.

little (if any) room for competition either due to natural monopolies or due to the predominant regulatory arrangement. As a consequence, for a number of the government services that will be considered in this book, there is one institution providing the service, making it relatively easy to determine which one is the dominant institution.

The idea of a dominant institution becomes slightly more complicated in cases where there is no monopoly in service provision. The more openness there is for new entrants to begin offering services or performing functions and successfully attracting users, the less relevant the idea of an institutional bypass becomes. By contrast, an institutional bypass is a particularly attractive reform strategy where the state possesses a *de jure* or *de facto* monopoly or quasi-monopoly, and where change and innovation are thus not naturally happening as a result of competitive forces. In sum, a dominant institution is most easily recognized in circumstances where the idea of an institutional bypass is most relevant.

While a monopoly or quasi-monopoly is required, a bypass does not require exclusive public provision: it can be also implemented where there is mixed public and private provision. For instance, many countries have public and private education and health care systems operating simultaneously. In some cases, the public system will be the dominant one and the private system could be considered a bypass. In other cases, both the public and private systems may be the dominant institution. In these cases, a bypass could be a small pilot project created to overcome existing deficiencies in the existing mixed public-private system.[4] Similarly, if the main route in Figure 2.1 is run by the government, whereas the alternate route is a toll road managed by a private company, the bypass route could be bypassing the main route or both.

The existence of a bypass is dependent upon the existence of a previous and dominant institution that "remains in place," that is, remains operational. For example, if the main route is demolished or closed to traffic after the bypass route is built and there is no alternate route, the bypass route is no longer a bypass. It becomes the main route. In contrast, if the main route was open and operational when the bypass route was built, then the bypass route is a bypass. However, if the main route is subsequently closed, from that point on, the bypass route can no longer be considered a bypass.

A more difficult situation arises where the main route is re-activated at any point in time after it ceases to be operational. Assuming the bypass route became the dominant one during the closure of the main route, there are two possible scenarios in such a case. On the one hand, the bypass route may regain its status as a bypass if the main route also regains its status as the dominant one, after being re-opened. On

---

[4] The fact that some institutional bypasses will be spearheaded by the government, such as *Poupatempo*, while others may not, is not a relevant distinction for the definition of the concept. For a detailed discussion about the importance and implications of this distinction, see Chapters 4 and 5.

the other hand, the bypass route may remain dominant even after the original main route is re-opened. In this case, the newly re-opened route could be considered a bypass (as long as it meets all the defining criteria discussed in this chapter). This suggests that the concept of institutional bypass is intrinsically relational, and the status of being a bypass can be temporary.

2.1.2. *The Bypass Creates an Alternative Institutional Pathway Through Which to Discharge Functions Performed by the Dominant Institution*

Choice is central to the idea of a bypass. Actors need to be able to choose between the dominant institution and the bypass. It is possible that the choices are constrained (e.g., it is necessary to pay tolls to use the bypass route) or restricted to a certain group (e.g., trucks are not allowed to use the bypass route). These constraints are not an obstacle to classifying an initiative as a bypass.

If the constraints and limitations effectively reduce the group of potential beneficiaries significantly, one may question the efficacy of the bypass as a strategy to promote change. Nonetheless, it remains a bypass. For example, if the bypass route in Figure 2.1 is built to allow emergency vehicles to reach City A faster, it would be restricted to a limited and relatively small group of users, but would still be a bypass. However, the accessibility is so restricted that it may not have much potential to change outcomes in the existing transport system or to force the dominant institution to improve its performance.[5]

To be considered a bypass, the new option needs to serve at least as a partial substitute for the dominant institution. The road analogy helps illustrate this. The entity managing the main route could build express lanes and physically separate them from existing lanes (which would be called collectors) in order to reduce the overall travel time of those in the express lanes. While this could achieve the objective of reducing travel times to reach City A, the express lanes cannot be considered a bypass because their function is to complement, not offer an alternative to the main road even if they are physically separated from one another.

Despite serving as a substitute, the bypass can be designed as either a cooperative or a competitive arrangement vis-à-vis the dominant institution. On the one hand, a bypass route can be built and managed by another company that aggressively tries to steer traffic away from the main route in order to collect the revenues generated by tolls. On the other hand, a bypass route can be designed and constructed to operate in tandem with the main route, offering an alternative that will not only help reduce traffic jams on the main route when needed, but will also reduce the overall number of accidents by creating an alternative for those inclined to travel at higher speeds. Regardless of whether it is cooperative or competitive, it is important that the bypass performs at least some of the same functions as the dominant arrangement.

---

[5] For a discussion of the potential for bypasses to promote change, see Chapter 1, Section 1.4.

The idea of "same function" is intrinsically subjective for the purpose of this book. To illustrate the subjectivity of the concept of "same function," imagine a communication system (e.g., videoconferencing) that eliminates the need to travel to City A for meetings. This could, of course, eliminate the aggravation one faces with long travel times on the main road. Communicating with other people may be the reason why some people seek to reach City A. For this group, the communication system may be even more desirable than a bypass road, and it could be classified as a bypass, because, for them, it serves the same purpose as the main route. Other groups, however, may be using the road to transport goods. For them, the communication system cannot be considered a bypass of the main road, as it does not perform the same function as the main road.

In sum, the concept of institutional bypass does not depend on an objective definition of the function (or "same function") that is being performed by the dominant and bypass institutions. Instead, that function is defined by the actors (or at least by a particular group of actors) who use the system. Similarly, any assessment of improvement in the performance of that function will also be subjective. This avoids the normative question of which functions should or should not be performed and how, and instead focuses on the question of what the actors perceive the function to be and what kind of improvements they seem to prefer (by choosing to use the bypass instead of the dominant system), as we discuss next.

2.1.3. *The Bypass Has at Least One Distinctive Feature That Aims at Addressing Perceived Dysfunctionalities or Limitations in the Dominant Institution*

Having a distinctive feature is what differentiates a bypass from being a mere replica of the dominant institution. Thus, creating another road to City A that goes through the urban core of City B simply creates an alternate route (see Figure 2.1). The alternate route may help resolve some problems. For example, by providing increased capacity, it may effectively reduce volume of traffic on the main route, allowing drivers on both routes to move faster. This solution would be satisfactory if users were content with the existing speed limits but not with the high volume of traffic on the main road. In other words, an option that simply increases capacity may be the solution in some cases. In other cases, however, users may be seeking the possibility of travelling at higher speeds than the ones imposed by the current urban zone's speed limits. In this case, the alternate route does not address this perceived dysfunctionality of the main route.

As these examples illustrate, the distinctive feature of the bypass is intrinsically connected with perceived dysfunctionalities in the pre-existing arrangement. What is functional and what is not will be determined by users and will, therefore, be subjective. For example, different groups may use the road for different purposes but may still agree on what is more functional. This is exemplified by the distinction between those who are driving to City A to connect with people versus those driving there to deliver goods. While the two groups may disagree as to whether a communications system is a good substitute for the functions performed by the road, as discussed in the previous section, they may both agree that, in the absence of such a communications systems, a road that allows them to reach City A faster is preferable to a road that reaches the same destination but has more restrictive speed limits.

There may be disagreement about what is more functional even within a group with the same objective. For example, for those people who are trying to reach City A to connect with others, some members of the group may want to reach it as fast as possible. Others may want to have a more leisurely drive with easy access to restaurants. For the latter, a high-speed highway outside the urban core may be the dysfunctional option. By the same token, older or younger drivers, for lack of experience or confidence, may prefer to drive at lower speeds, even if this implies longer travel times. All of this suggests that it is difficult to objectively determine what is functional and what is not, and there may be disagreement even within a group that uses the institutional arrangement for the same purpose.

Those perceiving the dysfunctionality of the dominant arrangement may be the ones creating the bypass or the ones using it.[6] In the latter case, the bypass may not be created with the aim of fixing anything in the dominant arrangement, but may still become attractive to a particular group of people as an alternative option to what they now perceive as a dysfunction in the pre-existing arrangement. For instance, imagine that two parallel roads are built, connecting Cities A and C. The roads are functionally identical and offer the same travel time between the two cities. Over time, however, what was once a small village becomes City B, a large urban sprawl that ends up engulfing one of the roads. This may force authorities to require reduced speeds on one road, while maintaining high speeds on the other one. For those who prefer to travel at higher speeds, the latter may then become a bypass of the former, even if it was not originally conceived as such.

Here is another example that reinforces the idea that dysfunctionality is subjective and that users' preferences and their behaviours determine whether a certain arrangement is operating as a bypass. Imagine a new road designed with the specific aim of reaching a particular waterfall – a function that is not performed by the main road, which was designed to connect cities (Figure 2.2). The new road and the main road were not designed to perform the same function. Nonetheless, it is possible that in performing another function (access to the waterfall), the new road may offer a feature that unintentionally addresses some dysfunctionality in the existing system. For instance, the road designed to provide access to the waterfall may not have been built to allow for higher speeds than the main route, but, due to the high volume of

---

[6] Institutional bypasses can be divided into spontaneous and intentional bypasses. See Chapters 4 and 5.

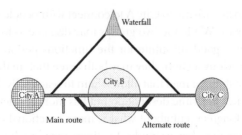

FIGURE 2.2. Waterfall route

traffic on the main route, the waterfall road becomes the fastest way to drive from City C to City A. In this case, the waterfall road becomes a bypass of the main route.

Whether the waterfall road is addressing a dysfunctionality in the dominant system is determined by whether drivers perceive it as a preferred option to the main system and, as a consequence, are using the new road as a bypass.

2.1.4. *The Bypass Is Separated from the Dominant Institution from a Governance Perspective*

There are many institutional solutions to dysfunctional performance, as we will discuss in greater detail in Chapter 3. These solutions are distinct from an institutional bypass in many ways, but one important distinguishing factor is that, unlike many other institutional solutions, there is some level of governance separation of the bypass from the dominant institution. However, having separate governance structures that operate side-by-side, and perhaps even compete with each other, is largely counter-intuitive in the domestic sphere. This is because, as previously mentioned, sovereign states are often assumed to hold a monopoly on the provision of certain services and the performance of certain functions at the domestic level, as is notably the case with policing.

How much separation is required for it to be considered a bypass? Taking the example of policing, which is often conceived as a monopoly of the state, one of us has argued that creating a new police battalion is not a bypass, but a separate police force is a bypass.[7] Both police forces are governed by the same legal system and will ultimately be reporting to the same authority (e.g., the state governor). However, the fact that they operate independently of each other on a daily basis seems to offer enough separation to consider the new police force a bypass of the old one. A new battalion, by contrast, is still embedded in the same governance structure and potentially the same institutional culture as the old police force. Thus, it would be more analogous to an express lane than to a bypass route.

7   Graham Denyer Willis & Mariana Mota Prado, "Process and Pattern in Institutional Reforms: The Police Pacifying Units in Brazil as an Institutional Bypass" (2014) 64 *World Dev* 232, https://doi.org/10.1016/j.worlddev.2014.06.006

That being said, institutions with the requisite level of governance separation to qualify as bypasses can take many different forms. The creation of a brand-new institution to perform the same function as a dominant institution is perhaps the clearest example of a separate governance structure. It is possible, however, that the alternative materializes by re-purposing an institution that was designed to perform another function (similarly to the route to the waterfall). This "conversion" can be classified as a bypass as long as it still maintains the required separation from a governance perspective.

It is also possible that this separate governance structure is created through a contractual arrangement among actors. Imagine, for instance, that a group of drivers decides to do some work on an off-road trail in order to enable its use as another route to travel to City A. When this group of people agrees to facilitate and maintain the use of that alternative, it becomes a bypass, as long as it addresses the perceived dysfunctionality of the main route. In this case, the agreement that these individuals have reached offers a separate governance structure from the one that currently governs the main route. While the agreement among the individuals may break down, terminating necessary maintenance and the viability of the alternative route as a consequence, it still qualifies as a bypass, despite its precariousness.

In contrast to contractual agreements, individual actions require more careful analysis, as they may fail to meet the second requirement, that is, creating an "alternative institutional pathway." Individual actors can adopt behaviours that bypass dysfunctional institutions but do not amount to an institutional arrangement. These behaviours alone will not constitute an institutional bypass. Suppose that a lone driver decides to take an off-road path to reach City A. While this individual driver may have found a legal way of bypassing traffic, she or he has not created or enhanced an institution so as to enable others to benefit from this option. As a result, this kind of isolated behaviour cannot be classified as an institutional bypass. Contrary to the definition proposed here, Keith S. Rosenn uses the notion of "institutional bypass" to describe the "jeito" – a term that refers to the regular and widespread creation of informal "fixes" to inefficient or dysfunctional rules and norms in Brazil.[8] However, as most of these arrangements are adopted by individuals (and are often illegal), they do not meet the criteria of our concept of an institutional bypass.

2.1.5. *The Bypass Has Effects in the Same Jurisdiction as the Bypassed Institution*

For drivers who are unhappy with the travel times to City A, one option is to move to City X (i.e., live and work in a different place), where traffic congestion is not a problem and thus commuting times are lower. This means that users who

---

[8] Keith S. Rosenn, "The Jeito: Brazil's Institutional Bypass of the Formal Legal System and Its Developmental Implications" (1971) 19:3 *Am J Comp L* 514.

are seeking ways of avoiding the dysfunctionalities of the dominant institution could choose to resort to institutions located in different jurisdictions. While such institutions may meet all the requirements listed so far, for our purposes, they are not classified as bypasses unless they have effects in the same jurisdiction where the relevant dominant institution operates. Thus, the choice to simply move to another jurisdiction is not a bypass.

Imagine a scenario in which a company decides to invest in Country B because it does not trust the judicial system of Country A. The exercise of this choice does not transform Country B's judiciary into a bypass, since it is not performing the same function as the judicial system of Country A (i.e., it does not resolve investment disputes for companies investing in Country A). Thus, even if Country B decides to create a judicial system that is better than that of Country A and competes with it to attract investment, this new system is not considered a bypass because it does not produce effects in the same jurisdiction where the bypassed institution is located.

By contrast, an example of an institutional bypass would be one in which a company decides to invest in Country A but replaces the use of domestic courts with international arbitration to resolve any disputes related to its investment in Country A. In this case, the arbitration forum would be a bypass of domestic courts because it has effects in the same jurisdiction where the bypassed institution operates (Country A). Assuming that such arbitral awards can be enforced without resorting to Country A's court system, the international arbitration system performs the same function as the dominant system, as per the second requirement outlined earlier. Moreover, investors can choose to use either domestic courts or international arbitration to resolve disputes in Country A, but the systems operate independently, as per the fourth requirement.

It is important to note that simply producing effects in the same jurisdictions is not sufficient to be considered a bypass. It is also necessary that an institution offers an alternative to the existing system. Consider the hypothetical case of a company that invests in a particular country but fails to obtain a favourable resolution of a dispute in the domestic courts and then resorts to international courts in an attempt to reverse what was decided domestically. The international courts are not operating as a bypass of the domestic courts since the case proceeded through domestic courts first before reaching the international sphere. There is no choice if there is a requirement to go through one system in order to access the other (failing to meet the second requirement outlined earlier). This system is an added layer to the existing system, not a bypass.

The idea that institutional bypasses can be located in different jurisdictions and yet produce effects in the same jurisdiction is the basis for the idea of vertical bypasses. In vertical bypasses, the relevant institutions are located at different levels. For instance, in a federal regime, a federal institution can be bypassing a municipal one. In such cases, the federal institution may be trying to perform the same function as a local one (or vice versa). Both institutions will not be operating in the same jurisdiction, but one can still be operating as a bypass of the other, as long as the bypassing institution produces effects on the jurisdiction of the bypassed one. The fundamental criterion here is that the bypass has effects in the jurisdiction where the bypassed institution is operating. The concept of vertical bypass can also include instances in which international institutions bypass domestic ones, as the international arbitration example suggests.[9] In contrast, horizontal bypasses describe cases in which two or more institutions are located at the same level of government and perform the same function. In those cases, however, compliance with the requirement that the bypass produce effects within the same jurisdiction as the dominant institution amounts to a foregone conclusion.

2.1.6. *The Bypass Does Not Expressly Contradict the Requirements of the Legal System within Which It Is Operating*

Imagine the following example: to circumvent the lengthy travel times on the main route to reach City A, an organization could use motorcycles to offer the option of driving between lanes as a service to commuters. This solution could reduce travel times, but it could possibly violate speed limits and also traffic rules if motorcycles are forbidden from driving between lanes. Our focus is not on this kind of arrangement, but instead on those that would be considered legal, while offering a potential solution to those confronting problems (e.g., longer travel times) when using the dominant system.

As stated earlier, an institutional bypass is a particularly attractive reform strategy where the state possesses a *de jure* or *de facto* monopoly or quasi-monopoly in the provision of services or performance of functions. This means that the legality requirement needs to be considered both from a *de jure* and *de facto* perspective. A *de jure* state monopoly over service provision does not necessarily mean that there is a *de facto* monopoly. If new players are entering the market and offering an alternative to the dominant state system, and the state is not actively trying to curb this kind of activity, the monopoly does not exist *de facto*. These arrangements, although *de jure* illegal, are tolerated *de facto* and will be considered bypasses. In contrast, there are cases in which the state does not have a *de jure* monopoly and state provision of services or performance of functions occurs side by side with private provision. Such private providers may be considered bypasses or not, depending on whether they are part of or integrated in the dominant system. Not being part of the dominant system (offering an alternative) and trying to address one or more perceived dysfunctionalities in that system are the two conditions for such an arrangement to be considered a bypass. Therefore, the concept of bypass includes arrangements that are either

---

[9]   Mariana Mota Prado & Steven J. Hoffman, "The Concept of an International Institutional Bypass" (2017) 111 *AJIL Unbound* 231.

de jure or *de facto* legal, as long as they meet the other requirements outlined in this chapter.

While compliance with this requirement is comparatively easier to assess in the domestic sphere than in the international realm, we acknowledge that it may nonetheless present some important difficulties. Federal structures, which have already been discussed under the heading of the fifth requirement, are probably among the most important complicating factors in this respect, particularly where the various levels of government lack clearly delineated spheres of power.[10] For this reason, we propose that illegality be defined in minimalist terms even in the domestic context. A bypass will be properly recognized as such, as long as it does not expressly violate any other rules or norms that prevail within the jurisdiction in which it is operating, and these rules have not been waived by tacit acquiescence in their non-enforcement.

2.2. CASE STUDY: THE *POUPATEMPO*[11]

As outlined in Chapter 1, the *Poupatempo* (in English, "timesaver") is a one-stop shop for Brazilian citizens that allows them to interact with federal, state, and, in some cases, local administrations in one location that is easily accessible to the general public. We have argued that this initiative is characteristic of the institutional bypass concept. Having outlined its essential features in Chapter 1, we now turn to a more detailed account of *Poupatempo*, followed by an analysis of how it fits the definition of an institutional bypass.

2.2.1. *The Genesis of* Poupatempo

The *Poupatempo* is a one-stop shop for Brazilian citizens who need documents such as identity cards, drivers' licenses, and criminal records. Public utility companies also have offices at the *Poupatempo* units, where consumers can pay utility bills (electricity, water, and telephone), dispute charges, and settle debts with company representatives. In contrast to the pre-existing bureaucracy, with offices scattered throughout the city, *Poupatempo* places offices of the federal, state, and, in some cases, municipal administration in one location with easy access for the general public (normally in close proximity to subway and bus stations). This makes it easier for citizens to obtain a wide range of services. In 2017, *Poupatempo* was providing services to an average of 190,485 people a day.[12] The total number of people who

---

[10] The phenomenon of legal pluralism may also provide additional complications, as we discuss in Chapters 3 and 5.

[11] This section is largely based on Mariana Mota Prado & Ana Carolina Chasin, "How Innovative Was the Poupatempo Experience in Brazil? Institutional Bypass as a New Form of Institutional Change" (2011) 5:1 *Brazilian Political Sci Rev* 11–34.

[12] Portal Poupatempo, "Histórico de Atendimentos desde 1997: Dados Estatísticos," online: www .poupatempo.sp.gov.br

benefited from services provided by *Poupatempo* from 1997 to 2017 was approximately 530 million.[13] The project is not the only nor the first one of its kind. One-stop shops for bureaucratic services have enjoyed a significant boom in the last decade both around the world[14] and within Brazil. As of 2015, twenty-three out of twenty-five of Brazil's states had one-stop shops.[15]

The project was an initiative of the executive branch of the state of São Paulo.[16] In 1994, Mario Covas was elected governor of the state of São Paulo with an agenda of improving the provision of services to citizens and reforming the public administration. In January 1995 he was inaugurated, and one year later the project was proposed by a strategic team in charge of designing reforms.[17] In order to implement the *Poupatempo* project, Covas assembled a team of professionals with diverse backgrounds in September 1996. This team was comprised mainly of civil servants from different governmental departments, but it also included some political appointees and private sector professionals.[18] The team was in charge of designing the first unit, which later became a model for new ones. They started with a case-by-case diagnosis of the problems in primary government services, and based on this decided which problems would be tackled by the project.[19]

Some government offices did not need improvements and became part of *Poupatempo* right away, with no changes to their existing processes. One example is the public utility company for water services (Sabesp), which had an efficient system

[13] Ibid.

[14] In Brazil, the first project of this kind seems to have been the one implemented in 1995 in Bahia, entitled Serviço de Atendimento ao Cidadão ("Citizen Assistance Service"); Daniel Annenberg, Odette Gabriela Tomchinsky, & Vera Lúcia Tokairim, *Reconstruindo Valores Públicos: Padrão Poupatempo em Recomendações* (São Paulo: Imprensa Oficial, 2006) at 29; see also John Halligan, "Australia's Administrative System" in Krishna K. Tummala, ed., *Comparative Bureaucratic Systems* (Lanham, KY: Lexington Books, 2005) at 134 (indicating that in the same year that the *Poupatempo* was created, 1997, Australia implemented a one-stop shop agency, Centrelink); "Programa Nacional de Gestão Pública e Desburocratização," discussion at the Fórum Internacional de Centrais de Atendimento Integrado (1–3 June 2009) Brasília (indicating that Portugal and Spain have also adopted the one-stop shop model for bureaucratic services).

[15] *Evolução Histórica de Implantação das Centrais No Brasil,* online: www.centraisdeatendimento .sp.gov.br

[16] Veronika Paulics, "Poupa Tempo: Central de Atendimento ao Cidadão" in Gabriela Spanghero Lotta, Hélio Batista Barboza, Marco Antonio Carvalho Teixeira, & Verena Pinto, eds., *Experiências de Gestão Pública e Cidadania* (São Paulo: Programa de Gestão Pública e Cidadania, 2003), online: www .eaesp.fgvsp.br/subportais/ceapg/Acervo%20Virtual/Cadernos/Experi%C3%AAncias/2002/18%20-% 20poupatempo.pdf

[17] Annenberg, Tomchinsky, & Tokairim, *supra* note 14 at 29–30.

[18] As the superintendent reported, some of the civil servants came from governmental departments, others did not. For instance, the first team had an IT person and a human resources person from the state-owned company for data processing of the State of São Paulo (Prodesp) and two architects from the state-owned company for metropolitan planning of the State of São Paulo (Emplasa). The manager and the person responsible for the information booklet, on the other hand, were from the private sector (Interview with Daniel Annenberg, 2009).

[19] Paulics, *supra* note 16 at 6.

of consumer services.²⁰ In contrast, other offices and departments required more careful analysis of why service times were long and whether improvements could be made to expedite their delivery. An example is the State Identification Department, which formerly took up to sixty days to issue identity cards (Registro Geral, also known as RG) for residents of the state of São Paulo.²¹ In this case, the *Poupatempo* team made a diagnosis and prepared proposals in collaboration with personnel in the pre-existing bureaucracy.

2.2.2. Poupatempo's *Innovative Strategies to Improve Service Delivery*

From the outset, *Poupatempo's* goal was to guarantee access to basic governmental services expeditiously, with quality and transparency. To achieve this goal, the project used a series of strategies that can be considered "distinctive features" for our purposes.²²

First, technology was used to improve the flow of the service and to eliminate bottlenecks caused by inefficient or redundant processes. Hardware played an important role in this respect, as adopting a scanner eliminated the need to physically transport files. Eventually, a new digital system allowed the complete substitution of paper files with electronic ones. As a result of the digitization process, issuing identification cards became faster, cheaper, and more secure.²³ The use of hardware (such as scanners) was coupled with sophisticated information technology, which enabled a more efficient flow of information. For instance, *Poupatempo* created a tracking system to measure how long a user had to wait in line, how long the line was, how long each user was in contact with customer services, how productive each employee was, etc. This system allowed the manager to allocate more resources (such as personnel) to the services in greater demand.

Second, *Poupatempo* sought to improve the communication between government departments and users. For this purpose, it prepared booklets indicating all the required documents and procedures to obtain services so that users could prepare in advance. Previously, users would have to travel to a department just to obtain information about what they needed, returning later with the appropriate

---

²⁰ Sabesp is partly state-owned, partly a private company. The assessment of its efficiency in the context of this project does not refer to the delivery of water services itself, but exclusively to its ability to communicate to consumers.

²¹ It is important to note that the identity card is the primary identification document for Brazilian citizens.

²² As the adjunct secretary of the State Secretary of government and Strategic Management says, a great deal of these innovations were being discussed in Brazil since the 1970s within two institutions: Fundap and the Red Tape Ministry (Interview with Dalmo Nogueira, 2009). The focus of the state administration in 1995 was on the use of technology to improve governmental services. For a detailed description of this process, see O. Sanchez, "O Poder Burocrático e o Controle da Informação" (2003) 58 *Lua Nova* 89.

²³ Annenberg, Tomchinsky, & Tokairim, *supra* note 14 at 148–9.

documents. This would often result in misunderstandings or a lack of accurate information, and it was not uncommon for users to make three or four trips to the same office just to place a request for services. In addition to the booklets, *Poupatempo* has a call centre providing information about the services available in each unit and a list of the required documents for each service. In 2002, attempts to reduce delays further led to the creation of the Internet service called e-*Poupatempo*.[24]

Finally, another concern of the reforms was appropriate infrastructure. The building structures of *Poupatempo* units were designed to be easily accessible and comfortable for those waiting for the service to be provided. When choosing the location to install a future unit, architects would look for places situated in central areas, easily accessible by public transportation. They also sought large ventilated buildings, with high ceilings and natural sunlight. Once a building was acquired or rented, they would divide areas of circulation from service areas, and each service area would be identified by different wall colours and coloured signs. However, no walls were installed to divide different departments and offices. Instead, the units were given half-walls in order to enhance the feeling of openness and transparency.[25]

Regarding human resources, an internal selection process was instituted to identify civil servants who were willing to be transferred to a *Poupatempo* unit. They were selected through a competitive internal process, which evaluated, among other things, their capacity to interact with people, to take initiative when needed, and to be flexible and open to change. The incentive to participate in this process was a marginal salary increase, a better work place, and a more dynamic environment.[26] After the selection process, these civil servants underwent intensive training to learn how to operate the new system, and once they became employees of *Poupatempo*, they were periodically retrained.

This internal selection process, targeted at motivated civil servants, was used in 1997 and 1998, but was largely discontinued in 1999 due to complaints from the heads of offices in the pre-existing bureaucracy from which employees were being selected. They claimed that *Poupatempo* was draining their core personnel, leaving them with fewer employees than they needed due to a hiring freeze that did not

---

[24] The call centre works from Monday to Friday from 7 AM to 8 PM, and Saturday from 6:30 AM to 3 PM, which are longer hours of operation than most of the *Poupatempo* units. For details about the call centre and e-poupatempo, see www.poupatempo.sp.gov.br/epoupatempo

[25] Annenberg, Tomchinsky, & Tokairim, *supra* note 14 at 123–45.

[26] As the superintendent reports, the salaries' increase varied according to the position that the civil servant exercised. The gratification was of R$500 (US$250) per month to the receptionists, R$700 (US$350) to the tutors and R$900 (US$450) to the supervisor; Daniel Annenberg, "Diretrizes e Estratégias Para a Implantação e Manutenção de um Padrão de Qualidade na Prestação de Serviços Públicos: a Experiência Paulista do Poupatempo" in *Proceedings of the VII Congresso del Clad Sobre la Reforma del Estado y de la Administración Pública* (Lisboa, Portugal: 2002). It is important to note that the staff emphasizes that there were greater incentives in going to work in a pleasant place and in a new and promising institution. Civil servants were proud of being part of *Poupatempo* (Interview with Dalmo Nogueira, 2009).

allow them to hire replacements. As a result, in around 2000, *Poupatempo* began outsourcing its services to create new units. The contracting-out process was initially used only for some services, but it expanded over time. Starting in 2006, some of the newly created units (Osasco and Santos) were fully contracted out (i.e., the management of the entire unit is provided by a private company). By 2009, around 45 percent of the employees of the *Poupatempo* (6,695) were contract employees,[27] and the numbers appear to have increased since then.[28]

2.2.3. *Governance Structure and Resistance at Different Levels of Government*

Poupatempo needed to be housed by an institution within the state government. Housing it in the office of the governor's chief of staff would have guaranteed that *Poupatempo* would be under direct control of the governor's office. However, according to the reformers, the bureaucratic structure of this particular office was ossified, and it would have been difficult to change practices and procedures to increase efficiency and effectiveness in the decision-making process. This would have been the case, they argued, despite the governor's strong commitment to the reform.

Due to these obstacles, the governor's team decided to house the project within a separate governance structure – that is, within a state-owned company in charge of information technology and data processing (Prodesp). This company had more flexibility in managing its budget and procurement processes than the governor's office. For example, rather than potentially taking six months to hire an architect through the public tendering process, it could do so within a day. The disadvantage of housing *Poupatempo* at Prodesp, however, was that the project could not be included as a formal item in the government's budget, making its budgetary situation precarious, with no guarantee of funding from year to year. In other words, the main advantage of *Poupatempo*'s separate governance structure – operating at arm's length from existing parts of the executive – also presented risks for the project.

As already noted earlier, *Poupatempo* began as a pilot project operating in the state of São Paulo, on instructions from the state governor. However, since the governor's powers were limited to the state bureaucracy, he could not remove or

---

[27] Information given by the Superintendência do Poupatempo, May 2009.
[28] For plans to expand the contracting out, see Alexandre Araújo, "O Poupatempo e sua Nova Forma de Gestão" (Jun 1–3, 2009) presentation at the Fórum Internacional das Centrais de Atendimento Integrado, Brasília-DF, Brazil, online: www.gespublica.gov.br/biblioteca/pasta.2010-12-07.7837648486/6_terceirizacao_poupa_tempo.pdf; For resistance to the expansion, see O Globo, "Poupatempo de Ribeirão é Proibido Pela Justiça de Terceirizar Atendimento" (June 3, 2014), online: Globo, http://g1.globo.com/sp/ribeirao-preto-franca/noticia/2014/06/poupatempo-de-ribeirao-preto-e-proibido-pela-justica-de-terceirizar-mao-de-obra.html referring to the decision of 1a Vara do Trabalho de Ribeirão Preto, Processo nº 0000818-10.2014.5.15.0004.

relocate bureaucrats attached to the federal or the local level of government. In these cases, bureaucratic resistance was not so easily overcome, as the state governor needed to convince bureaucrats to support *Poupatempo*.

At the federal level, the federal police force did not agree to have a passport-issuing office at *Poupatempo* units. It claimed that *Poupatempo*'s standards of expediency would compromise Federal Police security standards, but one might wonder whether the force was afraid of losing the monopoly over the services or whether it was resisting the idea of working longer hours, since the *Poupatempo* units had extended hours of operation. Additionally, there was a possible interest in retaining rents from corruption.

At the level of the local bureaucracy, there was also resistance, but largely motivated by a different set of problems. Local bureaucracies had very low standards of service provision, and they would require significant reforms before reaching the standards that would make it possible to consider their inclusion in the *Poupatempo* project. However, most municipalities could not afford these reforms. Moreover, since reformers would need support from mayors to include local services in the *Poupatempo* units, local services were offered only in the cities in which mayors were political allies of the governor.

Some civil servants who did not have self-interested reasons to resist the reforms were also not ready to support them. The reasons for this resistance are not fully clear, but risk aversion, due to the uncertain outcomes associated with the experimental nature of the reforms, may have played a role. To overcome this resistance, the reformers used meetings and a long consultative process, in which bureaucrats in the pre-existing bureaucracy were invited to voice their concerns and suggestions. To diagnose the problems of each department or office of the government, the *Poupatempo* team gathered information about service provision in that department and then reviewed concerns in meetings with representatives from each government office. The team used these meetings and the information produced by the assessments to convince bureaucrats of the importance of the project.

The reformers implementing *Poupatempo* had to adopt a series of strategies to overcome the resistance offered by certain groups at different phases of the implementation process. Most notably, they were able to create the *Poupatempo* project in a way that did not depend on legislative approval, while not violating laws or regulations applicable to public administration in Brazil.

2.2.4. Poupatempo *as an Institutional Bypass*

Considering its main features, *Poupatempo* is a clear example of an institutional bypass. The offices of the old bureaucracy were not eliminated or replaced at the time of *Poupatempo*'s creation, thereby giving users an option to continue using the pre-existing bureaucracy or to try the new service. Indeed, an opinion poll showed that 74 percent of the people who went to *Poupatempo* units in 2008 did not consider using the pre-existing bureaucracy, an increase from 67 percent in 2006 and 70 percent in 2007.[29] Unfortunately, this poll does not seem to have been repeated since then, making it hard to assess if the trend continued. It would be especially interesting to know if the numbers continued to rise along with the increasing contracting-out of the units.

In offering an alternative, it is clear that *Poupatempo* was seeking to address dysfunctionalities in the pre-existing bureaucracy. The project was conceived as an attempt to improve the quality of services provided through creative solutions along with regular feedback mechanisms for further improvements. Once in place, *Poupatempo* gave users an option to exit the pre-existing bureaucracy and go somewhere else, while at the same time keeping the traditional service providers in place. The increasing numbers of people attending *Poupatempo*, coupled with high reported levels of satisfaction, provided persuasive evidence that users were happy with the new alternative. Surveys conducted between 2001 and 2009 show that around 97 percent of the users supported the project and 95 percent said that it provided good services to citizens.[30] In addition, between 2010 and 2014, 99 percent of users were satisfied with the services provided at *Poupatempo*.[31]

While it is clear that *Poupatempo* was supplementing the pre-existing bureaucracy, whether it was designed with the intention to displace that bureaucracy is not so easy to discern. Although some of the offices of the pre-existing bureaucracy later faded away as the *Poupatempo* project expanded (e.g., identity cards), this was a consequence of *Poupatempo*'s success, rather than its direct objective. Indeed, interviews with reformers reveal their hope that innovations produced by these reforms would have feedback effects, being later incorporated by the traditional bureaucracy, creating a virtuous cycle of change. In some cases, this actually happened, such as the digitalization project at the identification card central office.

There was at least one case in which these changes to existing institutions were drastic: the complete modification of consumer services of the Company for Urban and Housing Development in São Paulo (Companhia de Desenvolvimento Habitacional e Urbano do Estado de São Paulo [CDHU]) to meet the standards of *Poupatempo* units. Before *Poupatempo*, the company had no standardized approach to consumer services: they were executed in different ways in each department within the same company. Moreover, consumers would receive conflicting information if they called more than one department within the company. To join the

---

[29] Portal Do Governo Do Estado De São Paulo, "Pesquisa Aponta que 98% Dos Usuários Aprovam o Poupatempo" (Feb 16, 2009), online: www.saopaulo.sp.gov.br/spnoticias/ultimas-noticias/pesquisa-aponta-que-98-dos-usuarios-aprovam-o-poupatempo/

[30] Poupatempo – Resumo 2015, *supra* note 12.

[31] Portal Do Governo Do Estado De São Paulo, "Poupatempo Recebe 99% De Aprovação Dos Usuários" (Jan 25, 2015), online: www.saopaulo.sp.gov.br/spnoticias/lenoticia2.php?id=239357

Poupatempo project, CDHU had to restructure, unify, and standardize its services.[32] This new system was eventually adopted within the entire company and was not restricted to the CDHU's offices at *Poupatempo* units.

2.3. CONCLUSION

This chapter began by using the road bypass analogy to introduce the defining characteristics of the institutional bypass. It then proceeded to review the example provided by a recent experience with bureaucratic reform in Brazil, namely the *Poupatempo* project, and connected it with each of these criteria. As we have suggested earlier, it is precisely because *Poupatempo* was framed as a bypass that it was able to overcome important obstacles to reform, including the issue of scarce resources. This example supports the view that institutional bypasses are alternatives to, not replacements of, existing institutions. They can be initiated as pilot projects with small start-up costs and may be subjected to reduced political resistance.

At the same time, the *Poupatempo* example shows that there are at least three more advantages to the non-disruptive nature of institutional bypasses. First, as we have already mentioned in Chapter 1, the bypass allows for experimentation because it does not bind the policy makers to the pre-existing institution or to the initial form of the bypass. Second, if successful, the bypass may provide useful feedback on potential improvements to the traditional system. Third, reformers can easily abort the reform and revert to the existing system if something goes wrong – an important trait, considering that even the best-intentioned institutional reforms are never assured of unqualified success. In sum, it helps reformers deal with obstacles to the unintended consequences of institutional change.

[32] Célio Noffs, "O Atendimento na CDHU Antes e Depois do Poupatempo," in Annenberg, Tomchinsky, & Tokairim, *supra* note 14.

3

Institutional Bypasses and Other Reform Strategies

The obstacles to reform of dysfunctional institutions have been extensively canvassed in the academic literature,[1] as have attempts to map strategies to overcome them. Therefore, it should not come as a surprise that an institutional bypass is closely related to, but distinct from, existing concepts in the specialized literature on institutional change. One of its distinguishing features is that a bypass is a remedial strategy. Reforming the dysfunctional institution is likely to be the preferred option in most cases. An institutional bypass becomes relevant where there are significant obstacles to promoting institutional change, while at the same time there is an acknowledgement that the functions performed by the dominant institution do not meet desired standards, as defined by users. It is in this very particular (albeit not uncommon) context that the idea of an institutional bypass becomes particularly relevant.

While being distinct from numerous reform strategies due to its remedial nature, by introducing an alternative pathway without a wholesale displacement of either the dominant institution or of its rules and procedures, the concept of institutional bypass still bears a good deal of resemblance to other reform strategies, such as institutional layering and regulatory dualism. Kathleen Thelen defines institutional layering as the "grafting of new elements onto an otherwise stable institutional framework."[2] Regulatory dualism, according to Henry Hansmann, Ronald Gilson, and Mariana Pargendler, is a reform strategy where actors can elect between the status quo regime and a reformed regime, hence mitigating resistance to reform by entrenched interests.[3] The first section of this chapter explores some of the similarities and differences between these concepts and others that bear close

---

[1] For an overview, see Chapter 1.

[2] Kathleen Thelen, *How Institutions Evolve: The Political Economy of Skills in Germany, Britain, the United States and Japan* (New York: Cambridge University Press, 2004) at 35.

[3] Henry Hansmann, Ronald J. Gilson, & Mariana Pargendler, "Regulatory Dualism as a Development Strategy: Corporate Reform in Brazil, the United States, and the European Union" (2011) 63:3 *Stan L Rev* 475.

resemblance to a bypass. For definitional purposes, we indicate how the concept of institutional bypass captures a unique type of institutional engineering that has not yet been extensively discussed in the institutional reform literature.

The institutional bypass may be novel from the point of view of institutional engineering, but one may still ask whether the concept provides any added value from an analytical point of view. The intuition behind an institutional bypass is in many respects similar to the analytical framework developed by Albert Hirschman in his well-known book, *Exit, Voice and Loyalty: Responses to Decline in Firms, Organizations, and States*, published in 1970.[4] In this book, Hirschman argued that responses to decline in the performance of firms, organizations, and states typically fall into two broad categories: those that strengthen voice and those that strengthen exit. He further argued that these two classes of responses reflect something of a disciplinary divide between political scientists, who often focus on the efficacy of various kinds of voice mechanisms, and economists, who typically focus on the efficacy of consumer or citizen exit as a source of discipline for under-performing institutions or organizations. While it is clear that institutional bypasses offer an exit option to users, in the second section of this chapter we will argue that the bypass concept also offers some important analytical insights that enrich and expand Hirschman's framework.

While the concept of institutional bypass offers something novel from both a strategic and an analytical perspective relative to other concepts in the specialized institutional reform literature, it cannot be so easily distinguished from the idea of institutional multiplicity. Institutional multiplicity is a concept that has long been used in organizational theory to explore the existence of more than one institutional arrangement or option within a certain institutional field.[5] The third section will attempt to distil the constitutive elements of what is often referred to as institutional multiplicity to argue that bypasses refer to a narrower phenomenon than the one described by the concept of multiplicity.

3.1. INSTITUTIONAL LAYERING, REGULATORY DUALISM, AND BYPASSES

Among the many different concepts in the institutional reform literature that closely resemble the idea of the institutional bypass, perhaps some of the closest are the four modal types of institutional change that often characterize incremental

---

[4] Albert O. Hirschman, *Exit, Voice, and Loyalty: Responses to Decline in Firms, Organizations, and States* (Cambridge, MA: Harvard University Press, 1970).

[5] See e.g., W. Richard Scott "Institutions and Organizations: Toward a Theoretical Synthesis" in W. Richard Scott, & John W. Meyer , eds., *Institutional Environments and Organizations: Structural Complexity and Individualism* (Thousand Oaks, CA: Sage Publications, 1994) at 55–80; Elisabeth S. Clemens & James M. Cook, "Politics and Institutionalism: Explaining Durability and Change" (1999) 25:1 *Ann Rev Soc* 441; Myeong-Gu Seo & W. E. Douglas Creed, "Institutional Contradictions, Praxis, and Institutional Change: A Dialectical Perspective" (2002) 27:2 *Ac Mgmt Rev* 222; Tom Goodfellow & Stefan Lindemann, "The Clash of Institutions: Traditional Authority, Conflict and the Failure of 'Hybridity' in Buganda" (2013) 51:1 *Commonwealth & Comp Pol* 3.

institutional reform presented by James Mahoney and Kathleen Thelen.[6] First, displacement describes a scenario in which "existing rules are replaced by new ones."[7] Sometimes this kind of change may be abrupt, but displacement can also be a slow-moving process when new institutions are introduced and directly compete with pre-existing institutions. Second, "layering occurs when new rules are attached to existing ones, thereby changing the ways in which the original rules structure behaviour."[8] Third, drift takes place "when rules remain formally the same but their impact changes as a result of shifts in external conditions."[9] Finally, "conversion occurs when rules remain formally the same but are interpreted and enacted in new ways."[10] Between these four concepts, institutional layering and displacement are probably the most similar to an institutional bypass, since they also refer to modes of institutional change that graft a new pathway onto an old system.[11] There are, however, important differences that distinguish both of these concepts from the institutional bypass.

Displacement, which occurs when existing rules are replaced by new ones, is the end result of a process of institutional change. This change can occur gradually, and this process *may* be associated with a bypass. After a certain period of time, an institutional bypass *may* lead to displacement of the dominant institution, although this will not always or even ideally be the case (see Chapter 1). However, not all displacements are necessarily preceded by bypasses. For instance, privatization can be defined as displacement of a public provider by a private one; but it is not a bypass, as the pre-existing institution does not remain in place.

For its part, institutional layering as defined by Mahoney and Thelen is distinct from a bypass because it involves the "grafting of new elements onto an otherwise stable institutional framework"[12]; that is it "does not introduce wholly new institutions or rules, but rather involves amendments, revisions or additions to existing ones."[13] The example they provide is the introduction of a voucher option to an existing school system, which would not qualify as an institutional bypass since it does not offer an alternative institutional pathway (i.e., there is no separate governance structure performing the same function as the existing school system).

---

[6] James Mahoney & Kathleen Thelen, eds., *Explaining Institutional Change: Ambiguity, Agency, and Power* (Cambridge, MA: Cambridge University Press, 2010); the concepts were originally formulated by Wolfgang Streeck & Kathleen Thelen, eds., *Beyond Continuity: Institutional Change in Advanced Political Economies* (Oxford, UK: Oxford University Press, 2005).

[7] James Mahoney & Kathleen Thelen, "A Theory of Gradual Institutional Change" in Mahoney & Thelen, *supra* note 6.

[8] Ibid.

[9] Ibid.

[10] Ibid.

[11] See Chapter 2.

[12] Thelen, *supra* note 2 at 35.

[13] Mahoney & Thelen, *supra* note 7.

Another important difference is that some types of layering simply superimpose "amendments, revisions or additions" onto the system instead of maintaining two parallel institutions that perform the same function and offer a choice to users.[14] A good example is the creation of budget committees in the United States, which Eric Schickler describes as layering: "The Congressional Budget and Impoundment Control Act of 1974 superimposed the new budget committees on a decades-old structure of authorization, appropriations, and revenue committees. The budget committee task of integrating fiscal policy was complicated because they had to work with committees that did not have a stake in the success of the new process."[15] While the budget committee keeps certain elements in place, it also changes the way the system works. To be a bypass, one would have to imagine a system where the new budget committees operate independently and in parallel to the pre-existing committees, with both systems performing the same function.[16] Thus, this example is not a bypass because it does not offer an alternative pathway while maintaining the dominant institution in place.

Despite these distinctions, there are still conceptual similarities between the concept of layering and bypass, such as political economy factors, which in both cases involves "a partial renegotiation of elements of a given set of institutions while leaving others in place."[17] As a result of this similarity, it is possible that layering may result in the creation of an institutional bypass as illustrated by the example that Thelen provides of Germany's vocational training system in the late nineteenth century. The system was centred on master artisans, whose apprenticeship was the sole means of obtaining a "skilled worker" certificate. The artisans (in the handicraft sector) therefore had absolute control over the supply of skilled labour – a source of frustration for the machine industry that employed most of the certificate-bearing youths in their factories. The industry therefore sought to establish its own training process (one bearing official government recognition) and was successful, resulting

---

[14] Graham Denyer Willis & Mariana Mota Prado, "Process and Pattern in Institutional Reforms: The Police Pacifying Units in Brazil as an Institutional Bypass" (2014) 64 *World Dev* 232. https://doi.org/ 10.1016/j.worlddev.2014.06.006 at 235

[15] Eric Schickler, *Disjointed Pluralism: Institutional Innovation and the Development of the U.S. Congress* (Princeton, NJ: Princeton University Press, 2001) at 16.

[16] It is unclear whether such a bypass would be possible in the context of fiscal policy, or any other rule-making process for that matter. While institutions that deliver services to users can easily function in a parallel fashion and even compete with each other, it is unclear how such competition could manifest in a rule-making context. To be sure, democracies do have a competitive process in which parties can compete to control the rule-making institution, but we have not designed a system wherein two rule-making institutions compete with each while engaging in the rule-making process. This is one of the reasons why we have defined the alternative pathway created by the bypass as solely related to delivery of government services and discharging of government functions.

[17] Kathleen Thelen, "The Political Economy of Business and Labor in the Developed Democracies: Agency and Structure in Historical Institutional Perspective" in Ira Katznelson & Helen Milner, eds., *Political Science: The State of the Discipline* (New York: American Political Science Assn, 2002) at 225.

in a layering of an alternative accreditation pathway on the existing one offered by the handicraft chambers. The outcome, Thelen concludes, is that Germany's vocational training system underwent an institutional change, as its developmental trajectory pulled away from a decentralized and non-standardized system under the apprenticeship model towards a uniform and centralized management of skill formation. The establishment of the alternative accreditation committee by Germany's machine industry, as described by Thelen, could be characterized as an institutional bypass as the new entity performed the same function (offering accreditation) as the handicraft chambers. In sum, while bypasses cannot be described as institutional layering, the process of layering could involve or result in an institutional bypass.

Regulatory dualism is another concept that is very similar to institutional bypasses.[18] Henry Hansmann, Ronald Gilson, and Mariana Pargendler describe it as the creation of a second regulatory regime (the reformist regime), while maintaining the pre-existing regime.[19] They distinguish regulatory dualism from regulatory diversification by the fact that diversification is used when the regulated actors are not homogeneous and thus need a menu of regulatory options to satisfy different needs. By contrast, regulatory dualism is used when the actors are homogeneous, but the regime has been captured by a subset of these actors for their private benefit. In this case, regulatory dualism provides an exit option to those actors that do not benefit from the existing regime, while reducing resistance to reforms from those that captured the system for their benefit. Like institutional bypasses, instances of regulatory dualism aim to create alternatives to those trapped in a dysfunctional system that is hard to reform. Both bypasses and dualism keep a pre-existing and dysfunction regulatory or institutional arrangement in place to reduce resistance to reform, while offering a new option to users.

The main conceptual difference between institutional bypasses and regulatory dualism is the latter's lack of a separate governance structure. Bypasses are characterized by the existence of distinct institutions operating independently. By contrast, the cases of regulatory dualism discussed by Hansmann, Gilson, and Pargendler seem to involve a single institution offering a menu of regulatory regimes from which actors can choose. While this may be an effective strategy to overcome resistance to reform and promote change, it is feasible only in cases where there is willingness and power to reform the institution from the inside, as was the case of the Brazilian Stock Exchange that implemented a menu of governance structures for companies publicly trading their shares (known as "New Market" or "*Novo Mercado*"). Institutional bypasses become an appealing reform strategy when there is insufficient political support inside the institution to promote change through regulatory dualism, or when the functions performed by the dominant institution cannot be translated into a menu of options. An example of the latter arises in policing, which is by definition

---

[18] Hansmann, Gilson, & Pargendler, *supra* note 3.
[19] Ibid. at 481.

coercive, and therefore presents limited opportunities for preferences to be voiced on an individual basis.

It is important to note that the separate governance structure in bypasses does not require a completely independent institution. In many cases, the bypassing and the bypassed institutions are both answering to and housed within the same umbrella institution. For instance, the units of *Poupatempo* are within the executive branch in the state of São Paulo, reporting to the office of the state governor, as is the old bureaucracy. This is, however, different from the arrangement described under the label "regulatory dualism": while bypasses are still answerable to the same central authority, they are operationally independent of the pre-existing institution. In contrast, in the New Market reforms described by Hansmann, Gilson, and Pargendler, those applying the old rules are also managing the new ones.

The distinction between institutional bypasses, layering, and regulatory dualism can be illustrated with judicial reforms. An example of layering in the judicial context is the creation of special "judicial bancs" (*varas especializadas*) to evaluate money-laundering cases in Brazil. The initiative was implemented as an option for federal tribunals in 2003,[20] and these specialized judicial bancs became mandatory for federal appeals tribunals in 2013.[21] This is a case of layering because it adds a new tier into the system, but it does not create a separate governance structure. A separate governance structure may be created with new courts, but if they have exclusive jurisdiction, they are not bypasses, because they are not alternatives to the pre-existing institution. For instance, debt recovery tribunals (DRTs) were established by the government of India under an Act of Parliament (Act 51 of 1993)[22] as an executive arm of the government. DRTs fall under the purview of the Ministry of Finance, unlike civil and criminal courts, which are part of the judiciary. Yet they have exclusive jurisdiction to deal with debt owed to banks and financial institutions, along with the Debt Recovery Appellate Tribunals.[23] DRTs and other courts with exclusive jurisdiction may be a case of layering designed to expedite debt recovery,[24] but they are not cases of institutional bypasses, as there is no choice to take the claim to one system or another.

New courts will only be bypasses if they have partial or complete overlapping jurisdiction with pre-existing courts. An example of a judicial bypass could be found in Indonesia where the creation of a Corruption Eradication Commission (Komisi Pemberantasan Korupsi or KPK) was accompanied by a specialized parallel anti-corruption court (The Indonesian Court for Corruption Crimes or Tipikor Court).[25]

---

[20] CJF Resolutions 314/03 and 517/06.

[21] CJF Resolution 273/13.

[22] *Recovery of Debts Due to Banks and Financial Institutions Act*, 1993, online: Debt Recovery Tribunal, www.drt.co.in/

[23] *Recovery of Debts Due to Banks and Financial Institutions Act*, 1993, ss 17, 18.

[24] Sujata Visaria, "Legal Reform and Loan Repayment: The Microeconomic Impact of Debt Recovery Tribunals in India" (2009) 1:3 *Am Econ J: Applied Econ* 59.

[25] Simon Butt, "Indonesia's Anti-Corruption Drive and the Constitutional Court" (2009) 4:2 *Comp L J* 186; Sofie Arjon Schütte, "Appointing Top Officials in a Democratic Indonesia: The Corruption

Created in 2002, the court's purpose was "to circumvent entirely a judicial system known to be complicit in protecting corruptors, and – at the very least – capable of being unresponsive or incompetent in the administration of justice."[26] However, the centralized anti-corruption court has ceased to be a bypass, as the jurisdiction to hear anti-corruption cases now rests exclusively in new specialized courts located in the capitals of each of Indonesia's provinces, rather than in Jakarta.[27] This 2009 reform was in response to an Indonesian Supreme Court decision that declared the anti-corruption court unconstitutional because the dual-track system was considered a violation of "equality before the law."[28] The Indonesia case before the 2009 reform shows that where new courts and regular courts have overlapping jurisdiction, they can be considered institutional bypasses.

Regular courts can also adopt different procedures for cases above or below a certain amount. This is not a case of an institutional bypass because there may be no choice, and there is no separate governance structure. These distinct rules of procedure can be classified as either regulatory diversification or regulatory dualism, depending on whether they aim at serving the different needs of a heterogeneous constituency or serve as a strategy to bypass resistance to reform by a relatively homogeneous constituency.

The example of regulatory diversification or regulatory dualism also illustrates one of the important limitations of institutional bypasses, namely that it is difficult to conceive how an institutional bypass can be used for policy-making or rule-making institutions. While there is much debate as to whether competition in the provision of public services is desirable or not, it is at least conceivable that service providers can run parallel operations (even if this may lead to inefficiencies in those cases involving natural monopolies, such as electricity transmission and distribution), and even compete with each other. By contrast, it is conceptually harder to envision the same type of duplication and parallel operation in the rule-making and policy-making context, unless the institutions are located in different jurisdictions. To use a bypass in this context, it would be necessary to design a system where two

---

Eradication Commission" (2011) 47:3 *Bull Indonesian Econ Stud* 355; Sofie Arjon Schütte, "Against the Odds: Anti-Corruption Reform in Indonesia" (2012) 32:1 *Pub Admin & Dev* 38.

[26] Stewart Fenwick, "Measuring Up? Indonesia's Anti-Corruption Commission and the New Corruption Agenda" in Tim Lindsey, ed., *Indonesia: Law and Society* 2nd edn. (Leichhardt: Federation Press, 2008) at 413. Despite being formally a chamber of the Central Jakarta District Court and lacking financial autonomy, the Indonesian Court for Corruption Crimes was physically located outside of the District Court, followed different procedural rules, and had a mandated majority of ad hoc (rather than career) judges, who were recruited from outside the judiciary; Simon Butt & Sofie Arjon Schütte, "Assessing Judicial Performance in Indonesia: The Court for Corruption Crimes" (2014) 62:5 *Crime L Soc Change* 603 at 609–10.

[27] Butt & Schütte, *supra* note 26 at 609–10.

[28] Simon Butt, "Anti-Corruption Reform in Indonesia: An Obituary?" (2012) 47:3 *Bull Indonesian Econ Stud* 381; Simon Butt & Sofie Arjon Schütte, "The Indonesian Court for Corruption Crimes: Circumventing Judicial Impropriety?" (Sep 2013) *U4 Brief* 5.

rule-making institutions can operate simultaneously in the same jurisdiction, while citizens can freely choose which set of rules to follow.[29]

To be sure, democracies do have ex-ante competitive processes to choose their representatives, but the winner obtains a "monopoly" in law-making functions. Yet in many developing countries there are parallel, informal, and unofficial systems of rules and norms that tend to offer an alternative to citizens. The seminal study of the Brazilian slums (*favelas*) conducted by Boaventura de Souza Santos documents the complexities but also the importance of these arrangements.[30] However, there are conceptual and practical difficulties in conceiving of alternative rule-making regimes as bypasses. This is beyond the scope of this book, which focuses on bypasses for the delivery of government services.

Ben Ross Schneider is one of the few authors who explicitly uses the concept of "institutional bypass" to describe the creation of a state-owned company (*Açominas*) during the military dictatorship in Brazil.[31] Despite opposition to the creation of the company by experts in the sector, the president decided to move ahead with the project to obtain political support in the region where the company operated. Schneider concludes that if the technical concerns voiced by bureaucrats had been taken into consideration and a compromise between political interests and technical concerns had been reached, the project could have avoided many of the problems it faced. In Schneider's book, the notion of a bypass is used to mean a process by which not all the stakeholders and relevant actors are consulted. This phenomenon is different from the one described in this book, because it refers to the process of bypassing relevant groups, stakeholders, and public opinion without producing two separate institutions performing the same function.

However, Schneider's analysis does call attention to the fact that while a bypass can help overcome undesirable (and often self-interested) resistance to reforms, it can also be used to overcome desirable and legitimate resistance. As mentioned in Chapter 1, this risk requires caution in evaluating when and why institutional bypasses are desirable strategies to overcome resistance to reforms.

3.2. THE VOICE-CHOICE NEXUS

In analyzing the concept of an institutional bypass, one is confronted with the question of whether the use of bypasses as an exit option for public services raises similar issues to those analyzed by Albert Hirschman in *Exit, Voice and Loyalty*. In his map

---

[29] For a discussion of this possibility in the international sphere, see Mariana Mota Prado & Steven J. Hoffman, "The Concept of an International Institutional Bypass" (2017) 111 *AJIL Unbound* 231.

[30] Boaventura de Sousa Santos, "The Law of the Oppressed: The Construction and Reproduction of Legality in Pasargada" (1977) 12:1 *L & Soc Rev*, online: www.boaventuradesousasantos.pt/media/The%20law%20of%20the%20oppressed_1978.pdf

[31] Ben Ross Schneider, *Politics within the State: Elite Bureaucrats and Industrial Policy in Authoritarian Brazil* (Pittsburgh, PA: University of Pittsburgh, 1991) ch. 7 at 122–45.

of the complex interaction of voice and exit mechanisms as sources of discipline for institutional or organizational shortcomings, Hirschman describes the possible interactions between the public and private provision of government services, aiming to build a bridge between the efficiency focus that often informs economic analyses and the legitimacy concerns embedded in a political science perspective.

For example, if exiting the system is possible, in the case of public services, the most influential and articulate citizens with alternative sources of service provision more readily available to them may exit first. This leaves poorer, less articulate, and less influential citizens trapped in a dysfunctional public service regime, which may deteriorate further, given the attenuation of voice by more influential and articulate citizens. In such a case, exit may in fact exacerbate institutional decline. On the other hand, Hirschman recognized that if all citizens were trapped in a dysfunctional public provision regime lacking even the threat of exit, exclusive reliance on voice mechanisms to discipline what would, in effect, be a public monopoly over the relevant class of goods or services may induce anemic or minimal responses by public authorities. This would perhaps be conditional on the responsiveness of the broader political system in the country to citizen concerns, the worst-case scenario being one in which the political system does not create incentives for the government to be responsive to citizens' concerns. In other words, voice and exit are sometimes substitutes and sometimes complements.

While the conceptual framework of exit-voice is extremely useful, and its application extends far beyond the limited confines of the debate about the public and private provision of government services, several early reviewers of Hirschman's book (e.g., Joseph Reid, Gordon Tullock, Louis Schwartz, and Brian Barry)[32] make the point, in one form or another, that his implicit model of a socially optimal mix of voice and exit in reducing or mitigating organizational slack or decline is seriously under-specified and indeterminate.

Even in purely private markets, there is a great deal of structural indeterminacy as to the pre-requisites for effective competition. There is a vast industrial organization literature that attempts to evaluate theoretically and empirically the welfare implications of alternative market structures. In an anti-trust or competition policy context, this literature seeks to evaluate the competitive implications of exit by existing firms through bankruptcy or merger or acquisition, and barriers to entry for new firms. Other strands of literature attempt to evaluate the impact of technological

---

[32] Joseph D. Reid Jr, "Book Review: Albert O. Hirschman (1970). Exit, Voice, and Loyalty: Responses to Decline in Firms, Organizations, and States" (1973) 81:4 *J Political Econ* 1042; Gordon Tullock, "Book Review: Albert O. Hirschman (1970). Exit, Voice, and Loyalty: Responses to Decline in Firms, Organizations, and States" (1970) 25:5 *J Fin* 1194; Louis B. Schwartz, "Book Review. Albert O. Hirschman (1970). Exit, Voice, and Loyalty: Responses to Decline in Firms, Organizations, and States" (1972) 120:6 *U Pa L Rev* 1210; Brian Barry, "Book Review: Albert O. Hirschman (1970). Exit, Voice, and Loyalty: Responses to Decline in Firms, Organizations, and States" (1974) 4:1 *Brit J Pol Sci* 79.

innovation on competitive dynamics in a market and sometimes seek to distinguish sustaining innovations pursued by incumbents from disruptive innovations often introduced by new entrants.[33] As to whether highly concentrated markets seriously deviate from perfectly competitive ideals, there are literally dozens of models of oligopolistic markets that predict behaviour ranging from tightly explicit or tacit collusion (in effect, monopolistic behaviour) to perfectly competitive behaviour.

Once one moves away from purely private markets to public–private arrangements, which are one of Hirschman's concerns, the indeterminacy is even more acute, as the state is both provider and regulator. Thus, whether enlarging the range of choices open to consumers (and hence their exit options) will lead to recuperation of the dominant or incumbent provider or further degeneration in the quality of services will largely be determined by the terms that the state itself (i.e., the controller of the dominant provider) chooses to impose on alternative suppliers (whether public or private). In other words, the state largely controls the relative domains of voice and choice in this context and hence the potential social welfare outcomes of adjusting the voice-choice mix is endogenous to the decision calculus. This is analogous to a monopolist in private markets being vested with legal authority to determine the terms in which it will permit competitive challenges to its monopoly, although a monopolist's objective function may be relatively clear (profit maximization), while that of the state is likely to be much more complex (ranging from the virtuous to the venal, and everything in between). In sum, there is an intrinsic tension in the state's role as provider and regulator, and the political economy factors involved in resolving this tension make it quite uncertain as to which institutional arrangement (if any) will lead to socially optimal outcomes.

These charges of indeterminacy are applicable to Hirschman's framework because his analysis seems driven by a quest for an optimal once-and-for-all voice-choice arrangement to prevent institutional decay. We do not embrace this quest, as we do not see any reason to make a once-and-for-all decision on a particular institutional arrangement. Instead, we embrace indeterminacy. Both Hirschman's book and our book begin with the premise that state provision of services may become dysfunctional, raising the question of what remedies can be used to address such dysfunction. The difference is that Hirschman's analysis focuses on preventing such decay and the existence of permanent mechanisms (exit or voice) that could potentially discipline service providers on an ongoing basis. The institutional bypass concept, by contrast, is remedial and may be purely experimental and transitional. Rather than preventing decay, it comes into play when the decay has already occurred. As a remedial solution, the institutional bypass is the second-best option, since reforming the dysfunctional institution may be the preferred course of action whenever feasible. While the bypass may aim at ultimately reversing the decay that characterizes the existing

---

[33] See Clayton M. Christensen, *The Innovator's Dilemma: When New Technologies Cause Great Firms to Fail* (Boston: Harvard Business School Press, 1997).

institutional arrangement, the bypass itself is not offered as a solution, but instead as a mechanism to search for such solution. And this search for solutions can be experimental in nature. Bypasses can proceed incrementally, in a trial- and error fashion, and can be modified over time to adapt to new information or changing circumstances. In some cases, bypasses will be solely a temporary solution that will ignite the process of institutional change. Reformers could use the bypass to disturb a stable equilibrium where there were significant obstacles to reforms, or to explore possible alternatives through experiments. In either of these cases, the institutional bypass may be only useful for a period of time.

We also depart from Hirschman's excessively narrow concept of voice, which ignores a range of voice mechanisms, especially in the private sector. Complaints regimes, consumer product and service ratings, and generous return policies are opportunities for voice in the private sector. These become especially relevant where technological innovation, such as electronic forms of communication, re-define and re-structure traditional forms of interaction and change the dynamics of long-existing governance structures. Thus, firms are not only constrained by the prospect of exit but also by opportunities of voice for their consumers. This suggests that most sectors operate with a complex mix of exit and voice at play. Moreover, as a regulator, the state may not only determine the range of choices for consumers (as discussed earlier) but also the voice options. For instance, return policies may be governed by consumer protection laws. Thus, in many contexts, the scope of consumers' voice is not exogenously determined but dictated by the state itself as the regulator.

By adopting this broader concept of voice, we reject the sharply drawn distinction between exit and voice. A bypass may offer enhanced voice through the exit option. While an institutional bypass may attract users simply by virtue of its offering a higher-quality service or superior performance, it may also be able to attract them by offering a comparable service in an institutional setting that offers mechanisms for consumers/citizens to exercise voice. In such cases, the decision of users to exercise the exit option (that is, to leave the dysfunctional institution in favour of the bypass) may be determined not only by the actual quality of the product/service offered but also by the institutional mechanisms that allow them to influence performance and avoid decline. The voice mechanisms may be important to signal to citizens/consumers the commitment to maintain continuous improvement of the services or products. This, in turn, could create loyalty to the bypass. Hirschman's theory of loyalty assumes that voice and loyalty are self-reinforcing features: higher levels of loyalty may increase the likelihood that the member of an organization may use voice, while the likelihood of voice increases the degree of loyalty. Institutional bypasses can therefore build in voice mechanisms that reduce the willingness of users to return to the pre-existing institution. The *Poupatempo* may be an example of voice options for citizens/consumers: new units were often created during electoral years; and there was constant improvement of the services based on consumers' feedback.

Another way in which our analysis differs from Hirschman's framework is by considering a factor that is largely neglected in Hirschman's analysis: the possibility that the exit option is provided and operated by the state itself, generating public–public competition. This possibility is not addressed by Hirschman, and it is at the heart of the concept of institutional bypass. Indeed, the *Poupatempo* case discussed in Chapters 1 and 2 of the book is an example of an exit option where the institution offering more efficient bureaucratic services (identity cards, drivers' licenses, etc.) is state-funded and state-run. The possibility of the state providing the exit option significantly changes the dynamic of the interaction between the two institutions, as the state has much more control over the choices offered and how the dynamic interaction may unfold than is the case in those scenarios that Hirschman contemplated. We call these intentional bypasses, and they will be discussed in greater detail in Chapter 4.

Despite these differences, a number of important features of Hirschman's analysis are relevant to the discussion of institutional bypasses. One is his cautionary note about the consequences of offering an exit option. This, according to him, could end up undermining any voice mechanism in the existing system. The same applies to bypasses: alternative pathways may be provided by a group of well-intentioned policy makers who want to empower a diffused and disorganized group of users who are oppressed by a concentrated and organized group of bureaucrats within a particular institution. But it can also be provided by a group of reformers who are using exit or exit with voice as a way of mitigating the most pressing problems, while at the same time reducing pressures for more radical and essential reforms.[34] These issues illustrate an important set of concerns: when the state determines the choices that it will make available to users, political economy considerations substantially complicate any predictions as to the long-term social welfare implications of particular voice-choice mixes, as is equally true of institutional bypasses.

3.3. INSTITUTIONAL MULTIPLICITY AND BYPASSES

This section turns to yet another concept that bears strong resemblance to institutional bypass: institutional multiplicity. This notion has been defined as a means of

---

[34] For example,

> people have criticized the idea of a "notarial citizenship" that is promoted by *Poupatempo*. The claim is that the Brazilian state requires too many documents, stamps and seals of approval from its citizens (i.e. citizens depend on notary services for most of their activities). It might be argued then that we should not be providing these services in a more efficient way. Instead, we should be getting rid of the need for Brazilian citizens to have so many government documents. Thus, the reform should be aiming at eliminating the requirement, not allowing citizens to obtain them faster. And the problem is that the creation of *Poupatempo* might just reinforce this "notarial" system, making it more difficult to implement reforms that eliminate it down the road

Mariana Mota Prado, "Institutional Bypass: An Alternative for Development Reform" (Apr 9, 2011), online: SSRN, https://ssrn.com/abstract=1815442

understanding multiple rule systems "that confront economic and political actors providing distinct and different normative frameworks and incentive structures in which they act."[35] It has been employed in a wide variety of contexts, including in the analysis of whether and how traditional authorities are integrated into the structure of modern state structures in Africa. For example, Goodfellow and Lindeman argue that cases in which traditional authorities have retained the power over customary or local affairs can be described as institutional multiplicity. Institutional multiplicity, thus allows for the coexistence of formal and informal institutions separated from each other. Multiplicity is distinct from cases in which informal rules and procedures are integrated or embedded within those associated with the state; these are described as institutional hybridity. According to Goodfellow and Lindeman, some types of multiplicity – those in which non-state and state institutions have overlapping functions, which they call discordant institutional multiplicity – are more likely to generate conflict than others.[36] Another example of institutional multiplicity involves the strategic use of formal and informal institutions by authoritarian regimes to adapt to and resist change.[37]

The political science literature has tended to use multiplicity in the manner evinced by the earlier examples – that is, to analyze the mechanisms, patterns, and processes of institutional change and stability.[38] Many sociologists, in turn, have relied on the concept to analyze heterogeneity in models of action, especially those in processes that culminate in the loss of social order or growth of social entropy.[39] While the focus of these analyses may be distinct, these two strands of the literature largely seem to explore the same phenomenon: the possibility that the existence of more than one institutional option may change individuals' choices and behaviours, and in turn may promote change (or further reinforce the status quo).[40]

Focusing on cases in which institutional multiplicity generates change, Clemens and Cook argue that a lack of institutional alternatives can generate regularities of social action, which are then taken for granted.[41] In this context, the creation or

35 Gabi Hesselbein, Frederick Golooba-Mutebi, & James Putzel, "Economic and Political Foundations of State Making in Africa: Understanding State Reconstruction" (2006) LSE Crisis States Research Centre Working Paper No. 3 at 1.
36 Goodfellow & Lindemann, *supra* note 5.
37 See e.g., Frederick Golooba-Mutebi & Sam Hickey, "The Master of Institutional Multiplicity? The Shifting Politics of Regime Survival, State-Building and Democratisation in Museveni's Uganda" (2016) 10:4 *J E Afr Stud* 601 at 601–2.
38 Thelen, *How Institutions Evolve, supra* note 2; Mahoney & Thelen, *Explaining Institutional Change, supra* note 6; Streeck & Thelen, *supra* note 6.
39 Clemens & Cook *supra* note 5.
40 See e.g., Anne Tempel & Peter Walgenbach, "Subsidiary Managers and the Transfer of Human Resource Practices in Multinational Companies – Institutional Work at the Intersection of Multiple Institutional Frameworks" (2012) 64:3 *Schmalenbach Bus Rev* 230; Anne-Claire Pache & Filipe M. Santos, "When Worlds Collide: The Internal Dynamics of Organizational Responses to Conflicting Institutional Demands" (2010) 35:3 *Ac Mgmt Rev* 455.
41 Clemens & Cook *supra* note 5 at 446.

existence of alternative institutional paths can generate contradictions that destabilize these existing regularities of action.[42] More specifically, institutional multiplicity has the potential to generate an external contradiction, that is, the behavioural regularities observed in one institution are challenged by contradictory behavioural patterns followed by another institution. As discussed by Clemens and Cook, two potential mechanisms can effect change in behavioural patterns: socialization and institutional incentives.[43] Thus, while the creation of formal institutions that offer alternative paths may modify behaviour, it does not exclude the possibility that these changes may also be caused at least in part by informal mechanisms, such as the socialization of actors in a different institutional culture.

From a legal perspective, the concept of multiplicity is evident in multiple forms of legal pluralism. Scholars who embrace this concept emphasize that many, if not most, societies embrace contending normative orders (e.g., formal state laws, religion/ethics/morality [natural laws] and customary norms of behaviour) that interact with each other in complex and dynamic processes entailing constant adjustments and accommodations.[44] Some argue that pluralistic legal systems may borrow liberally from one another to achieve a mixture of rules and procedures that will attract popular support, thus emerging as the most "legitimate" system in the eyes of the public.[45] This dynamic, however, seems to largely depend on how the interaction between the coexisting legal systems is structured. An example previously explored by one of us is the British colonies.[46] Colonizers were forced to make calculated decisions concerning the potential confluence and contradictions among the British and indigenous legal institutions. Across the empire, the British processes of establishing and developing jurisdictional allocation arrangements resulted in divergent approaches to the integration/separation of native and transplanted institutions. In so-called integrated jurisdictions, the legal systems, while still functioning semi-autonomously, regularly interacted, drawing on one another and promoting the creation of a relatively consistent corpus of law that could be retained by the colony post-independence. In contrast, in parallel jurisdictional models, the segregation of the British and native legal regimes impeded mutually advantageous institutional adaptation and thwarted the realization of robust rule of law outcomes.[47]

---

[42] Seo & Creed, *supra* note 5; Tammar B. Zilber, "Institutional Multiplicity in Practice: A Tale of Two High-Tech Conferences in Israel" (2011) 22:6 *Org Sci* 1539.

[43] Clemens & Cook, *supra* note 5.

[44] Werner Menski, *Comparative Law in a Global Context: The Legal Systems of Asia and Africa* (New York: Cambridge University Press, 2006); Michael Barry Hooker, *Legal Pluralism: An Introduction to Colonial and Neo-Colonial Laws* (Oxford, UK: Carendon Press, 1975).

[45] Donald L. Horowitz, "The Qu'ran and the Common Law: Islamic Law Reform and the Theory of Legal Change" (1994) 42:2 *Am J Comp L* 233.

[46] Ronald J. Daniels, Michael J. Trebilcock, & Lindsey Carson, "The Legacy of Empire: The Common Law Inheritance and Commitments to Legality in Former British Colonies" (2011) 59:1 *Am J Comp L* 111 at 152.

[47] Ibid.

The concepts of legal multiplicity and legal pluralism describe a multiplicity of legal orders. While both are relevant for our analysis, these concepts describe a much broader phenomenon than the one captured by the concept of institutional bypass. These co-existing legal orders may have competing institutions performing the same function, which can be characterized as bypasses. In other words, we are focusing on a narrow sub-set of cases of multiplicity and legal pluralism. Among the case studies in this book, the concept of multiplicity or legal pluralism is most evident in the *Lok Adalats* in India, which are traditional forms of informal dispute resolution that have provided an alternative to the formal court system for personal grievances.[48] The multiplicity exists because *Lok Adalats* are not adjudicating cases and applying existing laws in the same manner as courts, focusing instead on facilitating the parties to reach a compromise/settlement amicably.[49] Yet they serve as bypasses because they are conceived as institutions that offer an option to citizens seeking mechanisms to resolve disputes.[50] Indeed, their revival has been partly a response to dysfunctions in the formal legal system. One may also view the case study of *centrais sindicais*, or central unions, in Brazil[51] in the early 1980s as exemplifying a kind of bypass that would involve legal pluralism. The central unions were parallel institutions that tried to bypass indirectly dysfunctional labour unions controlled by an autocratic state by offering workers' groups an option of effective and legitimate labour representation and rights protection. Thus, these institutions were performing the same functions as the dominant institutions but did so by providing access to a different set of rules and norms than the ones prevailing in the dominant system.

As the concept of bypass is focused on the institution delivering services (rather than on the normative order that informs it), it is possible that informal institutions will serve as bypasses of formal ones, and vice versa. For instance, one could imagine a case in which the pre-colonial informal institutions were displaced by formal systems imposed by the colonizer. The dysfunctionalities that the formal system may develop over time, however, may force the government to implement reforms to revive the informal institutions. In such a case, informal institutions are initially bypassed by formal ones, but if these formal institutions become dysfunctional, the revival of the informal institutions become bypasses themselves.

The concept of institution adopted in this book is also narrower than the one adopted by those using the concept of institutional multiplicity. While the latter refers to the expansive new institutionalism concept of "the rules of the game," we prefer to use the concept of institutions to refer to entities that enact, implement,

---

[48] See Chapter 5.

[49] *The Legal Services Authorities Act*, 1987, s 20(5).

[50] Hon'ble Dr. Justice Bharat Bhushan Parsoon, "Domain and Sweep of Lok Adalats and Legal Literacy: An Indian Perspective" (2015) XVI: 1 Nyaya Deep: The official journal of NALSA, online: NALSA https://nalsa.gov.in/sites/default/files/publication%20pdf/Nyaya%20Deep-January,%202015.pdf

[51] See Chapter 4.

administer, and adjudicate these rules and norms, as discussed in Chapter 2. In light of this distinction, there may be institutional bypasses where there is institutional multiplicity: the bypasses would be the organizations that provide an alternative to the existing system of rules and norms (and thus provide access to the alternative system).

Despite the differences between the concepts of institutional multiplicity and bypass, these arrangements have particular advantages in overcoming entrenched barriers to institutional change. The establishment of an alternative communicates to parties both within and outside a pre-existing institution that the status quo is not inevitable or immutable.[52] It thus introduces the possibility of a new institutional framework that may lead to stronger performance and superior outcomes. Moreover, outright and abrupt institutional displacement – the supplantation of one institution by a new one – may generate intense opposition from constituencies invested in (or who benefit under) the current framework. Institutional bypasses and multiplicity can create displacement over time and in the long term, but in the short term they leave intact existing institutions and provide alternative paths for achieving the same or similar objectives.[53] For this reason, these arrangements may provoke less direct antagonism.[54] Finally, the presence of multiple institutional referents "enlarges the toolbox from which reformers can draw in crafting new solutions, facilitating deeper change."[55]

3.4. CONCLUSION

In this chapter, we provided an overview of concepts that have similarities with the institutional bypass but yet are distinct from it. The concept of institutional bypass exhibits many features of important concepts developed in the academic literature, while offering something conceptually and strategically different on institutional change and institutional reform. The next two chapters turn to concrete examples of bypasses with a series of case studies.

---

[52] See Zilber, *supra* note 42 at 1540.

[53] See Mahoney & Thelen, *Explaining Institutional Change, supra* note 6, describing slow-moving displacement: "[D]isplacement exists when existing rules are replaced by new ones. This kind of change may well be abrupt, and it may entail the radical shift that is often featured in leading institutional theories. Yet, displacement can also be a slow-moving process. This may occur when new institutions are introduced and directly compete (rather than supplement) an older set of institutions."

[54] See Schickler, *supra* note 15 at 252.

[55] Matt Andrews, *The Limits of Institutional Reform in Development: Changing Rules for Realistic Solutions* (Cambridge, UK: Cambridge University Press, 2013) at 182 (citing Elinor Ostrom, "Design Principles of Robust Property-Rights Institutions: What Have We Learned?" in Gregory K. Ingram & Yu-Hung Hong, eds., *Property Rights and Land Policies* (Cambridge, UK: Cambridge University Press, 2008) at 25–51).

4

Intentional Bypasses

While a multitude of conditions may favour the creation of a bypass, and while these may vary from case to case, observable patterns seem to emerge when individual examples are aggregated and compared. Using a small set of case studies, we try to map some of these patterns by offering a distinction between intentional and spontaneous bypasses. The first category represents conscious, planned, and centralized attempts to fix what are perceived as dysfunctionalities in the dominant institution. By contrast, spontaneous bypasses are scattered and uncoordinated solutions that emerge independently of each other but collectively amount to an arrangement that offers an alternative institutional pathway to the dominant system. In this chapter, we will focus on intentional bypasses and the conditions that may favour their creation and turn to spontaneous bypasses in the next chapter.

Because bypasses are designed to perform governmental functions, it may be tempting also to classify and distinguish them depending on the sector in which they originate or operate (i.e., public or private). This distinction, however, proves problematic when one considers the intricate and dynamic interactions between public and private actors. Some intentional bypasses may be primarily public or primarily private, while others may be a result of coordinated efforts between public and private actors. Moreover, while bypasses may be primarily located in one sector, the public and private dichotomy should be avoided because it falsely implies that there would necessarily be different levels of state control over the process of institutional change precipitated by an institutional bypass, depending on the primary sector in which a bypass operates.

Even in those cases spearheaded by private actors, the presence of the state will be felt in a number of different ways. For example, if the dominant state supplier suffers no adverse consequences from users choosing the alternative provider (e.g., continues to receive the same level of taxpayer-financed support as in the past), it is hard to identify any incentive that the management or employees of such an entity would have to improve their performance. Indeed, they may welcome the exit of the most disgruntled and assertive users, who might otherwise make life less comfortable for those working for and managing the dominant institution. Similarly, even when users choose a private provider, the state typically has at least the potential to exercise a great deal of control over the terms according to which this private option will be available. In this regard, the state is able to determine how easy or hard the exit option may be. In light of these complex interactions, the public–private dichotomy becomes not only fluid but also conceptually problematic.

Focusing on institutional bypasses that are *intentional*, we present three case studies in this chapter, discussing the conditions under which they were created and implemented while noting that the *Poupatempo* (discussed in Chapters 1 and 2) also falls into the category of an intentional institutional bypass. The first case study is the creation of a new police unit in the state of Rio de Janeiro, in Brazil, called *Unidade de Polícia Pacificadora* (UPP). The case illustrates how even intentional bypasses do not need to be based on a pre-designed and well-conceived plan. On the contrary, the evolution of this project shows how it came about due to a particular set of circumstances and was characterized by a trial-and-error approach with respect to its purpose and goals for a significant period of its existence. Nonetheless, the final result of this experiment was the creation of a separate governance structure, which classifies the UPP as an institutional bypass.

The second case study is a reform of the public health care system in Brazil, called *Unidade de Pronto Atendimento* (UPA). The units provide access to low- and medium-level emergency services. Unlike the UPP case study, the pilot project in this case did not involve much experimentation, as the goals were clear from the beginning and the initial setup was very close to what prevailed in the end. The experimentation here happened at a different level: after the pilot project had demonstrated positive effects, the federal government used it as a model for reforms in other states, scaling the project up.

The third case study is an innovative institutional arrangement adopted by a civil society movement to reform a state-centred and state-controlled labour system in Brazil. The *Central Única dos Trabalhadores* (CUT) was the first central union in the country, created during the military dictatorship by a labour movement known as New Unionism (*Novo Sindicalismo*). CUT tried to indirectly bypass dysfunctional labour unions controlled by an autocratic state, by offering workers' groups an option of effective and legitimate labour representation and rights protection. This case study differs from the previous two because, unlike UPPs, there was little experimentation in the implementation phase and, unlike UPAs, there was disagreement within the labour movement regarding the institutional design more likely to foster change, especially regarding how detached this parallel institution should be from the pre-existing system. The option of preserving some connections while maintaining some independence from the pre-existing system prevailed. Today, some regard this arrangement as the reason for the CUT's failure to successfully promote structural change within the labour system.

In the conclusion to this chapter, we point to a common set of conditions that may lead to effective implementation of intentional bypasses, which are very similar to those often present in other kinds of institutional reforms: a window of opportunity for change (e.g., times of crisis), political will (and alliances) to promote reforms, and the availability of resources. While conditions may be ripe for change, the obstacles to internal institutional reforms may be insurmountable and/or previous attempts at promoting such reforms may have failed. Due to these obstacles, in the three cases presented here, intentional bypasses become an attractive strategy for reformers. The cases also point to the fact that availability of resources is a key dimension both in the creation and the maintenance of bypasses, and drying up of resources can prove fatal.

4.1. CHOOSING POLICE SERVICES: THE UNIDADES DE POLÍCIA PACIFICADORA (UPPS)[1]

The first Police Pacifying Unit (UPP) began as a small-scale pilot experiment initiated by the governor of the state of Rio de Janeiro and his public security secretary in 2008. Over time, it was replicated in a number of low-income and marginalized communities known as *favelas*, following a military clearance of often violent, gang-based forms of social ordering. The project was frequently adjusted in its modus operandi in an ad hoc fashion, with the modifications implemented reflecting and reacting to the experience on the ground through reflective planning. This informal feedback process influenced how UPPs were scaled up from their inception in one or two *favelas* to much larger numbers. In its later form, the project acquired a separate governance structure from the regular police force, and personnel was recruited exclusively for the new UPP units, receiving special training and modest additional compensation relative to members of the regular public police force. UPPs not only enabled the newly hired police officials to significantly distance themselves from the prevailing organizational culture in the public police force, but they also created mechanisms for these officers to be more responsive to the needs and demands of citizens. These later features characterize the UPP project in Rio de Janeiro as an institutional bypass of the traditional police force in this Brazilian state.

4.1.1. A Pilot Project

Effectively, the UPP project began with an episode of torture that gained major prominence in the mass media. On May 14, 2008, in a *favela* community on the far eastern suburbs of Rio de Janeiro known as *Jardim Batan*, a journalist, a

[1] This section is largely based on Graham Denyer Willis & Mariana Mota Prado, "Process and Pattern in Institutional Reforms: The Police Pacifying Units in Brazil as an Institutional Bypass" (2014) 64 *World Dev* 232. https://doi.org/10.1016/j.worlddev.2014.06.006

photographer, and a driver were tortured by a para-police organization known as a *milicia*. As a result of the sudden and unexpected state and media attention, most of the *milicianos* fled the community. The overnight departure of the *milicia's* leaders left a stark security vacuum in the community. The *milicia* was a system of securitized governance and revenue, in the same way that other drug trafficking organizations have controlled many of Rio's *favelas* since the late 1980s.[2] It operated much like a protection racket, charging for security while monopolizing the sale of propane cooking tanks, illegal cable television, and telephone hook-ups. Before the rise of the *milicia*, Jardim Batan had been governed by the *Amigos dos Amigos* (ADA) – one of Rio de Janeiro's big three drug trafficking organizations.

In light of the power vacuum, the Public Security Secretary Jose Mario Beltrame created a new Community Police Post (*Posto de Policiamento Comunitario*) in early June 2008. Beltrame made it clear that this *posto* was different. It would be manned only by police living in the community and led by a lieutenant from Rio's revered and purportedly incorruptible SWAT-style police squad known as BOPE (*Batalhão de Operações Policiais Especiais*). As Beltrame put it, this effort would mark a decisive departure from a policing system that had allowed many of Rio's informally built communities to be controlled first by heavily armed drug trafficking organizations and increasingly by para-statal militias.[3]

Six months after the incident in *Jardim Batan*, similar initiatives were implemented in two other *favelas*. In October 2008, police fought their way into two well-known *favelas*, *Santa Marta* in the wealthy Botafogo neighbourhood and the City of God (*Cidade de Deus*) on the west side, made famous by the film of the same name. While following a similar pattern and producing similar *postos*, the justification for each of these "occupations" (as they are known in Brazil) was different. Santa Marta was a medium-sized *favela* of roughly 10,000 residents with clear boundaries and exits flowing out of the steep terrain. It would be easy to contain and implement a program in this defined space with a clear and relatively small constituency. The occupation force of Santa Marta was comprised of a specialized "community police squad" retrained from the local battalion's troops that, from the beginning, were doing something experimental and unprecedented. By contrast, City of God had been embroiled in a spate of violence as the so-called "cradle of the *Comando Vermelho*," Rio de Janeiro's oldest drug trafficking organization. The battalion commander was growing tired of making regular incursions into the community to deal with the problem. Among police leaders, it was decided that the area would be permanently occupied as a means of dealing with the chronic destabilizing influence

---

[2]　Elizabeth Leeds, "Cocaine and Parallel Polities on the Brazilian Urban Periphery: Constraints on Local Level Democratization" (1996) 31:3 *Latin Am Research Rev* 52.

[3]　Ignacio Cano e Carolina Ioot, "Seis por Meia Dúzia? Um Estudo Exploratório do Fenômeno das Chamadas 'Milícias' no Rio de Janeiro" in Justiça Global, *Segurança, Tráfico e Milícias* (Rio de Janeiro: H. Boll, 2008); Aluizio Freire, "Favela da Zona Sul é Modelo de Ocupação da Polícia" (Dec 6, 2008) online: Globo http://g1.globo.com/Noticias/Rio/o,,MUL913118-5606,00.html

of the area – a move that would also deflate the powerful international narrative of City of God's violence.[4]

In both the *Santa Marta* and City of God cases, a coherent public message was lacking as to why the occupation was happening. References were made to the banishment of illegal economies – drugs, unlicensed motorbike taxis, the sale of unregulated propane, illegal television hook-ups, and slot machines – that were proliferating in both places. Nonetheless, both of these operations were tagged from the beginning as a different kind of police incursion into *favelas*. As police said, they would depart from the routine in-and-out approach. This time the police would stay for an undetermined period. In interviews, Secretary Beltrame admitted that these efforts were a work-in-progress.

While it was undeniable that the three experiences – *Jardim Batan, Santa Marta,* and City of God – had much in common, they also had many differences. In each, the government had installed a rubric – if in rhetoric only – of "community policing." But the on-the-ground community policing efforts in these three spaces also had little in common. The training of their police was different, the rationale for their creation was different, and so were their reasons for being part of a "new model." And yet in a span of a few months, Jardim Batan, Santa Marta, and City of God would be united together under a new banner of police reform premised on one simple, flexible, but powerful idea: building state legitimacy in marginalized spaces.

In sum, the nascent project operated loosely around the aim to retake urban space, a model taken from Medellin, Colombia, which Beltrame and other senior political figures visited. In February 2009, more than ten months before Rio de Janeiro would be named the official host of the 2016 Olympics, these three communities became the first three units of the city's new *Unidades de Policia Pacificadora* (UPPs). As of February 2016, the number of units had increased to thirty-eight, serving in excess of 1.5 million citizens.[5]

While embraced by the government, the UPPs were characterized by flexibility and a "laboratory" approach that attracted some scepticism from residents. The apparent unplanned approach to where, when, and why UPP units were installed left it open to a common critique that it was not even a policy of any kind. To the everyday observer, the development of UPP units seemed to be nearly random, often reactive, and usually without much evidence of foresight or planning. They were, if nothing else, an unconventional approach to policing. Thus, the biggest challenge facing the UPP project during its early years was that it lacked a clear definition and a defined agenda.

4.1.2. *Scaling Up and Gathering Support*

As with the genesis of the project, the institutional arrangement that came to characterize the UPPs also evolved over time. UPPs were an informal arrangement, until

---

4 Willis & Prado, *supra* note 1.
5 UPP – *Unidade de Polícia Pacificadora* (nd), online: www.upprj.com

January 2009, when the governor of Rio de Janeiro enacted an executive decree that formally "created" the UPPs. In the decree, the UPPs were described as units subordinated to the hierarchical command of the military police in Rio de Janeiro, but specialized in operations in low-income communities.[6]

Despite this formalization, there were still a series of informal organizational mechanisms that placed the UPPs outside of the traditional structure. Though technically subordinated to the battalion heads, they received calls directly from citizens and orders only from superiors in the UPP command structure. These superiors, in turn, were authorized to use a great deal of experimentation in directing their subordinates, without having to report directly to, or ask permission from, the head of the battalion.[7]

Bit by bit, pieces began to fall into place. By mid-2009, the Secretary of Public Security made it clear that there were two phases to every pacification effort. An initial occupation and removal of drug trafficking groups, undertaken by the tactical squad known as BOPE (the *Batalhão de Operações Policiais Especiais*), was followed by the introduction of a new model of policing. This new model of policing was the crux of the reform: a new corpus of specially trained police defined largely in opposition to the old model. It emerged partly from a corpus of existing police officers who had taken community policing courses with the federal secretary for public security and who had seen firsthand the failure of previous reform efforts.

The introduction of this new model of policing represented the beginning of a key strategic shift for the UPP project, where the primary goal of the policy changed from a broad focus of retaking urban space from drug traffickers to a defined effort to reform the public security system with the creation of a new, more democratic, and citizen-oriented police institution that was separate from traditional police agencies.

The new model would become known as "proximity" policing, an approach based on the idea of having patrolmen and patrolwomen walking the street, visible and serving as an open and accessible conduit for forming new state–society relationships. Proximity denotes fewer patrols in vehicles, greater decentralization, and special training in community communication techniques. Most importantly though, the new model began to imply a new mission largely outside of the distrusted accountability structures, bureaucracy, and authority vested in the fiefdom-like policing of old. It did so not just in rhetoric, but by distinctly altering training, strategies, and pay and introducing a new kind of accountability: to the citizen.

Once the new model was defined, the changes were fast and significant. In the early days, UPP police were drawn from the traditional force, via local police battalions. By 2010, UPP police began to be recruited independently. Their training focused on community accountability, "proximity" to the public, and prevention, while sidestepping the training methods of the traditional police. UPP police

---

[6] Article 1, Decree No. 41.650 of Jan 21, 2009.
[7] Willis & Prado, *supra* note 1.

officers began to work in units with smaller numbers and received a salary top-up, equivalent to a roughly 25 percent raise. More importantly, though, this new system sought to enhance trust directly between citizens and UPP officers by creating an orientation towards the public as opposed to superiors and by incentivizing citizens to direct their emergency calls or preventative concerns directly to the UPP station via email, telephone, or face-to-face contact.

As the UPP project gathered momentum, it also gained support from important political and economic actors. In 2010, five major companies came together to create an investment fund to be administered by the government. These companies all paid to build new police headquarters in places like City of God. Shortly after that, the project received federal support that was essential to carry out large scale-ups of the UPP efforts. The first such scale-up occurred in *Complexo do Alemão* – a group of *favelas* with around 65,000 residents, followed by the occupation in late 2011 of two important *favelas* adjacent to the wealthiest neighbourhoods in the city: Rocinha and Vidigal. Home to somewhere between 80,000 and 150,000 residents, the occupation of Rocinha had the potential to throw the entire city into turmoil. These large-scale operations relied on amphibious armoured vehicles, as well as logistical and troop support from the federal navy.

The UPP has also managed to overcome a series of potentially fatal crises of legitimacy. On at least two occasions in 2013, UPP unit commanders had been removed following revelations of corruption and collusion with drug traffickers. But the response from UPP leaders was decisive, with the perpetrators ending up as ignominious public examples, subject for the first time to civilian justice.[8] In the same year, the *favela* of Rocinha erupted in controversy after it was revealed that police tortured and killed a man from the community. In response, and after a detailed investigation, twenty-five officers were charged with torture, murder, and associated crimes, including the UPP unit commander – formerly a high-profile member of the BOPE tactical police squad.[9] These types of killings remained common with the "old" police, but what differentiated the experience of Rocinha was that, under the UPP, citizens were active in voicing their dissent, and the state, via the UPP, showed itself to be highly responsive.

4.1.3. *A Separate Governance Structure*

As the number of UPP units grew, those in charge increasingly sought greater independence from the old police. In 2011, a new decree from the governor formalized

---

[8] João Bandeira de Mello, "Ex-chefe de UPP é Condenado por Associação para o Tráfico no Rio" (Mar 18, 2013) online: Globo http://g1.globo.com/rio-de-janeiro/noticia/2013/03/ex-chefe-de-upp-e-condenado-por-associacao-para-o-trafico-no-rio.html

[9] Rafael Soares, "Caso Amarildo: MP Revela que Tortura era Recorrente na Rocinha" (Nov 27, 2013), online: O Globo http://oglobo.globo.com/rio/caso-amarildo-mp-revela-que-tortura-era-recorrente-na-rocinha-10894912

FIGURE 4.1. UPP's place in the organizational structure after January 2011

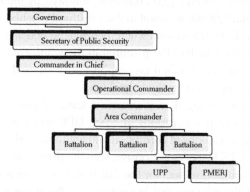

FIGURE 4.2. UPP's place in the organizational structure before January 2011

and more fully enshrined the separation of the UPP units from the traditional police force. This new decree placed UPPs higher up in the hierarchy of the military police and virtually eliminated their subservience to the local police battalion system (Figure 4.1). In the decree, the group in charge of coordinating the UPPs was made subordinate only to the commander in chief of the military police, who in turn reports directly to the public security secretary and the governor.[10]

This decree effectively removed the UPP units from the long and obfuscating hierarchical chain where they had been initially placed within police battalions (Figure 4.2), giving them bureaucratic and moral distance from the unpopular existing police units. After this change, no official below the commander in chief of the police had legal authority to interfere with the UPP units.

In 2013, the separation of UPPs from the established police was further reinforced with the creation of a special accountability unit that investigates and prosecutes

[10] Article 3, Par 1, Decree No. 42.787 of Jan 6, 2011, online: www.silep.planejamento.rj.gov .br/decreto_42_787_-_060111.htm

abuse and misconduct by UPP officers.[11] This gradual separation of UPP units from the police battalions seemed to reinforce the idea that UPPs operated as a parallel institution to the traditional police in Rio de Janeiro.

As the project advanced, police leaders became increasingly vocal that the idea of "proximity policing" and the UPP model were actually distinct. The UPP project, they argue, is a spatial strategy to retake parts of the city from the openly armed domination of Rio's drug trafficking groups. By contrast, and more importantly for the long-term public security outlook of Rio, "proximity policing" is about pacifying *the police* itself. In fact, the general strategy for the UPPs, formulated in a strategic plan scheduled to continue until 2016, was to institutionally overtake the "old" methods of policing, by a process of spatial expansion and the dilution effect caused by incoming officers trained in the new proximity policing methods. According to these leaders, traditional police training – which is seen as a factory of violent methods and clientelistic relations – would slowly diminish. As a result, the percentage of police trained in proximity policing would increase, and the model would expand spatially by reaching out of pacified areas and into places that have been (under-) policed by the existing police institutions. This process started in some places, with the areas adjacent to Jardim Batan on the west side of the city serving as an early example.

Nonetheless, at least some authors have expressed doubts as to whether the distinction between this "new" model of policing and the old one was sustainable – if it ever existed at all – as the project increased in scope.[12] Indeed, the positive results that were achieved in earlier stages of the project did not prove sustainable over time. A 2015 Amnesty International Report indicates that there are numerous complaints of abuses committed by UPP officers, including unnecessary and excessive use of force and extra-judicial executions, that follow the same pattern encountered in both the civil and military police, which have been lax in prosecuting officers involved in extra-judicial killings – with only 1 out of 220 such cases opened in 2011 actually being prosecuted.[13] The report nevertheless acknowledges that there has been progress, as observed by the reduction in homicide rates: there was an 85 percent decrease in deaths as a result of police interventions in UPP areas from 2008 to 2014 (declining from a total of 136 to 20 fatalities per year). However, some argue that this reduction was observed across the entire city (including areas without

---

[11] Isabel Kopschitz, "Policia Militar Receberá R$1,4 Bilhão em Investimentos" (Oct 2, 2012), online: Governo do Rio de Janeiro www.rj.gov.br/web/imprensa/exibeconteudo?article-id=1252512

[12] Rogerio F. Pinto & Maria Scarlet do Carmo, "The Pacifying Police Units of the State of Rio de Janeiro (UPPs): Incremental Innovation or Police Reform?" (2016) 36:2 *Pub Admin & Dev* 121; see also Juliana Corrêa et al., "Poor Youths and 'Pacification': Dilemmas between Discourse and Practice from the Perspective of Young People about Policing in Rio de Janeiro's Favelas" (2016) 31:1 *Int'l Soc* 100.

[13] Amnesty International, *You Killed My Son: Homicides by Military Police in the City of Rio de Janeiro* (Rio de Janeiro: Amnesty International, 2015) at 8.

UPPs) since 2009/2010, making any comparisons between UPP units and the old police unreliable.[14]

The objective of pacifying the old police was certainly never clear in the aftermath of the torture in Jardim Batan or in the early days of Santa Marta's "laboratory" occupation. At that time, the only obvious consequence of the effort was that the drug traffickers and the *milicia* were gone – temporarily at least. That the UPP project has transformed itself into a reform of police in the midst of creating a new and independent police institution was certainly not expected. It is an outcome of a process of learning by doing, learning from doing, and learning while doing. But just as leaders had doubts about the way that the UPP project had unfolded, they continued to do so with respect to the project's future. At the time of its creation, some feared that after the 2016 Olympics, it could come to a close. And these fears seem to have materialized: in the aftermath of the Olympics, Rio de Janeiro was plunged into one of the worse fiscal crises of its history, which was accompanied by a dramatic surge in violence. In 2017, while the UPP and "traditional" police have continued to operate alongside of each other, the lines dividing the two were becoming increasingly blurred: UPP police officers have been increasingly resorting to violence, reflecting a more "traditional" kind of policing,[15] and some of these officers have been deployed to patrol areas that were particularly affected by the violence to work with the old police force.[16]

4.1.4. *UPPs as Institutional Bypasses*

The UPPs eventually collapsed, for a number of reasons that included the lack of resources caused by the state of Rio de Janeiro's fiscal crisis, combined with one of the country's worst recessions.[17] Yet it remains a unique example of police reform in developing countries, where extra-judicial violence, corruption, and a deep lack

---

[14] Pinto & do Carmo, *supra* 12 ("In effect, the police precincts in areas with UPPs had lower monthly homicides than those without UPPs but in 2009/2010 the difference shrank to 2 homicides per 10000 population for those without UPPs and to 1–1.5 in those with UPPs.").

[15] See e.g., Jornal o Dia, "Sete Anos de Pacificação: Moradores Relatam Aumento de Confrontos na Providência" (Apr 26, 2017), online: http://odia.ig.com.br/rio-de-janeiro/2017-04-26/sete-anos-de-pacificacao-moradores-relatam-aumento-de-confrontos-na-providencia.html

[16] O Globo, "Polícia Militar vai Enviar 3 Mil Policiais das UPPS para as Ruas" (Aug 22, 2017), online: https://extra.globo.com/casos-de-policia/guerra-do-rio/policia-militar-vai-enviar-3-mil-policiais-das-upps-para-as-ruas-21735026.html; The Rio Times, "Rio de Janeiro Restructures UPP Program, Cuts One Third" (Aug 23, 2017), online: http://riotimesonline.com/brazil-news/rio-politics/rio-de-janeiro-restructures-upp-program-cuts-one-third

[17] Stephanie Nolen, "How Brazil's Big Policing Experiment Failed to Make Rio Safer for the Olympics" (Aug 2, 2016, updated on Nov 12, 2017) *The Globe and Mail*, online: www.theglobeandmail.com/news/world/how-brazils-big-policing-experiment-failed-to-make-rio-safer-for-theolympics/article31222945

of transparency characterize most understandings of police.[18] Though the field is crowded with proposed models for change, many police reforms focus too heavily on top-down conceptions of police forces, assuming that these institutions are both coherent and reasonable transmitters of policy innovation from top to bottom.[19] As a result, attempts to promote institutional reform in police organizations have an unimpressive track record.[20] The lack of successful police reform has in turn almost certainly perpetuated and deepened struggles of urban insecurity throughout the developing world, which is now witnessing a myriad of attempts to establish "order" via alternative means such as vigilantism, lynching, organized crime and community justice patrols.[21] This is very much the background conditions under which the UPP project started in Rio de Janeiro.

Instead of trying to change the institutional culture of the old police, and to fight against embedded self-reinforcing mechanisms that kept such a culture in place, the UPPs tried to perform the same functions as the traditional police force independently of them. One of the most important ways in which the project attempted to accomplish this was through experimentation, which was feasible because UPPs operated as a parallel structure, securing a relatively autonomous policy space where

[18] Paul Chevigny, *The Edge of the Knife: Police Violence in the Americas* (New York: New Press, 1999); Mark Ungar, "Police Reform in Argentina: Public Security versus Human Rights" in Niels Uildriks, ed., *Policing Insecurity* (Lanham, MD: Lexington Books, 2009); David H. Bayley, *Changing the Guard: Developing Democratic Police Abroad* (Oxford, UK: Oxford University Press, 2006); Daniel M. Brinks, *The Judicial Response to Police Killings in Latin America* (Cambridge, UK: Cambridge University Press, 2008); Andrew Goldsmith, "Police Reform and the Problem of Trust" (2005) 9:4 *Theoretical Criminology* 443; Diane E. Davis, "Undermining the Rule of Law: Democratization and the Dark Side of Police Reform in Mexico" (2006) 48:1 *Latin Am Pol & Soc* 55; Claudio A. Fuentes, *Contesting the Iron Fist: Advocacy Networks and Police Violence in Democratic Argentina and Chile* (New York: Routledge, 2004); Monique Marks, *Transforming the Robocops: Changing Police in South Africa* (KwaZulu Natal: University of KwaZulu Natal Press, 2005); Hugo Frühling, "Research on Latin American Police: Where Do We Go from Here?" (2009) 10:5/6 *Police Practice & Research* 465; Beatrice Jaregui, "Beatings, Beacons and Big Men: Police Disempowerment and Delegitimation in India" (2013) 38:3 *L & Soc Inquiry* 643.

[19] Nicole Ball, "Transforming Security Sectors: The IMF and World Bank Approaches" (2001) 1:1 *Confl, Sec & Dev* 45; Graham Denyer Willis, "Antagonistic Authorities and the Civil Police in São Paulo, Brazil" (2014) 49:1 *Latin Am Research Rev* 3.

[20] John Bailey & Lucía Dammert, *Public Security and Police Reform in the Americas* (Pittsburgh, PA: University of Pittsburgh Press, 2005); Ball, *supra* note 19; Michael J. Trebilcock & Ron Daniels, *Rule of Law Reform and Development: Charting the Fragile Path of Progress* (Cheltenham, UK: Edward Elgar Publishing, 2008); Elizabeth Leeds, "Serving States and Serving Citizens: Halting Steps Toward Police Reform in Brazil and Implications for Donor Intervention" (2007) 17:1 *Policing & Soc* 21; Mariana Mota Prado, Michael J. Trebilcock, & Patrick Hartford, "Police Reform in Violent Democracies in Latin America" (2012) 4 *Hague J Rule of L* 252.

[21] Angelina Snodgrass Godoy, *Popular Injustice: Violence, Community, and Law in Latin America* (Redwood City, CA: Stanford University Press, 2006); Kevin Lewis O'Neill & Kedron Thomas, eds., *Securing the City: Neoliberalism, Space, and Insecurity in Postwar Guatemala* (Durham, NC: Duke University Press, 2011); Diane Davis & Graham Denyer Willis, "Anticrime Movements in Latin America" in David A. Snow et al., eds., *The Wiley Blackwell Encyclopedia of Social and Political Movements* (Oxford, UK: Blackwell Publishing, 2013).

officers could try new ideas. Since there was ample room for experimentation and the program was imbued with flexibility, it could adapt to different circumstances and hence be more effective.[22] This openness to experimentation was complemented by the fact that the traditional police did not make effective use of formal mechanisms of hierarchical control over the UPPs.

As a result of such experimentation, the UPPs adopted strategies to create and restore a respectful dynamic between police officers and members of the community. The strategies to create proximity in the UPPs included both specialized training and a system of financial incentives where police officers received bonus payments for region-wide reductions in rates of crime and police abuse. They also included a greater concentration of police officers, more foot patrolling, and a push to have citizens communicate directly with the local unit.[23]

This last strategy in particular suggests that UPPs also offered, at least in the beginning of the project, a de facto alternative or an option for those requiring police services. The UPPs encouraged citizens to direct their emergency calls or preventative concerns directly to the UPP station via email, telephone, or face-to-face contact, as opposed to contacting a central dispatcher. This additional way of communicating with the police, which was not offered before, ensured that potential problems in the centralized communication system would not undermine the possibility of UPP units acting effectively within the communities where they operated.

The changes promoted by this arrangement, albeit temporary, were significant. While the UPPs were bypassing the traditional police force, they also sought to replace powerful localized forms of governance and security that were historically common under *favela* drug trafficking regimes.[24] They often replaced these decentralized forms of security with a form of security provided by central state authority. To do so, the UPPs sought to regain the trust of the communities in which they operated, and through the relationship forged from proximity sought to overcome the initial suspicion of police forces that is commonly found in these communities. The choice for citizens at that point was not only between the new and the old police but also between the decentralized security of non-state armed groups and a more complete provision of public security by police. This underscores a more substantial shift for residents of these communities, who previously experienced police only

[22] Stephanie Gimenez Stahlberg, "The Pacification of Favelas in Rio de Janeiro: Why the Program Is Working and What Are the Lessons for Other Countries" (2011) paper presented at the Conference Violence, Drugs and Governance: Mexican Security in Comparative Perspective, organized by CDDRL, CISAC, FSI Stanford, Stanford, at 29.

[23] Ibid. at 13–14, 27.

[24] Robert Gay, *Popular Organization and Democracy in Rio de Janeiro: A Tale of Two Favelas* (Philadelphia: Temple University Press, 1994); Leeds, *supra* note 2; Donna M. Goldstein, *Laughter Out of Place: Race, Class, Violence and Sexuality in a Rio Shantytown* (Berkeley, CA: University of California Press, 2013); Enrique Desmond Arias, *Drugs and Democracy in Rio de Janeiro: Trafficking, Social Networks and Public Security* (Durham, NC: University of North Carolina Press, 2006).

as a fleeting and violent "force." Under the UPP, the policy offered policing as an accessible public service.

UPPs were not initially created as an institutional bypass. As indicated earlier, the first units were informal arrangements. During this period, reformers managed to overcome obstacles partly through reflective planning, that is, constant adaptation and an organic, incremental, and spontaneous elaboration of goals and strategies. It was through reflective planning that the institutional bypass came about.[25]

Since its inception, the UPP project has taken many turns. Even during its most promising phase, the project was far from being comfortably classified as a success, but the UPP has distinguished itself from previous reform attempts by finding some traction. We have argued here that this result can be explained by the UPP project's structure as an institutional bypass, which opened up room for experimentation. As the history of the project shows, it was not the brainchild of technocrats, foreign observers, or even the progressive and eager-to-help federal government of Brazil. The strategy instead grew directly out of the insecurity that existed in the city where the project began. As fissures appeared, solutions were designed to address particular problems. These problems invited creative solutions from those involved, which were fed back into the project to strengthen its positive outcomes.

In sum, UPP units started as informal pilot projects. As a result of experimentation, they eventually evolved into a body formally detached from the old police force, allowing for a continuation of the experimental nature of the project despite its ongoing institutionalization. The formalization of the UPPs into a separate governance structure not only turned it into a bypass but also underscored our belief that such a structure was essential for the project's advancement and expansion. Discouragingly, the UPPs initiative seems largely to have collapsed in the wake of the fiscal crisis in Rio de Janeiro (and a country-wide recession), and gangs have now reoccupied many of the *favelas*.[26] Yet if the state decides to find new ways to reestablish an effective and constructive presence in the *favelas* in the future, reforms could potentially follow the same pattern adopted by the UPP model, and the lessons learned from this initiative should inform any future efforts. In other words,

---

[25] A push toward pragmatism among urban planners brought a cold reckoning with the likelihood that plans would never get it right with the first shot. Plans, and more importantly those overseeing them, needed greater flexibility and the ability to adapt and revisit assumptions and surprises along the way. Much of this shift was captured by Schon, who coined the term "reflective practice" to refer to the importance for planners to learn by doing, learn from doing, and learn while doing. Donald A. Schon, *The Reflective Practitioner: How Professionals Think in Action* (London, UK: Temple Smith, 1983). This new notion of planning encouraged professionals to revisit their own assumptions and normative positions, particularly when exposed to unforeseen surprises during policy implementation, or in uncertain, culturally dissimilar and unstable environments; Raphaël Fischler, "Reflective Practice" in Bishwapriya Sanyal, Lawrence J. Vale, & Christian D. Rosan, eds., *Planning Ideas That Matter: Livability, Territoriality, Governance, and Reflective Practice* (Cambridge, MA: MIT Press, 2012) at 313–31.

[26] Nolen, *supra* note 17.

the factors that led to UPP's ultimate fate should not be confused with the strategic and structural dimensions of the project that contributed to its many achievements.

4.2. CHOOSING EMERGENCY HEALTH CARE SERVICES:
THE *UNIDADES DE PRONTO ATENDIMENTO* (UPAS)

Brazil's "Emergency Care Units" (*Unidade de Pronto Atendimento* or UPA) provide twenty-four-hour emergency health care services, seven days a week. They are distinct from hospital emergency rooms (ERs) because they only deal with low- and medium-level emergencies, such as high blood pressure, high fever, fractures, cuts, heart attacks, and strokes.[27] High-level (i.e., more complex) emergencies are re-directed to hospitals. Despite not providing all the services that an ER would, UPAs emerged as a response to dysfunctional services provided by public hospitals in general, and ERs in particular. Specifically, the system was being overloaded by the kinds of health care demands being brought to ERs, reducing efficiency, and, in some cases, preventing the ER from providing adequate services to patients.

The creation of UPAs offers an alternative to those who would otherwise seek urgent care in hospitals, and the design of these units aims at addressing some of the deficiencies of the existing system (such as long waiting times, lack of personnel, and inadequate equipment). While UPAs may currently serve as an option for patients (i.e., they would to some extent be competing with ERs), the ultimate goal of this initiative is to provide a division of labour: UPAs intend to reduce the overloading of emergency hospitals, thus altering their demand profile. Urgent clinical cases should be served by a UPA, and those that are more complex by the hospitals.[28] In practice, however, a UPA is a bypass because it operates as a parallel institution, performing many of the same services or functions as the dysfunctional dominant institutions.

4.2.1. *A Historical Overview of Health Care Policies in Brazil*

Brazil has a two-tier health care system, and Brazilian citizens can elect to receive care from both public and private (i.e., paid) health care providers. Citizens do not need to opt in or subscribe to the public health system (*Sistema Único de Saúde –* SUS). SUS is free and accessible to all Brazilians, who simply need to provide a government-issued identification document to have access to public hospitals

---

[27] PAC, Ministério do Planejamento, "UPA – Unidade de Pronto Atendimento," online: www.pac.gov .br/comunidade-cidada/upa-unidade-de-pronto-atendimento. www.pac.gov.br/infraestrutura-social-e -urbana/upa-unidade-de-pronto-atendimento

[28] Luciana Dias de Lima et al., "Interdependência Federativa na Política de Saúde: a Implementação das Unidades de Pronto Atendimento no Estado do Rio de Janeiro, Brasil" (2015) 20:2 *Ciência & saúde coletiva* 595.

managed by federal, state, or municipal governments. Despite its aspiration to provide adequate health care services to the entire population, the system is underfunded, under-staffed, and lacks adequate infrastructure.[29] It is not uncommon for the media to report cases of patients dying while waiting for surgery or ambulances.[30] As a result, those who can afford to pay for private insurance or care have generally opted out of the public system.

With significantly more resources than the public system, private health care services in Brazil often provide higher-quality and more efficient care.[31] The disparity between public and private health services makes private health care coverage highly coveted, but only about 20 percent of the Brazilian population have private health care insurance.[32] Those who have subscribed to private health care continue to have access to the public system, as one cannot opt out of the public health care system. As a result, in subscribing to private health insurance plans, individuals are subscribing to double coverage: they can still use the resources of the public system at any point in time for any kind of service.

In brief, the Brazilian health care system operates with two pillars. First, all citizens have access to the public health care system at all times (indeed, the Brazilian constitution secures a constitutional right to health, and access to health care services to all citizens is guaranteed by free access to SUS, which is also established by a constitutional provision). There is no opt in or opt out. Second, individuals elect to use the private health care system, either by paying directly for services or by buying private health insurance. The private system operates its own network of health care services and facilities, mostly independent and in parallel with the public system.

---

[29] Jairnilson Paim et al., "The Brazilian Health System: History, Advances, and Challenges" (2011) 377:9779 *The Lancet* 1778; Michele Gragnolati, Magnus Lindelow, & Bernard Couttolenc, *Twenty Years of Health System Reform in Brazil* (Washington, DC: World Bank Group, 2013); Gerard M. La Forgia & Bernard F. Couttolenc, *Hospital Performance in Brazil: The Search for Excellence* (Washington, DC: World Bank Publications, 2008) at 291.

[30] See e.g., O Globo, "Pelo Menos 60 Pacientes Morreram em Filas de Espera por Cirurgia em Cinco Hospitais Federais" (Jan 11, 2015), online: https://oglobo.globo.com/rio/pelo-menos-60-pacientes-morreram-em-filas-de-espera-por-cirurgia-em-cinco-hospitais-federais-15021575; similar stories can be found with respect to ambulances: see e.g., O Globo "Homem de 59 Anos Morre Após Esperar Ambulância por Quase Duas Horas em São José" (Mar 23, 2017), online: http://g1.globo.com/sp/vale-do-paraiba-regiao/noticia/homem-de-59-anos-morre-apos-esperar-ambulancia-por-quase-2h-em-sao-jose.ghtml; A Notícia, "Polícia de Mafra Investiga Morte de Bebê Após 15 Horas de Espera por Ambulância" (Jun 14, 2017), online: http://anoticia.clicrbs.com.br/sc/geral/noticia/2017/06/policia-de-mafra-investiga-morte-de-bebe-apos-15-horas-de-espera-por-ambulancia-9816630.html

[31] Mariana Mota Prado, "Provision of Health Care Services and the Right to Health in Brazil" in Colleen Flood & Ayeal Gross, eds., *The Right to Health at the Public/Private Divide: A Global Comparative Study* (New York: Cambridge University Press, 2014); Robert Marten et al., "An Assessment of Progress Towards Universal Health Coverage in Brazil, Russia, India, China, and South Africa (BRICS)" (2014) 384:9960 *The Lancet* 2164.

[32] A reported 37 million people had private insurance in 2007 (19 percent of the total population). The number increased to 47 million in 2017 (23 percent of the total population). Data from Agência Nacional de Saúde Suplementar, "Dados Gerais: Beneficiários de Planos Privados de Saúde, por Cobertura Assistencial (Brasil − 2007–2017)" online: www.ans.gov.br/perfil-do-setor/dados-gerais

Those who can afford it (often wealthier citizens) elect to use the private system mostly by buying insurance (rather than paying service fees),[33] and the only option available to the poorer 75 percent of the population is the under-funded and over-crowded public health care system.

There are, however, significant obstacles to changing the public health care system, and especially emergency care in hospitals. Hospitals are often administratively independent from the government and have a great deal of autonomy.[34] In addition, public hospitals in Brazil are generally funded from general tax revenues collected by all three levels of government.[35] This makes any reform dependent on the political (and often financial) support of all levels of government, which has been rare in Brazilian history. Most attempts to implement emergency care units by one level of government alone have not been successful.[36] Cooperating on reforms is also difficult, as no single level of government can claim the electoral benefits.

Because UPAs are part of the public health care system, they are accessible to all citizens free of charge. This means that they could potentially become the primary source of emergency care for more than 175 million people – three-quarters of Brazil's population – who depend on the public system to meet their health care needs. Those who have access to a private network of emergency care are also entitled to use the services provided at UPAs, but it is not clear that they will do so. While a UPA could in theory have an impact on the private health care system by attracting patients who would otherwise be able to pay for services and/or insurance, the project seems primarily designed for those who do not have the option of using the private system. Indeed, many UPAs in the state of Rio de Janeiro are located in low-income neighbourhoods where the provision of medical care is limited.[37]

4.2.2. *Another Layer in Emergency Care Policies in Brazil*

One of the greatest challenges to improving the public health sector in Brazil is in the area of emergency services. ERs in the public health systems are often over-crowded, with few diagnostic and therapeutic resources. They also lack basic infrastructure, such as beds.[38] Due to the inadequate services offered by the

---

33 Gragnolati, Lindelow, & Couttolenc, *supra* note 29.
34 La Forgia & Couttolenc, *supra* note 29.
35 Ibid.
36 Gisele O'Dwyer et al., "The Current Scenario of Emergency Care Policies in Brazil" (2013) 13:1 *BMC Health Services Research* BMC Health Serv Res 70, online: http://bmchealthservres.biomedcentral .com/articles/10.1186/1472-6963-13-70 at 2; See also Gisele O'Dwyer & Ruben Araujo de Mattos, "O SAMU, a Regulação no Estado do Rio de Janeiro e a Integralidade Segundo Gestores dos Três Níveis de Governo" (2012) 22:1 *Physis* 141.
37 Dias de Lima, *supra* note 28.
38 Gustavo Pereira Fraga, Mario Luiz Quintas, & Simone de Campos Vieira Abib, "Trauma and Emergency: Is the Unified Health System (SUS) the Solution in Brazil?" (2014) 41:4 *Revista do Colégio Brasileiro de Cirurgiões* 232, online: https://dx.doi.org/10.1590/0100-69912014004001

public health care network, public hospitals are the primary provider of the full range of services offered by SUS, from emergency to preventive and clinical care.[39] As a result, public hospitals are the main hub of health care services and where most (if not all) emergency care takes place, including preventable conditions that now have degenerated into serious conditions.[40]

UPAs have emerged as an alternative to these dysfunctional services, providing twenty-four-hour services, seven days a week and they can treat most low- and medium-level emergencies.[41] While UPAs can be considered a response to the precarious emergency health care situation in Brazil, they were not the first attempt by the federal government to improve the provision of these services. On the contrary, UPAs were the third phase of a series of attempts to address the problems in the public health care system: "from 1998 to 2003, federal regulation; from 2004 to 2008, major expansion of the Mobile Emergency Medical Services (or *Serviço de Atendimento Móvel de Urgência* – SAMU, in Portuguese); and from 2009 onwards, the implementation of stationary pre-hospital care facilities."[42] All these policies had one common goal: improving the situation of clogged ERs at larger public hospitals by setting rules and standards (phase 1), dispersing the provision of emergency care in Brazil across different institutions with mobile care (phase 2), and with pre-hospital care facilities, the UPAs (phase 3).

Between 1998 and 2002 (phase 1), Brazil focused on the regulation of health care services through the creation of a uniform set of country-wide rules and standards.[43] Following extensive debates between the government and the medical community, this first phase culminated in the National Emergency Health Care Policy[44] and the creation of the General Coordination of Emergency Services as a management organization within the Ministry of Health.[45] Between 2003 and 2008 (phase 2),[46] Brazil then implemented the National Emergency Care Policy (*Política Nacional de*

---

[39] La Forgia & Couttolenc, *supra* note 29 ("Many Brazilians seek basic care in hospitals partly because publicly financed primary care is deficient or absent. In sum, there is strong evidence that health care in Brazil is already heavily centered on hospital-based delivery and is not coordinated using existing direct administrative control instruments across facilities at different levels [primary care, diagnostics, hospitals].")

[40] Barbara Starfield, Leiyu Shi, & James Macinko, "Contribution of Primary Care to Health Systems and Health" (2005) 83:3 *Milbank Q* 457; Frederico Guanais & James Macinko, "Primary Care and Avoidable Hospitalizations: Evidence from Brazil" (2009) 32:2 *J Ambulatory Care Mgmt* 115; but see James Macinko et al., "Major Expansion of Primary Care in Brazil Linked to Decline in Unnecessary Hospitalization" (2010) 29:12 *Health Aff* 2149.

[41] Ministério do Planejamento, *supra* note 27.

[42] O'Dwyer, Emergency Care Policies, *supra* note 36 at 3; Cristiani V. Machado, Fernanda C. F. Salvador, & Gisele O'Dwyer, "Serviço de Atendimento Móvel de Urgência: Análise da Política Brasileira" (2011) 45:3 *Rev Saúde Pública* 519.

[43] O'Dwyer, Emergency Care Policies, *supra* note 36 at 3.

[44] Ministerial Order (*Portaria*) N° 2.048 of Nov 5 2002, online: http://bvsms.saude.gov.br/bvs/saudelegis/gm/2002/prt2048_05_11_2002.html

[45] O'Dwyer, Emergency Care Policies, *supra* note 36 at 3.

[46] Machado, Salvador, & O'Dwyer, *supra* note 42.

Atenção às Urgências – PANU)[47] and the Emergency Mobile Care Services (*Serviço de Atendimento Móvel de Urgência* – SAMU).[48] Prior to SAMU, individuals experiencing health emergencies had to call their local fire department.[49] SAMU is an emergency mobile medical service that provides paramedic care while transporting individuals to emergency care units at public hospitals. "It has the goal of ensuring care, adequate transportation and routing of patients to an SUS-integrated service. Emergency response is engaged through a toll-free phone number (192) from anywhere in Brazil."[50] In addition to the implementation of the SAMU, the National Emergency Care Policy proposed the creation of different emergency care systems by the municipal, state, and federal governments and formal financing mechanisms to finance emergency care policies in Brazil.[51]

Starting in 2008 (phase 3), UPAs were created by the federal Ministry of Health.[52] In this phase, the government sought to strengthen the national emergency care network by implementing stationary emergency care units (UPAs) across the country that are connected with SAMU and public hospitals.[53] While the federal government was responsible for financing the initial costs, the state and the municipal governments were responsible for implementing UPAs.[54] Once fully functional, UPA costs were to be shared between the federal, state, and municipal governments, and the federal government would be responsible for 50 percent of their total operational cost.[55]

Despite becoming an official part of the federal government policies for emergency health care services in 2008, the history of UPAs begins before this date. UPAs were originally a pilot project implemented by a state government. In 2005, Rio de Janeiro state had a "health crisis" which was "heralded by overload of the emergency systems, the precarious nature of the municipal service and the city government's difficulties in managing health policies and services."[56] In 2006, federal and state elections brought to power political allies who decided to join forces to deal with the health crisis in the state. As a result of this political alliance between the federal and state governments, the first UPA was implemented in May 2007 in a poor district on the periphery of the municipality of Rio de Janeiro.[57]

---

[47]　National Emergency Care Policy (in Portuguese: Política Nacional de Atenção às Urgências or PANU), online: Biblioteca Virtual em Saúde: Ministério da Saúde, http://bvsms.saude.gov.br/bvs/publicacoes/politica_nac_urgencias.pdf

[48]　Machado, Salvador, & O'Dwyer, *supra* note 42.

[49]　O'Dwyer, Emergency Care Policies, *supra* note 36.

[50]　Ibid.

[51]　Machado, Salvador, & O'Dwyer, *supra* note 42.

[52]　Ministerial Order (*Portaria*) N° 2.922 of Dec 2 2008, online: http://bvsms.saude.gov.br/bvs/saudelegis/gm/2008/prt2922_02_12_2008_comp.html

[53]　Ibid. at art. 2.

[54]　Ibid. at art. 5.

[55]　Ibid. at art. 8.

[56]　Dias de Lima et al., *supra* note 28 at 598.

[57]　Ibid.

The importance of this serendipitous political alliance between the federal and state governments in Rio de Janeiro, as a result of elections, cannot be underestimated. Lack of political cooperation to improve existing health care institutions is generally pervasive in Brazil but was rampant in Rio de Janeiro, as illustrated by an episode in 2005. At this time, the hospitals of the municipality of Rio de Janeiro did not have enough beds or medical staff to treat their patients. The municipality blamed the health crisis on the lack of funding from the federal government.[58] Instead of transferring funds to the municipal government so that it could deal with the crisis, the federal government took a more "visible" approach (for electoral purposes) by taking administrative control of four municipal hospitals.[59] The municipal government appealed the decision to the federal Supreme Court, which reverted the administration of these hospitals to the municipality of Rio de Janeiro. This was not an isolated episode. In 2008, another crisis struck the municipality of Rio de Janeiro when it was hit with an epidemic of dengue fever. The ERs in public hospitals were overcrowded, and the municipal government blamed the other levels of government for not taking a proactive role in combating this epidemic. These examples illustrate how the structure of emergency care provision in Brazil creates a disincentive for governments to cooperate. It is interesting to note, however, that even when there was a political coalition among the federal, state, and municipal governments, they decided to create UPAs instead of reforming the existing system. And it is also important to note that this happened on the heels of the 2005 health crisis.[60]

After the success of this pilot project in Rio de Janeiro, the federal government decided to implement similar units and to create the institutional and budgetary framework to support the operation of UPAs across the country. UPAs began to receive financial support from the Ministry of Health: each UPA receives a minimum amount for start-up costs and a monthly allocation from the federal government that is matched by the state and municipalities.[61] These federal funds seem to operate as an important incentive for the creation of UPAs: as of 2017, there were 345 UPAs projects across different states of Brazil.[62] However, federal funding is accompanied by strict rules that are imposed top-down, not allowing states and municipalities to adapt UPAs to the particular circumstances in which they will be operating, potentially reducing their effectiveness.[63]

---

[58] John J. Crocitti & Monique Vallance, eds., *Brazil Today: An Encyclopedia of Life in the Republic* (Santa Barbara, CA: ABC-CLIO, 2011) at 369.
[59] Bruno Domingos, "STF Derruba Intervenção na Saúde do Rio – 21/04/2005" (May 2005), online: Folha de SPaulo – Cotidiano, www1.folha.uol.com.br/fsp/cotidian/ff2104200501.htm
[60] Dias de Lima, *supra* note 28.
[61] Ministerial Order N° 2.922, *supra* note 52 at art. 5–8.
[62] Ministério do Planejamento, *supra* note 27.
[63] Mariana Teixeira Konder & Gisele O'Dwyer, "As Unidades de Pronto-Atendimento na Política Nacional de Atenção às Urgências" (2015) 25:2 *Physis, Revista de Saúde Coletiva* 525.

4.2.3. UPAs as Institutional Bypasses

The core change produced by UPAs is the introduction of an alternate channel through which patients using the public health system can access acute care. Previously, access to emergency care, as with all other health care, was channelled through the public hospitals. The creation of UPAs did not promote any changes in the operation or policies of the ERs in public hospitals but did provide patients with a choice: for low- and medium-level emergencies, they could now elect between going to public hospitals or to an UPA. The latter were designed to be more accessible to patients by being located in areas with limited access to health care services, such as in low-income neighbourhoods away from the city centres.[64] This is possible because UPAs are smaller operations than a public hospital. As they only provide emergency care, UPAs have lower waiting times and are less crowded than ERs at hospitals. According to statistics, 97 percent of emergency cases that arrive at UPAs are treated by the institution.[65]

There are potentially two groups of people who may be served by UPAs. One is composed of those who would have sought services in a public hospital but have chosen to seek services at UPAs. The other group comprises those who would not otherwise have sought medical care, given the bureaucratic and burdensome process involved in pursuing these services at a public hospital. In this sense, UPAs "compete" with public hospitals for patients, addressing both the existing and latent demand for health care services. However, UPAs also serve a complementary function, since they have the potential to reduce the strain on public hospitals, thereby enabling them to function more effectively by reducing the number of patients at ERs.[66] This, of course, assumes that they are not drawing financial, operational, or human resources from public hospitals. In other words, if the government is reallocating resources from hospitals to UPAs, it is difficult to claim that they are performing a complementary function. While this does not seem to be the case, the federal government has faced challenges in attracting doctors to UPAs, and most of the UPAs hire doctors for short shifts (four to twelve hours a week), which allows them to keep their employment in the public or private sector and offer services at UPAs on the side. Since January 2017 the Ministry of Health has authorized some of these units to operate with fewer

---

[64] Dias de Lima, *supra* note 28.
[65] Ministério do Planejamento, *supra* note 27.
[66] Mariana Teixeira Konder, "Atenção às Urgências: a Integração das Unidades de Pronto Atendimento 24h (UPA 24h) Com a Rede Assistencial Domunicípio do Rio de Janeiro" (2013), online: http://157.86.8.70:8080/certifica/handle/icict/2298; Ythala Dellamary Feitosa De Gois, *Intervenções Para Solucionar a Superlotação no Setor de Emergência da Unidade Mista Elizabeth Barbosa do Município de Custódia–PE* (Recife, 2011), online: www.cpqam.fiocruz.br/bibpdf/2011-gois-ydf.pdf

personnel than initially planned.[67] Some commentators have claimed that these recent changes may significantly impair UPAs' potential to improve the quality and quantity of emergency care in Brazil.[68]

The implementation of UPAs in Brazil occurred in a unique socio-political context where the health care system was in crisis and the three levels of government were politically aligned. While these unique circumstances seem to explain why the reforms came about when they did, these same circumstances do not explain why the reforms were structured as a bypass. This case study may illustrate that while political will and alignment across multiple levels of government may be an important feature in promoting reforms, it may not be sufficient to overcome resistance (especially from inside the institution that needs reforms) and path dependence. It is in this context that a bypass may prove a useful strategy if there is a window of opportunity for reform. The challenge is how to scale up the bypass without losing its capacity to adapt to particular contexts in which they would be operating – UPAs seem to have faltered to some extent in this respect.

4.3. CHOOSING LABOUR ORGANIZATIONS: THE *CENTRAL ÚNICA DOS TRABALHADORES* (CUT)[69]

Brazil's Labour Law system has had an unexpectedly long life: before the 2017 reforms, it had not changed much from its inception in the 1930s.[70] More specifically, the traditional union structure in Brazil was almost ninety years old, despite radical changes in the Brazilian social, economic, and political environment. This resilience is especially surprising considering the multiple attempts to reform the system since its creation. Some of the most innovative strategies to this end were implemented in the late 1970s and were designed by the growing Brazilian labour movement known as New Unionism (*Novo Sindicalismo*). At least one of these strategies, the creation of the *Central Única dos Trabalhadores* (CUT), can be considered an intentional institutional bypass.

---

[67] Ministerial Order (*Portaria*) N° 10 of Jan 3 2017, online: http://bvsms.saude.gov.br/bvs/saudelegis/gm/2017/prt0010_03_01_2017.html

[68] EBC, "Entidades Temem que Nova Regra Reduza Interesse de Médicos em Trabalhar em UPA" (Feb 4, 2017), online: http://agenciabrasil.ebc.com.br/geral/noticia/2017-02/entidades-temem-que-nova-regra-reduza-interesse-de-medicos-em-trabalhar-em-upa

[69] This section is largely based on Ana Virginia Gomes & Mariana Mota Prado, "Institutional Bypasses in Brazil's New Unionism Movement: Central Unions and Workers' Committees" (unpublished manuscript).

[70] For a detailed description of the system and analysis of the multiple reasons for its resilience see Ana Virginia Gomes & Mariana Mota Prado, "Flawed Freedom of Association in Brazil: How Unions Can Become an Obstacle to Meaningful Reforms in the Labour Law System" (2011) 32:4 *Comp Lab L & Pol'y J* 843; for the recent reforms, see The Economist, "An Overhaul of Brazilian Labour Law Should Spur Job Creation" (Jul 20, 2017); Afonso de Paul Pinheiro Rocha & Ana Virginia Gomes, "The Fallout from the 2017 Labour Reform in Brazil for the Trade Union Movement" 2017 24:4 *Intl Union Rights* 9.

4.3.1. *The Rise of Brazil's New Unionism*

New Unionism is considered one of the most important (if not the most important) labour movements in Brazil.[71] The movement gained national and international prominence for organizing three general metal worker strikes in 1978, 1979, and 1980, which were the first general strikes since the beginning of the military dictatorship in 1964.

Many factors contributed to the rise of the movement in the late 1970s.[72] First, the implementation of a modern industrial cluster in São Paulo (in what is known as the ABC region[73]) resulted in the immigration of numerous workers. This led to the formation of a new working class, composed of a large group of workers (in 1972, this industrial cluster employed 69,132 workers in its 159 factories) working in the growing automobile manufacturing industry and concentrated in one small geographical region. Second, the existing trade union structure was incapable of dealing with the emerging and pressing labour issues affecting this working class and the tensions they were creating in the workplace. Third, there was increasing political opposition to the military dictatorship, and these opposition groups began to perceive the New Unionism fights against a government hostile to labour claims as part of a broader opposition to the autocratic regime.

The three general strikes in 1978, 1979, and 1980 were a response to the erosion of wages by inflation, repressive and abusive practices inside the factories, and authoritarian trade union laws.[74] During the 1970s, the military dictatorship manipulated wage policy to control the country's inflation, with the result that wage increases did not even offset the inflation rate. While the auto manufacturing industry was paying higher wages than other industries at the time, employers in that industry were also demanding long work hours and imposing draconian codes of conduct (such as eliminating any type of breaks during long shifts, prohibiting the use of washrooms, and preventing workers from talking to each other). In some cases, the measures adopted inside the factories violated existing labour law provisions. Rules would be created and imposed by managers, who not only imposed illegal sanctions for disobedience but also threatened workers on a regular basis. In sum, working conditions were often abusive, and workers who did not comply

---

[71] The term "new" differentiates the movement from the populist trade union movement, which took place before the military dictatorship; see Marco Aurélio Santana, "Entre a Ruptura e a Continuidade: Visões da História do Movimento Sindical Brasileiro" (1999) 14:41 *RBCS* 103 at 106; Luiz Werneck Vianna, "Atualizando uma Bibliografia: 'Novo Sindicalismo', Cidadania e Fábrica" in Luiz Werneck Vianna, *Travessia – da Abertura à Constituinte* (Rio de Janeiro: Livraria Taurus, 1986).

[72] Maria Hermínia Tavares de Almeida, "O Sindicalismo no Brasil: Novos Problemas, Velhas Estruturas" (1975) 6 *Debate & Crítica* (Revista Quadrimensal de Ciências Sociais) 49; Laís Wendel Abramo, *O Resgate da Dignidade (a Greve de 1978 em São Bernardo)* (Master's Dissertation, São Paulo: FFLCH-USP, 1987) at 185–92.

[73] ABC corresponds to three cities around Sao Paulo: Santo André, São Bernardo, and São Caetano. Some call it the ABCD region to include Diadema.

[74] Abramo, *supra* note 72 at 169; see also Tavares de Almeida, *supra* note 72 at 63–4.

with the rules were easily replaced, as reflected in the high turnover rate. For those subjected to these conditions, there was no dialogue or room for negotiation. This was complemented and reinforced by the repressive policies of the military government that were used to control trade unions, among the most notable of which was the general prohibition of strikes.[75] In addition to the rigid governmental control of trade unions and wages, the internal structures in factories that rigidly controlled the labour force were not aimed primarily at increasing productivity but were instead designed to avoid insurrections of any sort.[76]

It is interesting to note that the strikes and ensuing negotiations were not organized by formal unions but by a movement of workers. To be sure, some trade unions acted as intermediaries between workers and their employers, but the movement was mostly led by workers' strike committees inside the factories.[77] While in 1978 the military government seemed to be taken by surprise by the strike and was slow to react, in 1979 it reacted promptly, repressing the strike and blocking any collective negotiation.[78] One of the main repressive actions was the dismissal of the leaders of the trade union who were (or had been in 1978) acting as intermediaries between workers and employers. The government repression was particularly forceful during the forty-one day strike in 1980. The trade union leaders were removed and arrested. The police also arrested 290 workers, most of them for picketing.[79] The government forbade the workers from meeting in public spaces, forcing them to meet inside churches. In this strike, the movement adopted strategies to reduce the harsh financial impact that work stoppages had on workers and their families. For example, it used community networks to support workers during the strike (family, church, etc.); it also organized a strike fund, and it sought political support from other sectors of society. However, the strike was not successful: none of the workers' demands were met and the leaders of the movement were fired.[80]

These three strikes were a turning point because they gave the New Unionism movement a national profile. They also increased awareness among workers of the importance of trade unions and gave workers a sense of representation more directly connected with its base. Since the beginning of the military dictatorship, this was the first time many workers experienced actual dialogue and effective negotiation to address their demands.

---

[75] Statute 4.330 of Jun 1 1964, was supposed to regulate the right to strike but imposed so many conditions to its exercise that in practice made the right impossible to be exercised.

[76] Silvio Cesar Silva, "Experiências das Comissões de Fábrica na Reestruturação Produtiva da Autolatina" (1997) 2 *Lutas Sociais* 141 at 142.

[77] Abramo, *supra* note 72 at 218.

[78] Armando Boito Jr, "De Volta Para o Novo Corporativismo: A Trajetoria Politica do Sindicalismo Brasileiro" (1994) 8:3 *Sao Paulo Perspect* 23 at 24.

[79] Francisco Barbosa de Macedo, *A Greve de 1980: Redes Sociais e Mobilização Coletiva dos Metalúrgicos de São Bernardo do Campo* (Master's Thesis, São Paulo: USP, 2010) at 91.

[80] Ibid.

4.3.2. *The Origins of the* Central Única dos Trabalhadores

The New Unionism was not only fighting against oppressive and often abusive working conditions described earlier but also against a labour law system that allowed these to exist and remain in place. The structure of labour unions in Brazil is often described in the specialized literature as a corporatist system, which considers trade unions as organizations that must cooperate with the state, and therefore should be closely controlled and monitored by the government. [81] While it is possible to conceive of corporatist structures that foster cooperation between unions and the state to achieve public interest goals, such as economic development, in the Brazilian case the corporatist structure was characterized by a number of restrictions on freedom of association.[82] To fight this corporatist structure, the New Unionism movement, which emerged from workers' organization inside the factories, assumed combative positions against the government.[83]

The New Unionism marked the first time in Brazilian history that a labour movement challenged the pillars of the corporatist system, such as mandatory trade union dues and mandatory representation by a single, state-sanctioned union. The movement argued that trade unions should be created voluntarily by the workers themselves.[84] Despite being under a military dictatorship, members refused to wait for governmental changes in policy or state approval of their proposals. Instead, the movement promoted direct participation of workers in labour organizations.[85] For instance, the movement "established the celebrated *comissões de fábrica*, or workers' committees, which served as new vehicles for the negotiation of agreements and the resolution of labour disputes."[86] The grassroots movement was created and conceived outside of the corporatist system and state structures. Even when they worked with existing trade unions, as they did in the 1978, 1979, and 1980 strikes, the leaders of these unions emerged from spontaneous workers' organizations.[87]

While the movement was focused on improving working conditions and fighting for the most pressing workers' demands at the time, it was politically motivated and supported by strong political forces, while fiercely resisted by others. On the one hand, the movement derived a great deal of its support from opposition to the autocratic regime in power at the time.[88] Thus, its strategies were intrinsically

---

[81] For a detailed discussion of the features of Brazil's corporatist labour law system, see Gomes & Prado, *supra* note 70.

[82] Ibid.

[83] Stanley A. Gacek, "Revisiting the Corporatist and Contractualist Models of Labor Law Regimes: A Review of the Brazilian and American Systems" (1994) 16:1 *Cardozo L Rev* 21, at 82.

[84] Santana, *supra* note 71 at 109.

[85] Francisco Luiz Salles Gonçalves, *Duas Vertentes e Dois Projetos no Sindicalismo Brasileiro* (São Paulo: Cedec, 1985) at 42.

[86] Gacek, *supra* note 83 at 22.

[87] Santana, *supra* note 71 at 6.

[88] Boito, *supra* note 78 at 24.

associated with the broader aspirations of other political movements, especially the hopes for the return to a democratic system of government. On the other hand, there was strong opposition to the movement by the autocratic government, the employers, and the official trade unions. Moreover, groups genuinely interested in workers' rights and legitimate labour organizations alleged that workers were not prepared to handle freedom of association. These groups feared that freedom of association would weaken the labour movement, as "the proliferation of autonomous unions might eventually lead to deeper divisions within a heterogeneous working class and to a strictly 'economistic' activism (such as U.S.-style 'business unionism') on the part of a 'labour aristocracy' willing to play by the capitalist rules."[89]

One of the main proposals in the New Unionism agenda was to reform the corporatist trade union structure to create freedom of association in Brazil. In the pursuit of such reforms, the movement created an important institutional innovation in the Brazilian labour law system: the *Central Única dos Trabalhadores* (CUT), a central association for trade unions (*central sindical*), which allows unions to join forces and lobby for changes in the system. This was the first trade union central in the country[90] and was neither part of the traditional trade union structure nor was it authorized by the existing labour law system. At that time, the corporatist system did not allow for a national multi-sector association made up of multiple trade unions.[91] CUT was designed to operate very much along the lines of the federations and confederations in Brazil. Federations are top-level (or peak) organizations that aggregate the local unions of a certain professional category; confederations, in turn, aggregate federations of the same professional category.[92] A federation comprises at least five trade unions of a certain category, and a confederation comprises a minimum of three federations of a certain category. For instance, five labour unions of metal workers from five different municipalities in the state of São Paulo could form a federation of metal workers, and such a federation could then join federations in other

---

[89] Peter Swavely "Organized Labor in Brazil" in Lawrence S. Grahm & Robert H. Wilson, *The Political Economy of Brazil: Public Policies in an Era of Transition* (Austin, TX: University of Texas Press, 1990) 267; see also Tavares de Almeida, *supra* note 72 at 61.

[90] Today, there are more than ten trade union centrals in Brazil, such as *Força Sindical* (Union Strength), *Social Democracia Sindical* (Union Social Democracy), and the CGT (Workers' General Confederation), A 2001 survey indicates that 65.85 percent of the trade unions are associated with CUT, 19.49 percent with Força Sindical, 6.71 percent with Social Democracia Sindical, and 5.53 percent with CGT; IBGE, Departamento de População e Indicadores Sociais, "Sindicatos: Indicadores Sociais 2001 (IBGE, Rio de Janeiro, 2003) at 68 online: https://servicodados.ibge.gov.br/Download/Download.ashx?http=1&u=biblioteca.ibge.gov.br/visualizacao/livros/liv1416.pdf

[91] While CUT's operations were affronting the labour law provision that prohibited the organization of inter-categories institutions, the institution itself was legal, as the constitution 1967 authorized the formation of civil society organizations; Edson Gramuglia Araújo, *As Centrais no Sistema de Representação Sindical no Brasil* (Doctoral Dissertation, São Paulo: USP, 2012) at 16.

[92] For an explanation of the criteria and the process that define professional categories, establishing yet another limit into the freedom of association, see Gomes & Prado, *supra* note 70 at 109, FN 40.

states to form a confederation. This would all be authorized and closely monitored by the state under the corporatist structure.

Similar to federations, CUT also offers affiliation with unions. However, and in contrast to federations, the affiliation is not restricted by category. The idea was to allow a unification of the workers' movement across the sharply divided professional categories dictated by the corporatist system. The creators of CUT believed that an institutional arrangement uniting workers could potentially strengthen the political power of workers in their demands for change.

The movement perceived the creation of "new institutional spaces" as one of the most effective ways to overcome obstacles to labour law reforms.[93] CUT, in particular, was a strategy used to overcome two important obstacles, one external and one internal. The external obstacle was the existence of an authoritarian regime that was not open to internally driven reforms but which still allowed the CUT to be formed in 1983, during the last year of Brazil's military regime. The anticipated end of the regime may partially explain why the military government did not try to shut the organization down. As the country was preparing for a democratic transition, there was an increased fear of international criticism, combined with a desire to signal the new government's openness to change. Moreover, some authors suggest that the government believed that internal divisions in the movement were likely to weaken what had started as a strong and very confrontational labour movement in the late 1970s.[94] The internal obstacle was the existence of groups within the unions and the labour law system (Ministry of Labour and labour courts) that were interested in maintaining some of the power and benefits they had acquired through the existing system, while only promoting some changes at the margins.[95]

Both these obstacles imposed severe constraints on the possibility that existing trade unions could be instruments to foster change. The authoritarian regime had adopted laws imposing severe restrictions on strikes and effectively eliminating the possibility of collective negotiation.[96] Moreover, the regime had a strong hold over the union leadership, appointing people who were likely to protect its interests. These union leaders affiliated with the regime (known in Portuguese as *pelegos*), in turn, were interested in maintaining a system that empowered them, creating a group resistant to reform that was located inside the trade unions. Despite the fact that some unions had helped with the general strikes in the late 1970s, after the disappointing outcomes of the 1979 and 1980 strikes, the leaders of the movement realized that attempts to change the union system from within were significantly limited.

---

[93] Jeffrey Sluyter-Beltrão, *Rise and Decline of Brazil's New Unionism: The Politics of the Central Única dos Trabalhadores* (Oxford, UK: Peter Lang, 2010) at 41.

[94] Ibid. at 145.

[95] Ibid. at 41, 86–7 (dividing the "progressive Brazilian labor law field" into two large groups: the Reformists, who wanted gradual change through negotiation and sought marginal reforms in the system, and the Combatives, who wanted radical and rapid change to overhaul the existing structure).

[96] For a detailed description, see Section 4.3.1.

4.3.3. *The Governance Structure of CUT*

The idea of a central union had been circulating for many years before CUT was created, but gained support in the 1981–2 period due to a recession and high unemployment rates caused by government's austerity policies.[97] The internal disputes during this period reveal the importance of institutional design for all the groups participating in this process. More specifically, the governance structure of the central union was regarded as key to its success in changing the existing labour system in Brazil but was also a valuable instrument for different groups to seek control over such institutions.[98] The most important governance questions during this time related to the determination of which groups would be entitled to participate in the central union and how their delegations would be selected.

The major dispute over these questions was between two groups, called the Reformist bloc and the Combative bloc. The Reformists favoured authorizing only official institutions (unions, federations, and confederations). Their argument was that it was more important to unify all efforts against the military rule using the existing official institutions, rather than fragmenting their opposition by encouraging parallel labour organizations. The Reformists wanted to use the central union to denounce the repressive and abusive measures of the state apparatus, while at the same time maintaining most of the status quo.[99] While they seemed to perceive this as the most effective institutional strategy against the regime, it is no coincidence that most of their political support resided in these official institutions. In contrast, the Combative bloc favoured the inclusion of non-official entities in the central union, including new forms of shop-floor organizing. This proposal was based on a more radical concept of resistance, centred on confrontation with the military regime.[100] Not coincidentally, non-official organizations, often linked with broader social movements and with the Catholic Church, were the source of most of the Combative bloc's political support.[101]

The two groups could not reconcile their differences and, as a result, the Combative bloc created a central union, CUT, without the participation of the Reformist bloc. The Reformist bloc went on to create its own central union three months later, in November 1983, called CGT.[102] Reflecting their general preferences outlined earlier, CUT had a strong concern for the democratization of labour

---

[97] In the history of the Brazilian trade union movement, there have been some experiences with multi-categories organizations that for different reasons did not last much or had very restrict influence; Araújo, *supra* note 91 at 73.

[98] Sluyter-Beltrão, *supra* note 93.

[99] Maurício Rands Barros, *Labor Relations and the New Unionism in Contemporary Brazil* (Basingstoke, Hampshire and London, UK: Palgrave Macmillan UK, 1999) at 33.

[100] Ibid. at 32.

[101] Sluyter-Beltrão, *supra* note 93.

[102] Barros, *supra* note 99 at 35.

structures and representation of rank-and-file workers, while CGT was less inclined to empower rank-and-file workers or to oppose the existing structure in general.[103]

In addition to this dispute regarding *whether* non-official organizations should be included in the central union (Reformists vs. Combatives), there were important differences within Combatives (the group favouring the participation of non-official institutions) regarding *how* these institutions would be included in the central union. More specifically, there was a divergence of opinion regarding whether non-official groups (such as extra-official or independent workers' committees) would have direct representation in the central union, or whether they would only be able to participate through official unions. Those defending the direct participation of these non-official groups perceived this as a guarantee that non-union leaders (rank-and-file workers) and opposition groups to those running the official unions would be able to actively participate in the central union.

The final arrangement was a compromise among these groups within the Combative bloc.[104] While the first group within the Combative bloc managed to guarantee direct election and representation of rank-and-file workers in the annual deliberative meetings of CUT (as opposed to only union officials), the second group guaranteed that on a daily basis workers' committees would be subordinated to official unions, becoming arms of unions inside the factories.[105] This contradicted the preferences of part of the Combative bloc that wanted to use workers' committees as parallel union structures, with the right to participate directly in CUT. This would have effectively transformed the workers' committees into bypasses of official trade unions. However, CUT decided to adopt the other option, in which these workers' committees would be encouraged and supported, but their main mission was to obtain leadership positions within the existing trade unions. They believed that this would increase the possibility of changing the system from within.

One of the reasons why the leaders of the movement adopted this compromise solution was to legitimize CUT.[106] It is clear that CUT was operating outside the existing labour framework in Brazil, and its leaders did not want to compound its non-official status with forms of collective organization that were prosecuted by the state. Moreover, the severe backlash and state repression against the movement in

---

[103] For a useful comparison of the main differences in institutional preferences, see the table provided by Sluyter-Beltrão, *supra* note 93 at 124.

[104] For a more detailed and nuanced description of these disputes, see Sluyter-Beltrão, *supra* note 93 at 114–5.

[105] Sluyter-Beltrão, *supra* note 93 at 114, 127, 142.

[106] Maria Rosângela Batistoni, *Entre a Fábrica e o Sindicato: Os dilemas da Oposição Sindical Metalúrgica de São Paulo* (Doctoral dissertation, São Paulo: PUC – Department of Social Work, 2001) 387; Francisco Carlos Palomanes Martinho "Vargas e o Legado do Trabalhismo no Brasil: Entre a Tradição e a Modernidade" (2004–5) 12:2 *Portuguese Stud Rev* 161 at 172–3 (emphasizing how the New Unionism leaders have used the corporativist structure to make their own movement possible); Armando Boito Jr, *O Sindicalismo de Estado no Brasil* (São Paulo: Hucitec/Unicamp, 1991) at 153; see also Marco Aurélio Santana, "O 'Novo' e o 'Velho' Sindicalismo: Análise de um Debate" (1998) 10/11 *Revista de Sociologia e Política* 19 at 32.

the late 1970s made workers very wary of joining non-official organizations, as they feared state prosecution.[107]

4.3.4. *CUT as an Institutional Bypass of Federations and Confederations*

CUT is clearly a bypass of federations and confederations, as it offers official unions a choice between associating themselves under the umbrella of the official structure of the corporatist system or under the central union. Its main institutional innovation vis-à-vis the existing labour system was the unification of a diverse set of organizations across different professional categories, which empowered CUT to press the government for reforms. It did not, however, operate as an institutional bypass of trade unions. Despite the fact that it allowed worker representatives to participate in its annual meetings, where most decisions were taken, it did not allow the direct affiliation of workers. This remains true today. The representatives are chosen according to governance rules of CUT, and thus the central union does not serve as an alternative for workers who are questioning affiliation with an official union. According to the governance rules of CUT, there are both official union representatives and rank-and-file representatives, who are usually operating at the level of workers' committees.[108] In sum, what CUT has offered is a place that allows cross-sectoral alliances between unions and non-official institutions, such as workers' committees.

CUT initially created a virtuous cycle of changes in Brazil's union structures, and its importance cannot be overstated. The number and volume of strikes significantly increased in the 1980s.[109] While economic policies implemented by the government were the direct motivation for strikes, CUT was also indirectly strengthening the movement by reinforcing the decentralized pattern of mobilization that had begun before its creation, especially with the 1970s company-wide strikes.[110] Also, the upsurge in strike activities reflected the combative attitude of CUT, which had a strong influence on individual workers' attitudes and values.[111] Moreover, CUT registered significant achievements in reducing the dominance of a state-controlled system. For instance, it introduced a more combative type of collective bargaining in a system designed to avoid collective bargaining at all costs. The strike law imposed strict limits on workers' ability to organize strikes and was directly challenged during the late 1970 and early 1980s strikes. In 1990s, CUT introduced another institutional innovation, creating organic federations and confederations that allowed trade unions affiliated with CUT to be represented in the system even if their official

---

[107] Barros, *supra* note 99 at 66–7.
[108] For more details about the rules of representation, see Sluyter-Beltrão, *supra* note 93 at 142.
[109] Barros, *supra* note 99 at 59–60.
[110] Ibid. at 63.
[111] Giovanni Alves, "Do 'Novo Sindicalismo' à 'Concertação Social': Ascensão (e Crise) do Sindicalismo no Brasil (1978–1998)" (2000) 15 *Rev Sociol Polít, Curitiba* 111 at 114.

federations and confederations were not members of CUT.[112] These organic federations and confederations can be considered additional bypasses within the bypass
that was CUT. They revitalized workers' involvement and opened space for new
leadership in many unions in the country, despite the existence of a corporatist
system that was designed to prevent this.[113]

Over the long term, however, CUT did not create significant changes within
the corporatist structure of unions in Brazil. There were informal changes in the
internal governance structure of some unions (those in which the leadership was
affiliated with the Combatives) but no formal changes in the legislation and its
strongest corporatist elements.[114] Some scholars ascribe this failure to the particular
institutional choice to prevent informal institutions (such as workers' committees)
from operating independently from trade unions.[115] CUT itself was already operating outside the existing labour law structure and could have tapped into the potential of the movement to create an entirely parallel union structure and effectively
bypass the entire corporatist system. In other words, some claim that the bypass of
federations and confederations could have been more effective if coupled with a
bypass of the official trade unions.[116]

While a bypass of official trade unions could have enhanced the institutional
innovations, it could also have sparked much stronger repression of these newly
created institutions and the New Unionism movement overall. Considering the
uncertainties surrounding the political transition, and the fact that Brazil had not
yet fully established a democratic regime, this was a risky strategy. At least one
author suggests that CUT's implementation of a very ambitious structure that
was independent of the existing system would have likely led to its repression and
potential destruction rather than to its becoming a truly transformative force.[117]

---

[112] At the time of the creation of CUT, there was also a debate about whether the central union should be
open to official federation and confederation leaders. Some wanted to block the participation of these
leaders, arguing that they would ruin the purpose of the central union, because official federations
and confederations (and their leaders) were closely associated with the military regime and with very
undemocratic governance structures.

[113] Maria Herminia Tavares de Almeida, "Difícil Caminho: Sindicatos e Política na Construção da
Democracia" in Fábio Wanderley Reis & Guillermo O'Donnell, eds., *A Democracia no Brasil –
Dilemas e Perspectivas* (São Paulo: Vértice, 1988).

[114] Iran Jácome conducted a quantitative survey among trade unions affiliated with CUT on their
practices and concluded that there was a discrepancy between CUT's policy discourse and the
practice of its affiliated trade unions. For example, from all the trade unions surveyed only 70 percent
would receive the mandatory trade union due, contrary to CUT's orientation; Iran Jácome Rodrigues,
Sindicalismo e Política: A Trajetória da CUT (1983 a 1993) 2nd ed., (São Paulo: LTr, 2011) at 157.

[115] Boito, *supra* note 106; but see Batistoni, *supra* note 106 at 387–8 (describing a movement that tried to
do just that but failed, called Entões).

[116] The workers' committees before the creation of CUT can be considered a spontaneous institutional
bypass of trade unions. After CUT, however, their operation was not independent of the governance
structure of trade unions.

[117] Barros, *supra* note 99 at 66–7; see also Boito, *supra* note 106.

As these are all counter-factual speculations, it is difficult to determine whether a more ambitious approach would have indeed helped the movement succeed.

The result of these compromise solutions was a governance structure that operated independently of the corporatist regime but had strong ties with it. The New Unionism, on the one hand, had a discourse and practices that were directed against the official labour law system, but on the other hand CUT decided to use the corporatist trade union structure as a source of support.[118] The supportive relationship between the bypassing institution and the bypassed system culminated in the official recognition and incorporation of the central unions (CUT and similar organizations) into the Brazilian labour law system in 2008. One of the core elements of this change is the fact that all central unions became entitled to receive the mandatory dues collected by the corporatist trade unions.[119]

4.4. CONCLUSION

The three case studies analyzed in this chapter provide examples of intentional bypasses promoted either by the government or by civil society movements. The common element in all three case studies (along with the *Poupatempo* case study discussed in Chapters 1 and 2) is the fact that these are intentional interventions designed to provide an alternative to existing system and over time potentially change it. In all cases, bypasses allowed users to choose between different service providers. One may question whether individuals did have a choice of which security forces to use once the UPP was created. We would answer in the affirmative, even as we acknowledge that the availability of a choice in this case may not be as clear-cut as that observed in other cases, such as *Poupatempo*. One may also question whether workers indeed had a choice with the creation of CUT, which was primarily designed to replace federations and confederations. Although the choice may not have been as direct as choosing an alternative trade union, it did represent an option for union leaders and some rank-and-file workers in what was otherwise a monopolistic system.

All three cases also illustrate different ways in which the institutional bypass can be separated from the dominant institution from a governance perspective. While UPP started as a pilot project, deeply embedded in the dominant institution, over time it evolved to become separate from it from a governance and, most importantly, operational standpoint. In contrast, the case of CUT offers an example where a separate governance structure with connections to the dominant system existed until 2008, when the Brazilian legal system entitled all central unions to receive the

---

[118] Marcelo Badaró Mattos, *Novos e Velhos Sindicalismos no Rio de Janeiro* (1955–1988) (Rio de Janeiro: Vício de Leitura, 1998) at 80–1.
[119] Statute 11,648 of Mar 31, 2008.

mandatory trade union fee.[120] While this guarantees their financial independence vis-à-vis official unions, it is perceived as a reform that makes them even less prone to push for changes as the existing structure of the Brazilian labour system guarantees their survival.

The three cases also illustrate an aspiration to offer an alternative that is more functional than the dominant system. That being said, the case of UPAs illustrates some of the complexities raised by this kind of analysis. What kind of metrics should be used to assess the effectiveness of the bypass, since the choice of individual users may be motivated by incommensurable concerns like better quality health care, on the one hand, and geographical proximity and convenience, on the other? The concept of bypass does not offer an answer to this question, adopting instead a descriptive account of what users may or may not prefer when given the choice.

Some important threads also emerge from the three case studies. Acknowledging the limitations of producing a generalization from small sample sizes, it is interesting to note that all three initiatives seem to have emerged under very particular circumstances: they were immediately preceded by a crisis, which acted as a window of opportunity for reforms; they relied heavily on strong political will (and political alliances) to make them feasible; and they had, at least in the beginning, access to significant resources, especially financial resources. These commonalities among the case studies may point to conditions under which intentional institutional bypasses are more likely to come about, but further research would be required to affirm this more conclusively.

Despite the common traits in all three cases, the particular circumstances of each raises interesting questions about the importance of resources and their connection with political support for the creation and maintenance of an institutional bypass. For instance, in the cases of UPPs and UPAs, a political alliance between federal, state, and municipal governments made a significant amount of resources available to support UPPs and UPAs. UPPs also had financial support from the private sector. However, these resources (and the political support for these resources) may be limited and unsustainable, as some have argued to be the case with UPPs, which had access to a significantly larger amount of resources than the regular police force, in part due to the concern with security leading up to the mega-events of the World Cup and Olympics in Rio de Janeiro.

In other cases, the financial incentives may have driven the willingness to embrace the initiative rather than a fair and impartial assessment of the results. For instance, it is not clear whether the replication of UPAs across the country could be interpreted as evidence of their success in improving access to health care services, or whether the scaling up of the project has been driven primarily by the financial incentives provided by the federal government to municipalities that are often scrambling to find resources to provide health care services to citizens. The same question could

---

[120] Ibid.

also be raised regarding the creation of one-stop shops for bureaucratic services in most Brazilian states with the support of the federal government.

And last but not least, the viability of the bypass (politically and financially) may be dependent upon establishing connections and securing access to resources inside the dominant system. As an intentional bypass spearheaded by a civil society movement, CUT was confronted with this conundrum. In this case, the degree of separation of this parallel structure from the existing system was inversely connected with its ability to garner political support and obtain resources. UPPs, in turn, illustrate how a bypass may simply become infeasible once these resources are no longer available.

In sum, these three case studies not only provide examples of intentional institutional bypasses, but they also indicate some of the common trends that may characterize the creation and maintenance of these arrangements. While intentional bypasses seem predicated on the same conditions that often favour the implementation of other institutional reforms, they become attractive options primarily in cases where internal reforms are either not feasible or not promising. The attractiveness of this remedial arrangement, in turn, will vary from case to case depending largely on the amount of political support and resources available to sustain it.

5

Spontaneous Bypasses

5.1. INTRODUCTION

Spontaneous bypasses are scattered and uncoordinated solutions that emerge independently of each other but collectively amount to an arrangement that offers an alternative institutional pathway to the dominant system. In contrast to intentional bypasses, which are conscious, centralized, and planned attempts to fix what are perceived as dysfunctionalities in a system,[1] spontaneous bypasses lack the self-declared and official purpose of offering a structural solution to such dysfunctionalities. Instead, they are based on uncoordinated attempts to seek alternatives that will suit particular individuals in a defined context.

Isolated individual actors seeking solutions to their particular needs amount to a bypass only when they create an alternative institutional pathway. The concept of institutional bypass does not include the acts of one single individual trying to find a way around a dysfunctional system, unless these acts create some sort of institutional infrastructure that can enable others to benefit from this option.[2] Such infrastructure can be defined either as creating a pathway that others can also use, or simply creating an institutional arrangement that others can mimic and replicate on their own. In both these cases, the individual initiative has the potential to reach and benefit others, not being confined to its creator.

In this chapter, we illustrate the concept of spontaneous bypasses with three case studies: private security services in Latin America, low-cost private schools in India, and *Lok Adalat*, an informal dispute resolution system, also in India. The first case study analyzes the dramatic proliferation of private security forces in Brazil and other countries in Latin America. These initiatives are driven by users, partially motivated by exceptionally high crime rates in many of these countries, the ineffectiveness of traditional public police forces in responding to citizen concerns and failed police

---

[1] See Chapter 4.
[2] See Chapter 2.

reform efforts. As a result, firms, organizations, and citizens have increasingly come to view protection from criminal activity as a private rather than a public good, through contractual arrangements with private security providers (often small and informal entities that are *de facto* unregulated).

The second case study discusses low-cost schools in India that are accessible to families of modest means and operate informally in both rural and urban communities, largely without formal recognition or regulation by the state. Almost 30 percent of primary school age children in India now attend private schools, a phenomenon seen on a similar scale in a number of other developing countries. In large part, this trend appears to be driven by the appalling performance of the Indian public school system. In comparative tests of literacy and numeracy, many of these low-cost private schools significantly out-perform their public school counterparts, despite often modest and informal physical facilities, lower levels of teacher credentials or formal training and compensation, and much lower levels of revenues and expenditures per student.

The third case study discusses the *Lok Adalats* in India, which are traditional forms of informal dispute resolution that have provided an alternative to the formal court system for personal grievances. Despite being supported by the government, legitimate concerns have been raised as to whether these traditional forms of dispute resolution meet minimal understandings of due process and equality before the law (especially for women and marginalized minorities), while attenuating political pressures for reform of the formal court system to make it more accommodating of and responsive to often small scale (in monetary terms) personal grievances.

In analyzing these examples of spontaneous bypasses, we discuss conditions under which they are likely to appear and the role of the state in this process. In all three cases, we also inquire into the circumstances (if any) under which these spontaneous bypasses are likely to destabilize the dominant system and promote institutional change. All three case studies provide cautionary tales with respect to government reactions to spontaneously emerging bypasses. As indicated in Chapter 2, institutional bypasses cannot expressly contradict the requirements of the legal system within which they are operating. Therefore, the concept of spontaneous bypass would not include illegal initiatives that try to circumvent the dominant system. However, in all three case studies discussed in this chapter, the initiatives seem to be operating at the boundaries of legality (and some of them could be crossing the line). This raises an important question about the legality requirement for bypasses: Are governmental restrictions being imposed for principled reasons (e.g., to prevent derogation from the rule of law), or are these restrictions protectionist measures to favour certain groups to the detriment of others? If the latter, one is led to wonder whether these arrangements, even if initially illegal, are one of the few possibilities of promoting meaningful institutional change.

There are many examples of illegal initiatives that ended up promoting institutional change. These include the widespread evasion of Prohibition laws in the

United States, leading to their repeal; recent massive construction booms in many Chinese cities that were initially illegal but led to the reform of property laws; ride-sharing services entering heavily regulated taxi markets; and the informal curbside market in Taiwan for financing small business that is illegal but whose widespread use has led to government acquiescence.[3] These examples raise the question of what role the government can play in opening space for these spontaneous bypasses to flourish or not. While illegal *de jure*, some of these arrangements are tolerated *de facto*, since there are no government efforts to curb the initiatives. Considering the transformative potential of the arrangements operating at the boundary of legality, we will consider that *de facto* tolerance (i.e., law in action, as opposed to law in the books) also allows us to qualify a particular initiative as a bypass.

We conclude this chapter by acknowledging that the transformative potential of alternative institutional arrangements may be inversely proportional to their legality. This is not a reason to include clearly illegal arrangements in the concept of institutional bypass, as this would raise the risk of embracing arrangements that challenge and undermine the general public interest in law-abiding behaviour. However, it does suggest that there is a grey zone where *de jure* illegal but *de facto* tolerated arrangements are often those that most radically and visibly push for institutional changes. Indeed, while the three cases analyzed here may not be representative of the majority of spontaneous bypasses, they do indicate that these can often operate at the limits of legality. In light of this, the role of governments in the process of creation and replication of spontaneous bypasses should be carefully scrutinized in light of the particularities of each context. Specifically, the drivers of governmental constraints may reveal that these will be more justifiable in some circumstances than in others. An in-depth, contextualized analysis of the nature, reasons, and consequences of governmental regulations and restrictions on a case-by-case basis will therefore be necessary in the context of spontaneous bypasses.

5.2. CHOOSING SECURITY SERVICES: PRIVATE PROVISION IN LATIN AMERICA

Latin America is currently one of the most violent regions in the world, accounting for nearly one in three global homicides.[4] The causes of these high levels of

---

3 See Frank K. Upham, *The Great Property Fallacy* (Cambridge, UK: Cambridge University Press) [forthcoming in January 2018]; Shui-Yan Tang, "Informal Credit Markets and Economic Development in Taiwan" (1995) 23:5 *World Dev* 845.

4 David Luhnow, "Latin America is World's Most Violent Region" (Apr 11, 2014) *Wall Street Journal*, online: www.wsj.com/articles/SB10001424052702303603904579495863883782316. Latin America also has the highest mortality rate due to violence. Moreover, homicide rates in Latin America are more than double the world average. See Rodrigo Soares & Joana Naritomi, "Understanding High Crime Rates in Latin America: The Role of Social and Policy Factors" in Rafael Di Tella, Sebastian Edwards, & Ernesto Schargrodsky, eds., *The Economics of Crime: Lessons For and From Latin America* (Chicago: University of Chicago Press, 2010).

violence are complex and controversial, and are not the principal focus of this section.[5] Instead, we discuss one consequence of this persistent violence: the expansion of private security services for companies and for individuals in middle and upper social classes. Faced with unrelenting crime rates, Latin American companies have been increasingly reliant on private security services, and wealthy individuals are hiring bodyguards, moving to gated communities and driving bulletproof cars. These private security services seem to be operating as an institutional bypass in Latin America. Private security forces may perform a wide variety of functions, and in many countries they complement the services delivered by public security forces. However, in the case of Brazil and other Latin American countries, private security services are replacing public security forces, seeking to bypass ineffective state protection against crimes.

5.2.1. *The Problem: High Crime Rates and Failed Police Reforms*

Although data on crime and violence in Latin America are often incomplete and sometimes unreliable, most information available confirms that there was a steep rise in crime rates and violence in Latin American countries during the 1980s and 1990s.[6] The trend continued into the 2000s: this is the only region in the world where lethal violence increased between 2000 and 2010; homicide rates in most regions of the world have fallen by as much as 50 percent, but in Latin America they increased by 12 percent.[7]

The United Nations Development Programme (UNDP) recently highlighted citizen insecurity as an urgent human development challenge in Latin America.[8] Indeed, an average of 17 percent of those surveyed in the Americas Barometer 2014 study report being the victim of a crime in the past year, although this figure is

---

[5] For a discussion of the causes of violence in Latin America, see, for example, Alessandra Heinemann & Dorte Verner, *Crime and Violence in Development: A Literature Review of Latin America and the Caribbean* (Washington, DC: World Bank, 2006).

[6] United Nations Office on Drugs and Crime, *Global Study on Homicide, 2013: Trends, Contexts, Data* (United Nations Office on Drugs and Crime, 2013), online: www.unodc.org/documents/ data-and-analysis/statistics/GSH2013/2014_GLOBAL_HOMICIDE_BOOK_web.pdf; Kurt Weyland, "Political Repercussions of Crime and Violence in Latin America" (paper delivered at the Conference on Culture and Peace: Violence, Politics and Representations in the Americas at the University of Texas at Austin, Law School, Mar 24–25, 2003) at 1 [unpublished]; Mark A. Cohen & Mauricio Rubio, "Solutions Paper: Violence and Crime in Latin America" (paper delivered at the Consulta de San Jose [San Jose Consultation] of the Inter-American Development Bank, San Jose, Costa Rica, Oct 22–26, 2007) at 2 [unpublished].

[7] United Nations Development Programme (UNDP), *Human Development Report for Latin America 2013–2014: Citizen Security with a Human Face: Evidence and Proposals for Latin America* (New York: United Nations Development Programme, 2013), online: www.undp.org/content/undp/ en/home/librarypage/hdr/human-development-report-for-latin-america-2013-2014/ See also The Economist, Apr 5, 2018, "Shining Light on Latin America's Homicide Epidemic."

[8] UNDP, *supra* note 7.

as high as 30 percent in some South and Central American countries.[9] Although violent crime receives much of the attention in public reporting, non-violent crime is also pervasive. Robberies, which have become the most common crime in Latin America, have tripled in the past quarter century.[10] In general, those surveyed more commonly reported having seen in the past year burglary and the sale of illegal drugs than extortion and homicide.[11]

Latin American citizens have not been insensitive to these problems. Five out of ten Latin Americans perceive that security in their country has deteriorated: "Up to 65 percent stopped going out at night due to insecurity and 13 percent reported having felt the need to move to another place for fear of becoming victims of a crime."[12] A 2013 survey of public opinion across Latin America found that crime was listed as the most important problem, ahead of unemployment.[13] Similarly, the Americas Barometer survey (2014) found that security and the economy are considered the two top issues in the Americas (with 33 percent and 36 percent of respondents citing these issues as the most important problem, respectively), with a rise in the importance of security over the past decade.[14]

Moreover, there is growing scepticism across Latin America about the capacity of governments to reduce crime rates; confidence that the state can resolve this problem dropped from 61 percent in 2011 to 55 percent in 2013.[15] This concern has been translated into significant social pressure on political representatives for increased public security and police reforms,[16] and there have indeed been various attempts to implement police reform throughout the region.[17] Nevertheless, most studies show that the efficacy of these reforms has been either limited or nonexistent.[18]

---

[9] Elizabeth Zechmeister, ed., *The Political Culture of Democracy in the Americas, 2014: Democratic Governance across 10 Years of the Americas Barometer* (Nashville, TN: USAID, 2014). For example, the reported victimization rate was 30 percent for Peru, 28 percent for Ecuador, 24 percent for Argentina and Venezuela, 23 percent for Mexico, and 16 percent for Brazil. Victimization rates were lower in rural areas than urban areas.

[10] UNDP, *supra* note 7.

[11] Ibid.

[12] Ibid.

[13] Corporacion Latinobarometro, *Informe 2013* (Santiago, Chile: Corporacion Latinobarometro, 2013) at 61.

[14] Zechmeister, *supra* note 9. Notably, this survey includes Canada and the United States.

[15] Ibid. at 68.

[16] Saima Husain, "On the Long Road to Demilitarization and Professionalization of the Police" in Niels A. Uildriks, ed., *Policing Insecurity: Police Reform, Security, and Human Rights in Latin America* (Lanham, MD: Lexington Books, 2009) 47 at 53.

[17] Hugo Fruhling, "Research on Latin American Police: Where Do We Go from Here?" (2009) 10:5–6 *Police Prac & Research* 465 at 465; Mariana Mota Prado, Michael J. Trebilcock, & Patrick Hartford, "Police Reform in Violent Democracies in Latin America" (2012) 4 *Hague J on the Rule of L* 252.

[18] Lucia Dammert, "Dilemas da Reforma Policial na America Latina" in Haydee Caruso, Jacqueline Muniz, & Antonio Carlos Carballo Blanco, eds., *Policia, Estado e Sociedade: Pratica e Saberes Latino Americanos* (Rio de Janeiro: Viva Rio, 2007) at 145.

While social and institutional realities affecting violence levels and the feasibility of police reform in Latin America vary a great deal, depending on the country
and sector of society, there seems to be some common trends that help explain
the disappointing track record of reforms throughout the region. One constraint is
lack of resources. Police in the region are "often underpaid, under-qualified and
under-trained," lacking overall capacity to effectively investigate reported crimes
and support communities.[19] This constraint also fuels police corruption, further
undermining the ability of police institutions to provide a professional and effective
service.[20] Corrupt police officers are also likely to resist any type of reforms that
could reduce their rents. This is of special concern in Latin America, where the
rates of police corruption in the region are particularly high.[21]

Opposition to reform is derived not only from police forces themselves (especially
where this would entail greater public accountability) but also from political elites
imbued with a tradition of viewing the police as a para-military organization primarily designed to protect and preserve incumbent political regimes, and broad public
sympathy for *"mano-dura"* policing practices in the face of often high and rising
violent crime rates.[22] Historically, in much of Latin America "the predominant role
of the military and the implementation of National Security Doctrines to combat
civil unrest and guerrilla movements blurred the distinctions between the police
and the military and between common criminals and threats to the state."[23] As a
result, Latin American police forces have generally been better prepared to secure
social order and defend ruling interests than to prevent and address violence in democratic societies.[24] In addition, there is a popular preference for short-term reforms
in the form of *mano-dura* repressive policies that do not address the real causes of
violence.[25] Another consequence of this historical legacy is the fierce resistance of
many police officials to any kind of reform that will make police more accountable to society.[26] "Many studies show that lower-ranking officers are not supportive
of community policing or similar programs that have the potential for improving
officers' adherence to the law."[27]

---

[19] Michael J. Trebilcock & Ronald J. Daniels, *Rule of Law Reform and Development: Charting the
Fragile Path of Progress* (Northampton, MA: Edward Elgar Publishing Limited, 2008) at 108.
[20] Niels A. Uildriks, "Police Reform, Security, and Human Rights in Latin America: An Introduction"
in Uildriks, *Policing Insecurity, supra* note 16, 1 at 10.
[21] Corporacion Latinobaromentro, *supra* note 13; see also Uildriks, *Police Reform, supra* note 20 at 8–10;
Trebilcock & Daniels, *supra* note 19 at 123.
[22] Prado, Trebilcock, & Hartford, *supra* note 17.
[23] Trebilcock & Daniels, *supra* note 19 at 108.
[24] Ibid. at 109; see also Prado, Trebilcock, & Hartford, *supra* note 17.
[25] Mark Ungar, "The Privatization of Citizen Security in Latin America: From Elite Guards to
Neighborhood Vigilantes" (2007–8) 34:3–4 *Soc Justice* 20 at 25.
[26] See e.g., Trebilcock & Daniels, *supra* note 19 at 119.
[27] Hugo Frühling, "Recent Police Reform in Latin America" in Uildriks, *Policing Insecurity, supra* note
16 at 29.

In sum, ever-increasing crime rates and failed police reforms are creating a latent demand for enhanced security, which is fuelling a significant expansion of the private security sector.[28]

5.2.2. The Response: Bypassing Public Security with Private Security Services

The private security industry is large, and growing globally. An estimated 20 million private security personnel exist worldwide, and half of the world's population lives in countries where the number of private security workers is larger than the number of public police officers.[29] Global demand for private contract security services is projected to increase 6 percent annually and is expected to be worth US$240 billion in 2020 (up from US$180 billion in 2017).[30] This expansion has not only happened in Latin America and other developing countries with record crime rates, but also in the United States, Canada, and Western and Eastern Europe.[31]

In 2015 Latin America comprised just over one-tenth of the global private security industry, being worth approximately US$30 billion.[32] While the Latin American market for private security services may not be the largest in the world, it has experienced significant growth.[33] The industry is growing at 9 percent per year in Latin America, slightly faster than the worldwide average.[34] Brazil is driving a great deal of this growth with an annual average growth rate of 15–20 percent over the past eight years and annual sales (equipment and services) of approximately US$26 billion.[35]

---

[28] Ungar, *supra* note 25 at 20.

[29] Niall McCarthy, "Private Security Outnumbers The Police In Most Countries Worldwide" (Aug 31, 2017) Forbes, online: www.forbes.com/sites/niallmccarthy/2017/08/31/private-security-outnumbers-the-police-in-most-countries-worldwide-infographic/#76754769210f

[30] "World Security Services" (Jan 2017), *Freedonia Group*, online: www.freedoniagroup.com/industry-study/global-security-services-market-by-type-market-and-region-12th-edition-3451.htm; see also Claire Provost, "The Industry of Inequality: Why the World Is Obsessed with Private Security" (May 12, 2017) *The Guardian*, online: www.theguardian.com/inequality/2017/may/12/industry-of-inequality-why-world-is-obsessed-with-private-security

[31] Ibid.; see also Vera Institute of Justice, *The Public Accountability of Private Police: Lessons from New York, Johannesburg and Mexico City* (New York: Vera Institute of Justice, 2000) at 1; Geoffrey Li, "Private Security and Public Policing in Canada" (Dec 2008) *Statistics Canada*, online: www.statcan.gc.ca/pub/85-002-x/2008010/article/10730-eng.htm#a3; Nigel South, "Privatizing Policing in the European Market: Some Issues for Theory, Policy and Research" (1994) 10 *Eur Sociological Rev* 219 at 221; Mark Button, "Assessing the Regulation of Private Security across Europe" (2007) 4:1 *Eur J of Crim* 109 at 111.

[32] Adam Blackwell, "The Unregulated and Threatening Growth of Private Security in Latin America and the Caribbean" (2015) Wilson Center Latin American Program, online: www.wilsoncenter.org/sites/default/files/Private%20Security%20in%20Latin%20America.pdf.

[33] Ungar, *supra* note 25 at 20.

[34] Blackwell, *supra* note 32.

[35] "Brazil – Safety and Security" (Oct 8, 2017), online: www.export.gov/article?id=Brazil-Safety-and-Security; see also Juliana Mello, "Introduction to the Security Industry in Brazil" (Apr 3, 2012) *The Brazil Business*, online: http://thebrazilbusiness.com/article/introduction-to-the-security-industry-in-brazil

As a result, the ratio of private security guards to police officers in Latin America has been in general much higher than in other countries. For instance, while developed countries generally have 2:1 ratios, some Latin American countries have 11:1 ratios.[36] The largest clients in this market are financial and commercial institutions, as well as the federal government.[37]

In addition to elevated rates of growth, a unique feature of private security forces in Latin America is that these services are seeking to perform the same functions that are performed by the public police force. This goal contrasts with the situation in other countries (especially developed countries), where either *private parties* are using private security services to cater to their special security needs or *the state* is using privatization in exceptional cases to substitute for public security forces.[38] Neither of these options, however, can be classified as a spontaneous bypass, in light of the characteristics of an institutional bypass presented in Chapter 2. Hiring specialized private security services is not a bypass if the private security services perform specialized functions or respond to the special security needs of their clients. An example is private security for banks and companies.[39] These private security services do not perform the same function as the public police force. Thus, specialized private security services do not offer an "alternative pathway" to the delivery of services provided by the state. In turn, privatization of security forces is also not a bypass, as it does not keep the dominant institution in place. Outsourcing security services means that the public police force is replaced by private security.[40] In contrast

---

[36] Patricia Arias, *Seguridad Privada en America Latina: el Lucro y los Dilemas de Una Regulacion Deficitaria* (Santiago, Chile: Facultad Latinoamericana de Ciencias Sociales, 2009) at 25–7; Andre Zanetic, A *Questao da Seguranca Privada: Estudo do Marco Regulatório dos Serviços Particulares de Segurança* (Masters Thesis, São Paulo: USP, 2005) at 43–4 [unpublished]; see also McCarthy, *supra* note 29.

[37] Ibid.

[38] For a discussion of the specific reasons that could motivate this type of privatization, see Mariana Mota Prado, "Regulatory Choices in the Privatization of Infrastructure" in Simon Chesterman & Angelina Fisher, eds., *Private Security, Public Order* (New York: Oxford University Press, 2009) 107–32 at 110; Martha Minnow, "Outsourcing Power: How Privatizing Military Efforts Challenges Accountability, Professionalism, and Democracy" (2005) 46:5 *BC L Rev* 989; Jody Freeman & Martha Minow, eds., *Government by Contract: Outsourcing and American Democracy* (Cambridge, MA: Harvard University Press, 2009).

[39] This conceptual distinction may not be as stark in practice, as these services may interact with the functions performed by public police forces and could even generate positive externalities, such as reducing the overall level of crime in a region. See John M. MacDonald, Jonathan Klick, & Ben Grunwald, "The Effect of Private Police on Crime: Evidence from a Geographic Regression Discontinuity Design," (2016) 179:3 *J of the Royal Statistical Soc: Series A (Statistics in Society)* 831.

[40] There is one form of privatization that could be viewed as an institutional bypass: a private analogue to the example of the UPPs discussed in the previous chapter. This would involve the state contracting out the provision of security services to private security providers in particular neighbourhoods where public police forces have proven ineffective and impermeable to reform. In some respects, this approach could serve as an interim measure that may provide the political impetus for public security

to these two arrangements, the provision of private security services in Latin America keeps the traditional institution in place (i.e., the public police force is neither terminated nor removed from its function or deprived of its jurisdiction), while at the same time offering an "alternative pathway" to users seeking more security. A user can choose to rely on the police force or to hire private security instead to deliver the services that would otherwise be delivered by the police.

It is important to emphasize that a bypass does not arise where one private user hires a person to provide security services, as doing so does not create an infrastructure that allows other users to benefit from the same service. The existence of a market for private security services, with established institutions structured to provide such services to those willing to pay for their services, is what characterizes the phenomenon as an institutional bypass. In sum, the existence of a bypass depends on the existence of separate governance structures (that governing private companies and that governing the public police force), each of which has institutions performing the same function (providing public security).

Mexico and Brazil provide examples of this kind of spontaneous bypass. The disturbing security conditions in Mexico and inadequacies in the public police forces – notably, lack of capacity and corruption – have led to an explosion of the private security sector in Mexico as a response by citizens to problems that governments have proved incapable of tackling. Indeed, public trust in the police is "so low they are practically the last to be called when a crime is committed, in part because citizens fear further abuses at their hands."[41] Davis describes this reaction as citizens "effectively introducing their own 'bottom-up' police reforms, built on a rejection or repudiation ... of 'public' police's willful disenfranchisement from ascribed duties."[42] Another example is Brazil where, in 2015, the market for private security services was considered the fourth-largest in the world if measured by revenue,[43] with approximately 80,000 security companies employing over 500,000 people.[44] The type of private security being offered in Brazil and Mexico and other Latin American countries is a bypass because the growth of demand for private security services by citizens, private companies, and even the government is directly related to declining levels of trust in the police.[45] Moreover, these private security

---

service reforms along the lines of the UPP experience. However, it would amount to an intentional bypass, not a spontaneous one.

[41] Diane Davis, "Law Enforcement in Mexico: Not Yet Under Control" (2003) 37:2 *NACLA Report on the Americas* 17 at 17.

[42] Ibid.

[43] "World Security Services" (Jan 2013) *Freedonia Group*, online www.freedoniagroup.com/industry-study/2978/world-security-services.htm

[44] Kate Wilkinson, "Does SA Have the Largest Private Security Industry in the World?" (Jan 23, 2015) *Africa Check*, online: http://africacheck.org/reports/does-sa-have-the-largest-private-security-industry-in-the-world/

[45] See Katherine Corcoran, "Private Firms Filling Latin America's Security Gap Amid Distrust of Corrupt, Inept Police Forces" (Nov 30, 2014) *Japan Times*, online: www.japantimes.co.jp/news/2014/11/30/world/crime-legal-world/private-firms-filling-latin-americas-security-gap-amid

services are performing functions that would otherwise be assigned to the public police force.[46]

In sum, the phenomenon of growing private security services becomes an institutional bypass when there is an institutional infrastructure from which multiple agents can benefit. The growth of such services, as characterized by the rise of the number of private security companies performing the same functions as public security forces, not only consolidates the idea that this is an institutional bypass but also raises questions about the impact of such pervasive practices in these societies, as we will discuss next.

5.2.3. *The Conundrum: The Legality of Private Security Services*

It may be hard to envision how bypasses of security services could be designed without destabilizing the state's monopoly on violence. Parties (individuals and organizations) hiring private security services to operate in parallel with public security forces may eventually raise the empirical and theoretical stakes about who, within a country's territory, is the agent of legitimate use of force. In cases where private security services are not operating as bypasses but are complementing the functions performed by the public police or are performing functions outsourced by the state, the state's monopoly on violence may be preserved, as long as the provision of private security services is adequately regulated.[47] Some scholars argue that an increase in the number of private police officers may even be beneficial, as it substantially adds to the physical presence of law enforcement and frees up the public police from more mundane patrol duties, allowing them to focus on the business of fighting serious crime.[48] In line with this, improving law enforcement–private security collaboration has been a policy imperative in many developed countries.[49] Often, private security officers in developed countries operate in coordination with

---

-distrust-corrupt-inept-police-forces/; Guillermina Seri, *Seguridad: Crime, Police Power, and Democracy in Argentina* (New York: Continuum International Publishing Group, 2012); Uildriks, "Police Reform," *supra* note 20.

[46] See Markus-Michael Müller, *Public Security in the Negotiated State: Policing in Latin America and Beyond* (New York: Palgrave Macmillan, 2012).

[47] Freeman & Minow, *supra* note 38.

[48] Button, "Assessing the Regulation," *supra* note 31; Mark Button, "Private Security and the Policing of Quasi-Public Space" (2003) 31:3 *Int'l J Soc L* 227; Mark Button, *Security Officers and Policing: Powers, Culture and Control in Governance of Private Space* (Aldershot, UK: Ashgate Publishing Ltd, 2007); Jenny Irish, "Policing for Profit: The Future of South Africa's private Security Industry" (1999) Inst for Sec Stud Monograph No. 39.

[49] Andrew Morabito & Sheldon Greenberg, *Engaging the Private Sector to Promote Homeland Security: Law Enforcement – Private Security Partnerships* (Washington, DC: US Department of Justice Office of Justice Programs, 2005); Terrance Gainer, "Partnerships between Public Law Enforcement and Private Security Should become the Norm" (2014) *Securitas* (website), online: https://cdn2 .hubspot.net/hub/60387/file-1919249152-pdf/docs/benefits_of_public-private_security_partnerships_ securitas.pdf

public police – for example, in some Canadian policing jurisdictions, department store loss prevention officers are empowered to release shoplifters after conferring via telephone with police.[50] In such cases, regulation, though imperfect, is relatively stringent.

In contrast, in the cases where these private security services are operating as bypasses, there is a risk that public and private police will compete over the means of violence and legitimacy in using force. One might argue that even operating as bypasses, private security services may not present a problem for societies where the state has strong control over and indeed finances some private security activities. However, Latin America is characterized by the absence of effective regulations and controls by the state due to limited state capacity to monitor actions of the private security industry. This means that the growth of this industry potentially poses a threat to the state monopoly on the legitimate use of force,[51] generating further violence and insecurity. If the use of private security services becomes pervasive, there are significant risks that "violent 'resolutions' to questions of public insecurity become the norm."[52] Thus, without effective regulation, the existence of these services may have negative consequences, such as letting abusive and corrupt police off the hook by alleviating public pressure on the state, and raising troubling questions about equality, democracy, and the rule of law.

If the private security groups resorting to violence are illegally constituted and not tolerated *de jure* and *de facto*, they are not examples of spontaneous bypasses.[53] However, in many Latin American countries, the existence of private security forces *per se* is not prohibited, but their operation may not be fully compliant with regulations and/or their tactics may not be in accordance with the law. One could try to distinguish between those Latin American countries that simply lack any regulation, effectively making some of these arrangements legal, from those that have prohibitions and constraints that are not effectively enforced. We consider both as bypasses. In other words, if the laws on the books that prohibit a given institutional arrangement from operating are not enforced, this is sufficient for that institutional arrangement to qualify as a bypass. Nevertheless, in many cases the absence of prohibition or effective enforcement may be connected to the absence of a strong state presence. As a result, legal and illegal private security services end up having equally damaging consequences for the provision of public security in a country. Acknowledging this, we argue that both legal and illegal private security services

50   Edward J. Carroll, "The Blurring of Public Police and Private Agencies" (2003–4) written submission to the Law Commission of Canada discussion paper, *In Search of Security: the Roles of Public Police and Private Agencies* (Ottawa: Law Commission of Canada, 2002).

51   Blackwell, *supra* note 32.

52   Diane Davis, "Undermining the Rule of Law: Democratization and the Dark Side of Police Reform in Mexico" (2006) 48:1 *Latin Am Pol & Soc* 55–86 at 76.

53   See Chapter 2.

may be still operating in tension with public police forces and competing for scarce resources.

As the demand for private security services and competition in their supply has increased, companies have pursued strategies to provide more services at lower costs. Private security companies in Latin America have adopted two strategies in this regard.

First, a significant number of these companies provide services in the informal economy.[54] Some estimates suggest that the number of private security guards and agents in the informal sector could be double the number of private security officers and agents in the formal, regulated or licensed sector and that there is an informal company for each formal one.[55] The lack of reliable statistics for both formal and informal private security firms makes it difficult to assess the size of the sector with precision, but the number could be even higher than most estimates. Indeed, some suggest that although 20,000 private security companies are operating in Mexico, only 5,000 of them are officially registered, that is, it may be the case that 80 percent of the private security market in Mexico operates informally.[56]

Operating informally is a way of avoiding regulatory costs, which greatly increases the amount of capital required to start up and run a private security firm. For example, in Mexico the cost of compliance with regulatory and bureaucratic requirements, as well as the necessity of paying bribes to regulatory personnel, motivates small- and medium-sized private security entrepreneurs to avoid the formal security market by operating informally.[57] Private security businesses operating informally also avoid the costs of complying with labour laws; an estimated half of private security sector workers in the region operate informally and so lack these protections.[58] By reducing start-up and operational costs, these clandestine companies – operating without licenses or any type of regulation – are able to offer services for lower prices than companies in the formal sector, which often makes it difficult for larger, registered companies to compete.[59]

A second strategy that private security companies adopt to save costs is hiring security guards that were trained elsewhere. Often these companies hire police officers to work as private security guards in their off-duty hours. This reduces training costs. Officers who are still in the police force and work for private firms in their

[54] Arias, *supra* note 36 at 26.

[55] Ibid. at 27–8.

[56] Markus-Michael Müller, "Private Security and the State in Latin America: The Case of Mexico City" (2010) 4:1 *Brazilian Pol Sci Rev* 131–54 at 140.

[57] Ibid.

[58] Lucia Dammert, *Private Security: An Answer to Public Security Needs in Urban Centers?* (Organization of American States, 2008), online: www.oas.org/dsp/documentos/Publicaciones/PUBLIC%20 SECURITY-%20URBAN%20CENTERS.pdf

[59] Geoff Burt, "The Privatisation of Security in Latin America" (2010) Security Sector Reform Resource Centre Working Paper No. 3.

spare time ("moonlight") sell their services to complement their income.[60] This is permitted in some countries, as legislatures have not imposed any prohibition on active members of the police force working for private companies. This is the case in Bolivia, Ecuador, El Salvador, Mexico, Panama, Peru, the Dominican Republic, and Uruguay.[61] Other countries prohibit active police officers from working for private companies. Examples include Argentina, Brazil, Chile, Colombia, Costa Rica, Guatemala, Honduras, and Nicaragua.[62] However, in some of these countries, like Brazil, the practice exists despite a statutory prohibition due to lack of enforcement.[63] Monitoring these activities and imposing sanctions are especially difficult in the case of companies that are not formally licensed or registered.[64]

The informality of the sector allows for many of these companies to tap into state resources, such as public investments in training police officers, without paying for them (and sometimes without being authorized to do so). Moreover, these companies are imposing two major costs on public security services. First, police officers working double shifts are often less effective in the performance of their official duties.[65] Second, these officers are exposed to higher levels of risk in their private jobs because they normally work alone and often without proper equipment.[66] Casualties involving officers providing private services impose costs on the public security force, such as missed days at work or even losses in human resources if they die or become permanently incapacitated.

Curtailing informality and strictly enforcing regulations for the provision of these services, however, may have negative distributional consequences in the Latin American context. Regulation may increase the costs of providing such services, thereby making them less accessible. As a consequence, crimes may be simply displaced onto the sections of the population unable to afford similar protection.[67] Once criminality has been displaced onto poorer neighbourhoods, two possible consequences may follow. On the one hand, if public forces operate mostly in more marginalized areas, then those areas will be subjected to a greater proportion of police abuse.[68] On the other hand, if crimes are displaced to a region in which there is no public security, problems with vigilantism and militias may ensue.[69] In either

---

[60] Arias, *supra* note 36 at 23–4; Zanetic, *supra* note 36 at 92.
[61] Arias, *supra* note 36 at 24.
[62] Ibid.
[63] Zanetic, *supra* note 36 at 93
[64] Ungar, *supra* note 25 at 28.
[65] Adriana Czelusniak "PM Não Pode Prestar Serviço de Segurança Privada" (Aug 5, 2008) Gazeta do Povo, online: www.gazetadopovo.com.br/vida-e-cidadania/pm-nao-pode-prestar-servico-de-seguranca -privada-b3yvbsocmvoru2tgbb2dep7bi
[66] Ibid.
[67] South, *supra* note 31 at 230.
[68] Ibid.
[69] Ibid.; Desmond Arias, "Dispatches from the Field; Milicias and Police Corruption in Rio's Favelas" (2009) 3 Am Q 90 at 90; Michael Webster, "Civil War and Vigilantism Gripping Mexico" (Jan 18, 2009) *American Chronicle*.

case, investment in private security will impose significant costs on lower classes. As a result, the risk of becoming a victim of crime is influenced by income and/or place of residence.[70]

Such distributional concerns do not suggest, however, that attempts to curtail informality should be coupled with efforts to make such services more accessible. While tied demand-side subsidies (vouchers) might, in principle, ameliorate distributional concerns over the rapidly expanding role of private securities services in Latin America, by way of substituting for, rather than complementing, public policing, it is difficult to imagine how voucher systems might be designed so as to take account of the widely varying and contingent security needs of users in different communities in various countries in Latin America, or how individualized rather than collective underwriting of security services would not forfeit major economies of scale that collective provision can, at least in principle, achieve.

Moreover, the rise of private security services in Latin America could potentially reduce the range of political actors who are actively engaged and interested in improving public security, raising Hirschman's fears about the negative consequences of the exit option.[71] Even if it could be shown that diverting resources from private to public security would increase the overall level of security in the long run, there would still be obstacles to convincing users of private services to support this strategy. Ever-increasing crime rates, corruption, lack of transparency/accountability, and failed reforms have undermined hopes for effective change in the public sphere.[72] If those benefiting from private services did not have an exit option, they might be more open to the idea of increasing investments in public security. Thus, more accessible private security services may significantly decrease the likelihood of much needed public reforms.

In summary, it may be argued that public security has natural monopoly and public goods characteristics that require exclusive or predominant public provision, reinforced by the importance for the legitimacy and authority of the state in preserving a monopoly on force. If this is the case, an effective regulatory framework would strictly forbid private security services from competing with or performing the same functions as public police forces. If regulation effectively preserves the state's monopoly of force, it would be impossible to conceive of a spontaneous institutional bypass for security services.

In contrast, one might argue that it is possible for a spontaneous bypass of public security services to exist, as long as we can conceive of a regulatory framework that

---

[70] UNODC, *supra* note 6; Ignacio Cano & Eduardo Ribeiro, "Homicidios no Rio de Janeiro e no Brasil" in Marcus Vinicius Goncalves da Cruz & Eduardo Cerqueira Batitucci, eds., *Homicidios no Brasil* (Rio de Janeiro: Editora FGV, 2007) 51 at 59.

[71] Albert O. Hirschman, *Exit, Voice, and Loyalty: Responses to Decline in Firms, Organizations, and States* (Cambridge, MA: Harvard University Press, 1970).

[72] Uildriks, "Police Reform," *supra* note 20 at 6.

allows public and private security forces to perform the same functions and compete with each other, without undermining the state's monopoly on violence. It is not clear if such a framework exists. Latin America has private security companies operating legally, but this does not allow us to assess whether such a framework would be possible as legality may in some cases simply mean a lack of an effective state presence. Therefore, this option seems highly speculative.

5.3. CHOOSING EDUCATION SERVICES: LOW-COST SCHOOLS IN INDIA[73]

Substantial progress has been achieved in improving access to basic education in developing countries. While 58 million children of primary school age remain out of school worldwide, enrollment has risen substantially in recent decades, particularly since the international community agreed, as a Millennium Development Goal in 2000, to seek to achieve universal primary education by 2015.[74] Primary school net enrollment in low-income countries increased from 55 percent to 82 percent between 1990 and 2012.[75] Enrollment in secondary school has also increased across low-income countries, albeit at a slower pace: net enrollment in secondary school rose from 52 percent in 1999 to 65 percent in 2013.[76]

Unfortunately, however, despite remarkable improvements in primary school enrollment rates over the last half-century, learning outcomes in many developing countries remain appallingly bad.[77] The results of the Organisation for Economic Co-operation and Development's (OECD) 2009 Program for International Student Assessment (PISA) show that 90 percent of students in lower-middle-income countries and 73 percent of students in upper-middle-income countries failed to reach the threshold of the most basic numeracy skills (compared with 22 percent of

---

[73] For a detailed review of the case from which the following discussion is drawn, see Lindsey Carson, Joanna V. Noronha, & Michael J. Trebilcock, "Held Back: Explaining the Sluggish Pace of Improvement to Basic Education in Developing Democracies – The Cases of India and Brazil" (2015) 6:2 *J of Poverty Alleviation & Int'l Dev* 1.

[74] United Nations, "Goal 2: Achieve Universal Primary Education" *United Nations Millennium Development Goals and Beyond 2015*, online: www.un.org/millenniumgoals/education.shtml. Unfortunately, this goal has not been achieved. However, the MDGs will be succeeded by the Sustainable Development Goals, the proposal for which includes an education goal (Goal 4: "Ensure inclusive and equitable quality education and promote lifelong learning opportunities for all"); see United Nations Department of Social and Economic Affairs, "Open Working Group Proposal for Sustainable Development Goals" (2015) *UNESCO Sustainable Development Knowledge Platform*, online: https://sustainabledevelopment.un.org/sdgsproposal.html.

[75] Donald Baum, Laura Lewis, Oni Lusk-Stovei, & Harry Patrinos, "What Matters Most for Engaging the Private Sector in Education: A Framework Paper" (July 2014) World Bank Group SABER Working Paper Series 95570 No. 8 at 8; The World Bank, "World Development Indicators: Participation in Education" *World Bank Data*, online: http://wdi.worldbank.org/table/2.11

[76] The World Bank, "World Development Indicators," *supra* note 75.

[77] Lant Pritchett, *The Rebirth of Education: Schooling Ain't Learning* (Washington, DC: Center for Global Development, 2013).

students in OECD countries).[78] Thus, ensuring that children have access to quality basic education remains a key development challenge.

It is important to note that the choice between public and private schools may or may not be an institutional bypass, depending on whether it is part of the dominant system or an alternative to it. It is also important to acknowledge that within the public school system there is also some potential for intentional institutional bypasses: at least in some developed countries (most prominently the United States), in recent decades, publicly financed charter schools, with substantial degrees of institutional autonomy, have emerged as an alternative to the conventional public school system.[79] The focus of our analysis, however, is on a spontaneous bypass of education services as evidenced by the proliferation of low-cost private schools in many developing countries in recent years.[80]

The proliferation of such schools is part of a greater trend: the growing incidence of private education in low-income countries over the past two decades. Growth in enrollment has been faster for private schools than public schools. Across the world, enrollment in private primary schools grew by 58 percent between 1991 and 2004, while enrollment in public primary schools grew only by 10 percent. Globally, there are approximately 113 million students in non-government schools.[81] While this phenomenon of greater demand for private education seems relevant to the larger debate about the public and private provision of education services, we are particularly interested in the growth of private school enrollment in organizations that have organically emerged to meet existing demand. While a part of this growth is also associated with the fact that some governments have enacted policies to encourage expansion of the private education sector, this is not the focus of our analysis, since the sheer existence of a private education sector operating in parallel with a public sector will not necessarily be classified as a bypass. From a conceptual perspective, a private school will only be an institutional bypass of the public system if (1) the public system is conceived as the dominant one, and (2) it somehow offers something distinct from or superior to what is being offered in the dominant system.

Private schools have emerged organically to meet existing demand in areas where public education is either unavailable or of poor quality.[82] For example, Tooley's research surveying high-poverty regions of Nigeria, Ghana, Kenya, India, and

---

[78] Baum, Lewis, Lusk-Stovei, & Patrinos, *supra* note 75.

[79] See e.g., Margaret E. Raymond, "A Critical Look at the Charter School Debate" (Mar 27 2014) Education Week: Phi Delta Kappa International, online: www.edweek.org/ew/articles/2014/02/01/kappan_raymond.html

[80] See Stephen Heyneman & Jonathan Stern, "Low Cost Private Schools for the Poor: What Public Policy Is Appropriate?" (2014) 35 *Int'l J of Educational Dev* 3.

[81] Harry Anthony Patrinos, Felipe Barrera-Osorio, & Juliana Guáqueta, *The Role and Impact of Public-Private Partnerships in Education* (Washington, DC: The World Bank, 2009) at 3.

[82] James Tooley, *The Beautiful Tree: A Personal Journey into How the World's Poorest People Are Educating Themselves* (Washington, DC: CATO, 2009); James Tooley, "Educating Amaretch: Private Schools for the Poor and the New Frontier for Investors" (2007) 27:2 *Economic Affairs* 3743.

China revealed that the vast majority of children in urban and quasi-rural areas were enrolled in "budget" or "low-fee" private schools typically established by entrepreneurs from within the poor communities and employing teachers from those communities.[83] His research showed that the quality of these budget private schools usually exceeded that of rival public schools; private schools scored better on metrics such as test achievement, teacher absenteeism, teacher commitment, and infrastructure quality.[84]

To illustrate one prominent example of how school choice may operate as an institutional bypass, this section reviews the massive exodus to low-fee private schools in India. This has occurred as a result of demand by parents for higher-quality education (especially in English, in contrast to the vernacular languages that prevail in the public school system), in light of persistent challenges to improving learning outcomes in public schools.

5.3.1. *The Problem: The Quality of Public Education in India*

India is engaged in a long-standing effort to bring universal primary education to its citizens, as a result of which the Indian public education system is now the largest in the world, with nearly 1.1 million primary public schools serving 200 million children.[85] The country has made impressive strides in improving access to education in recent decades, with primary school enrollment rates climbing from 61.2 percent in 1971 to 93.1 percent in 2012.[86] While India has not achieved its goal of attaining universal primary education by 2015, the number of children ages six to fourteen out of school has dropped from 32 million in 2001 to 2.9 million in 2012–13.[87]

However, the quality of education remains a critical issue in India. Learning outcomes for students are low and learning trajectories largely flat.[88] The 2013 ASER survey found that only 37.2 percent of rural government school students aged six to fourteen were able to read a paragraph from a story designed for grade 2 students, while just 19.8 percent were able to solve a basic division problem.[89] India's students also perform extremely poorly on international assessments of learning outcomes.

---

[83] Ibid.

[84] Ibid.

[85] National University of Educational Planning and Administration (NUEPA), *Elementary Education in India: Progress towards UEE, Flash Statistics DISE 2013–2014* (New Delhi: NUEPA, 2014), online: www.dise.in/Downloads/Publications/Documents/Flash%20Statistics2013-14.pdf.

[86] The World Bank, "World Development Indicators," *supra* note 75; The World Bank, "School Enrollment, Primary (% Net)" (2014) World Bank Data, online: http://data.worldbank.org/indicator/SE.PRM.NENR/countries/1W-IN?display=graph

[87] The World Bank, "India: Third Elementary Education Project (SSA III)" (2014) Project Appraisal Document Report No. PAD743, online: www-wds.worldbank.org/external/default/WDSContentServer/WDSP/IB/2014/05/01/000333037_20140501103833/Rendered/PDF/PAD7430P144447010Box385199B00OUO090.pdf

[88] Ibid.; Pritchett, *supra* note 77.

[89] Pratham, *Annual Status of Education Report (Rural)*, 2013 (New Delhi: ASER Centre, 2014).

In the 2009 OECD PISA survey, fewer than 20 percent of fifteen-year-old students in the two Indian states tested, Himachal Pradesh and Tamil Nadu, were considered "proficient"[90] on tests of reading, math, and science literacy; of the seventy-five countries tested, including developing countries such as Azerbaijan, Brazil, Indonesia, Mauritius, and Peru, only Kyrgyzstan had comparably low levels of performance.[91] Further, India's youth literacy rates suggest that the country's schools continue to under-perform; only 81.1 percent of Indians between the ages of fifteen and twenty-four are literate in comparison to rates in excess of 98 percent in other rapidly growing Asian economies such as China, Indonesia, and Malaysia.[92]

There are three basic reasons for the poor performance of Indian public schools: insufficient and uneven funding for public education, poor administration and oversight of Indian public schools, and low teacher quality. We discuss each briefly in turn.

First, while studies on the relationship between financial inputs and student performance have generally concluded that increased resources are not closely associated with better learning outcomes,[93] there appears to be some minimum resource threshold that educational systems must meet in order to ensure that factors associated with student performance – the availability of textbooks, the existence of basic facilities including water and toilets, and having teachers present and engaged in teaching in the classroom – are present.[94] Data on the financing of basic education in India strongly suggests that the country's expenditures fall below this minimum financial baseline.[95]

Similarly, India has thus far failed to ensure that per-pupil expenditures are equivalent across states and villages.[96] This has resulted partially from the nature of the funding relationship between levels of government. The central and state governments share fiscal and administrative authority over education in India. However,

---

[90] "Proficiency" is defined as the baseline level needed to participate effectively and productively in life; see Maurice Walker, *PISA 2009 Plus Results: Performance of 15-Year-Olds in Reading, Mathematics and Science for 10 Additional Participants* (Melbourne: ACER Press, 2011) at xiii.

[91] Ibid.

[92] The World Bank, "School Enrollment," *supra* note 86.

[93] Paul W. Glewwe, Eric A. Hanushek, Sarah D. Humpage, & Renato Ravina, "School Resources and Educational Outcomes in Developing Countries: A Review of the Literature from 1990 to 2010" in Paul Glewwe, ed., *Education Policies in Developing Countries* (Chicago: University of Chicago Press, 2014) 13.

[94] Eric A. Hanushek & Ludger Wößmann, "The Role of Education Quality in Economic Growth" (2007) World Bank Policy Research Working Paper No. 4122.

[95] While domestic public spending on education has increased in the vast majority of countries in recent years, rising from a global average of 4.6 percent of gross national product (GNP) in 1999 to 5.1 percent in 2011, India's public expenditures on education dropped from 4.4 percent of GNP in 1999 to 3.3 percent in 2010; see United Nations Educational, Scientific, and Cultural Organization (UNESCO), *Overcoming Inequality: Why Governance Matters*, commissioned for the EFA Global Monitoring Report 2009 (Oxford, UK: Oxford University Press, 2008); Carson, Noronha, & Trebilcock, *supra* note 73.

[96] Ibid.

the division of fiscal responsibility for national education programs has often proven contentious, while confusion and mismanagement have led to waste and heightened geographic disparities. Moreover, funding for education is uneven across the country because states remain responsible for the majority of education funding. States vary enormously in terms of their fiscal capacity, as well as in their budgetary priorities, resulting in massive discrepancies in spending per student across states.[97] Some action has been taken by the federal government to narrow funding gaps through equalization grants, but these have barely covered 10 percent of the gap between the per-student elementary education expenditures of the eight states with the lowest educational outcomes[98] and the national average.[99] Finally, geographic disparities exist even within states, as state officials have the power to make strategic, often politically calculated, decisions with regard to resource allocations across districts and villages.[100] Thus, learning outcomes are hampered by insufficient overall funding for education, as well as uneven spending within and between states.

The second reason is poor administration and oversight of Indian public schools. As with financing, the administration and oversight of public education in India has been encumbered by problems of divided responsibilities amongst the different levels of government. All levels of government in India are involved in administering public education. Federal authorities establish national education objectives and standards (on, for example, student–teacher ratios, facilities, and school working days) and state governments are then responsible for implementing these requirements through hiring teachers, providing education infrastructure, and setting curricula. Education management is devolved to the local level. Locally, community education committees (i.e., school management committees, village education committees, and parent–teacher associations) are responsible for creating school development plans and, more generally, performing monitoring and management functions. These community-based organizations ostensibly provide a mechanism for oversight and accountability at the local level.

Studies on the effect of community-based education committees in other developing countries suggest that such organizations can improve student test scores, reduce teacher absenteeism, and decrease dropout rates.[101] However, evidence on

---

[97] Hanushek & Wößmann, *supra* note 94; Government of India, "Budget Briefs – Education Sector" (2012) *Accountability Initiative Government of India*, 2012–13, online: www.accountabilityindia .in/sites/default/files/sarva_shiksha_abhiyan_2012-13.pdf; Anuradha De & Tanuka Endow, "Public Expenditure on Education in India: Recent Trends and Outcomes" (2008) RECOUP Working Paper No. 18.

[98] Namely, these states are Assam, Bihar, Jharkhjand, Madhya Pradesh, Orissa, Rajasthan, Uttar Pradesh, and West Bengal.

[99] Santosh Mehrotra, "The Cost and Financing of the Right to Education in India: Can We Fill the Financing Gap?" (2012) 32 *Int'l J of Educational Dev* 65.

[100] Benjamin Crost & Uma S. Kambhampati, "Political Market Characteristics and the Provision of Educational Infrastructure in North India" (2010) 38:2 *World Dev* 195.

[101] Barbara Bruns, Deon Filmer, & Harry Anthony Patrinos, *Making Schools Work: New Evidence on Accountability Reforms* (Washington, DC: World Bank, 2011).

the impact of community education committees in India has been mixed to poor.[102] The cause of these results lies partially with problems in the implementation of specific programs. However, the broader policy context within which such committees operate has been a substantial obstacle. Three problems stand out in particular. First, as with the financing of education, there is a lack of clarity about the division of responsibility amongst different levels of government. Surveys suggest that there remains substantial confusion regarding the powers and responsibilities of community education committees, even among the members themselves.[103] Second, some powers that arguably should have been devolved to the local level remain with the state government. For example, members of these local community education committees perform some oversight of teacher attendance, training, and performance, but because most teachers are permanent state employees, state authorities make all critical decisions concerning their hiring, compensation, transfer, and dismissal.[104] Finally, insufficient resources have been afforded to the local level to engage in effective oversight. District inspectors are typically charged with ensuring that principals' reports on teacher attendance and performance are accurate, but inspectors are often responsible for dozens and sometimes hundreds of primary schools, and in-person monitoring visits are rare, rendering the threat of teacher dismissal for absence or poor performance largely non-existent.

The third reason for the poor performance of Indian public schools is poor teacher quality. Teaching quality is the cornerstone of a strong education system and is, unfortunately, one of the greatest challenges in India. First, high teacher salaries have made it difficult for some states to maintain manageable class sizes. Teacher salaries constitute the majority of educational outlays at the primary level, with an average of 77 percent of total basic education budgets invested in teacher and management costs.[105] The often-generous salaries paid to public-sector teachers can amount to thirteen times the average per-capita income in some states.[106] In order to accommodate teacher salaries many schools maintain high student-to-teacher ratios; while the *Right to Education Act*[107] established a maximum 30:1 pupil-to-teacher ratio, only 45.3 percent of rural public primary schools were able to meet this standard in 2013.[108]

Another persistent problem has been the lack of teacher engagement (teacher attendance and activity rates). Absenteeism rates run as high as 30 percent in many states, and the percentage of teachers' time, even when present, actually spent

[102] Abhijit V. Banerjee, Rukmini Banerji, Esther Duflo, Rachel Glennerster, & Stuti Khemani, "Pitfalls of Participatory Programs: Evidence from a Randomized Evaluation in Education in India" (2008) National Bureau of Economic Research Working Paper No. 14311.
[103] Ibid.; Government of India, *supra* note 97.
[104] Pratham, *supra* note 89.
[105] Ibid.
[106] De & Endow, *supra* note 97.
[107] The act is also referred to as the Right of Children to Free and Compulsory Education Act, 2009.
[108] Pratham, *supra* note 89.

teaching is often as low as 60 percent. Although permanent teachers hired through the Indian public school system have stronger formal qualifications than private school teachers, this has often not led to better engagement in the classroom. For example, contract teachers are often hired by village- or district-level authorities to fill staffing gaps created by the lack of qualified formal teacher candidates (the passing rate on the Central Teacher Eligibility Test has been woefully low, with only 11 percent of test-takers passing in 2013, for example).[109] These contract teachers do not meet the training criteria necessary to secure permanent teacher positions and are hired for terms ranging from one to three years at salaries far lower than regular teachers.[110] While the reliance of the public education system on teachers who lack formal qualifications may raise concerns about the quality of instruction, a recent study examining data from government primary schools in Uttar Pradesh and Madhya Pradesh found that contract teachers had higher attendance and teaching activity rates than regular teachers and that higher teacher effort rates were associated with better student performance.[111] This seemingly counterintuitive finding points to the centrality of flexibility in hiring and firing: while permanent teachers are extremely difficult to fire, contract teachers are employed based on renewable contracts that can be terminated if a teacher underperforms.

Thus, empowering local officials with the ability to hire and fire teachers on the basis of performance may offer one strategy for improving learning outcomes.[112] However, any initiative to decentralize teacher accountability mechanisms, promote innovative incentive structures or performance-based compensation and promotions, or reduce class sizes by cutting salaries is likely to face strong political opposition from powerful teachers' unions.[113] In fact, while an initial draft of the *Right to Education Act* would have delegated authority for appointing and dismissing teachers to local school management committees, this provision was omitted when the bill was presented to Parliament, reflecting the historically close relationship between educators – who constitute the largest civil service group in most states – and politicians in the country.[114] More generally, evidence suggests that Indian students taught by unionized or politically connected teachers have significantly lower achievement scores.[115]

Finally, the power wielded by school officials and teachers' unions poses a barrier to the oversight of school administration. For example, the selection of committee

[109] Manash Pratim Gohain, "11% Aspirants Pass CTET 2013" (Sep 4, 2013) *Times of India*, online: http://timesofindia.indiatimes.com/home/education/news/11-aspirants-pass-CTET-2013/articleshow/22276839.cms
[110] Sangeeta Goyal & Priyanka Pandey, "Contract Teachers in India" (2013) 21:5 *Educ Econ* 464.
[111] Ibid.
[112] Ibid.
[113] Geeta Kingdon & Mohd Muzzammil, "The School Governance Environment in Uttar Pradesh, India: Implications for Teacher Accountability and Effort" (2013) 49 *J Dev Stud* 251.
[114] Mehrotra, *supra* note 99.
[115] Kingdon & Muzzammil, *supra* note 113.

members, as well as the functioning of community education committees, is some-times subject to undue influence by school principals (whose performance these organizations are supposed to monitor).[116]

5.3.2. *The Response: Bypassing Public Education*
Through Low-Fee Private Schools

Confronted with the problems described in the previous section, Indian parents have made increasingly widespread use of private schools. Over 37 percent of the country's students in grades one to five and more than 41 percent of those in grades six to eight were enrolled in private schools in 2013–14.[117] This is much higher than for the other BRICS countries (Brazil, Russia, India, China, and South Africa),[118] but is similar to neighbouring Pakistan and Bangladesh.[119] Primary-level private school enrollments have grown particularly dramatically in rural areas, rising from 18.7 percent in 2006 to 29 percent in 2012.[120] Much of the expansion in private school enrollment has been driven by increasing demand from poorer households, rather than India's upper- and middle-income groups; accordingly, low-fee private schools have proliferated throughout the country, opening the doors of private edu-cation to broader segments of the population.[121]

There are generally three types of school management structures in India: govern-ment, private aided, and private unaided. Government schools are owned, funded, regulated, and managed by the government. Private schools are a mix of for-profit and non-profit organizations. Private aided schools are owned and managed privately but are usually fully funded (including 100 percent of teacher salaries) and regulated by the government. They are prohibited from charging tuition fees (although small fees are still sometimes charged), and in some states, they cannot recruit or dismiss their

---

[116] Ayokunle Abogan, *Lessons in Learning: An Analysis of Outcomes in India's Implementation of the Right to Education Act* (Princeton, NJ: Woodrow Wilson School of International and Public Affairs, 2013), online: www.princeton.edu/rpds/papers/Hammer_Policy_Workshop_Spring2013.pdf

[117] NUEPA, *Flash Statistics 2013–2014*, *supra* note 85.

[118] Of the other BRICS, China has the next highest proportion of private primary enrollment, at 6 percent of total enrollment in 2013. Private primary enrollment rates were 3.8 percent in South Africa and 0.7 percent in Russia in 2013; see The World Bank, "School Enrollment, Primary, Private (% of Total Primary)," (2015) World Bank Data, online: http://data.worldbank.org/indicator/SE.PRM .PRIV.ZS/countries/IN-BR-CN-ZA-PK-BD-RU?display=graph

[119] Ibid.; The data for Pakistan is from 2013, while the most recent data available for Bangladesh is from 2011.

[120] Pratham, *supra* note 89.

[121] Prachi Srivastava, "Neither Voice nor Loyalty: School Choice and the Low-Fee Private Sector in India" (2007) Research Paper Series, Occasional Paper No. 34; Tooley, "Educating Amaretch," *supra* note 82; James Tooley, Pauline Dixon, & S. V. Gomathi, "Private Schools and the Millennium Development Goal of Universal Primary Education: A Census and Comparative Survey in Hyderabad, India" (2007) 33 *Oxford Rev Educ* 539.

own staff.[122] Private unaided schools are privately owned and fully self-funded and have autonomy in relation to management, fees, hiring, and pedagogy.[123]

Private unaided schools can be further divided into two subcategories: recognized and unrecognized. Recognized schools have an "official stamp of approval" as they are deemed to have met state regulatory requirements, which enables students to sit board examinations.[124] However, few private schools actually fulfil all the conditions, and "the large numbers of unrecognized private schools suggest that parents do not take government recognition as a stamp of quality."[125] Indeed, parents are often largely unaware of whether a school is recognized or not, and often pay similar fees to both recognized and unrecognized private schools.[126] Unrecognized unaided schools are those that have either not applied for, or have not succeeded in gaining, recognition from the government.[127]

Private low-cost options have appeared organically, driven by the initiative of individuals who have seen an opportunity to address an unmet demand. These low-fee private schools can be classified as bypasses because they offer an alternative pathway to the dominant system which is characterized by either dysfunctional public schools, or unaffordable private schools.[128] Parents are particularly attracted to unrecognized schools, as many believe that these schools offer a better education as teachers are more committed and attentive to students and more accountable to parents than at government schools.[129] Moreover, often unrecognized schools offer "English-medium" education, unlike the government schools that may primarily teach in the vernacular.[130] In addition, teachers at unrecognized schools are often

[122] Anjini Kochar, "Emerging Challenges for Indian Education Policy" (2001) Standford Center for International Development Working Paper No. 97 at 12.

[123] Joanna Härmä, "Can Choice Promote Education for All? Evidence from Growth in Private Primary Schooling in India" (2009) 39:2 *Compare* 151 at 152; James Tooley & Pauline Dixon, "Private Schooling for Low-Income Families: A Census and Comparative Survey in East Delhi, India" (2007) 27:2 *Int'l J of Educational Dev* 205 at 207.

[124] Ibid.; Geeta Gandhi Kingdon, "The Progress of School Education in India" (2007) Global Poverty Research Group Working Paper No. 071 at 17.

[125] Ibid. at 17–18.

[126] Härmä, *supra* note 123.

[127] Tooley & Dixon, *supra* note 123 at 207; Härmä, *supra* note 123 at 152.

[128] Sharma & Ibrari, *infra* note 130; Manjuma Akhtar Mousumi & Tatsuya Kusakabe, "The Dilemmas of School Choice: Do Parents Really 'Choose' Low-Fee Private Schools in Delhi, India?" (2017) *Compare: J Comp & Int'l Educ*, online: www.tandfonline.com/doi/full/10.1080/03057925.2017 .1401451

[129] Mousumi & Kusakabe, *supra* note 128; Balutsav, "Why No One Sends Their Child to a Government School in India" (Jan 22, 2013), online: https://balutsav.org/education-for-children/government-school-in-india/; Alys Francis, "Why India's Landmark Education Law Is Shutting Down Schools" (Mar 6, 2014) *BBC*, online: www.bbc.com/news/world-asia-india-26333713; Balakrishnan Chandrasekaran, "The Unrecognized Schools Under RTE Regime" (Jun 21, 2014) *Swarajya*, online: https://swarajyamag.com/commentary/the-unrecognized-schools-under-rte-regime

[130] Krittika Sharma & Mohammad Ibrar, "Why Unrecognised Delhi Schools Are Still Trusted" (Feb 10, 2018) *The Times of India*, online: https://timesofindia.indiatimes.com/home/education/news/why-unrecognised-schools-are-still-trusted/articleshow/62857015.cms

considered better at instilling discipline in their students, when compared to government schools.[131] For instance, sometimes parents cite concerns that in government schools children learn to use foul language even at very young ages.[132] Sometimes distance is a factor: when the closest government school may be too far away for small children (due to physical distance or safety issues), parents may prefer to send their young children to an unrecognized private school that is closer to home.[133]

Despite the documented exodus to low-fee private schools, especially unrecognized ones, it is unclear who is the main provider of elementary education. Recent statistics published by the National University of Educational Planning and Administration show that around 80 percent of elementary schools are government schools, 6 percent private-aided schools, and 14 percent recognized private-unaided schools. In terms of enrollment, government schools account for about 71 percent of enrolments, private-aided schools 9 percent and recognized private unaided 20 percent.[134] However, it is worth noting that these figures may be underestimates of the role of private schools, as private unaided unrecognized schools operate in the informal sector of the economy and are not counted in official statistics.[135] As indicated earlier, other sources have suggested that over 37 percent of the country's students in grades one to five and more than 41 percent of those in grades six to eight were enrolled in private schools in 2013–14.

In contrast to the assumption that the state should have a monopoly on the use of force in its territory, the provision of educational services is rarely conceived of as a public monopoly, being often characterized by the parallel existence of public and private providers. Therefore, in countries where they are part of the dominant system, private schools will not be perceived as institutional bypasses. As indicated earlier, a private school will only be an institutional bypass if it somehow offers something superior to what is being offered in the dominant system. Similarly, a public school can also be a bypass, as is the case of charter schools in the United States, which offer an alternative governance structure to public schools. Similarly, low-cost private schools in India offer an alternative financial and operational model that addresses both dysfunctional public schools and unaffordable private schools. Thus, these low-cost private schools attempt to address perceived dysfunctionalities in the dominant system.

Do these low-cost private schools avoid expressly contradicting the requirements of the legal system within which they are operating? On the one hand, if private

[131] Ibid.; Mousumi & Kusakabe, *infra* note 128; Balutsav, *supra* note 129.

[132] Sharma & Ibrar, *supra* note 130.

[133] Ibid.; Mousumi & Kusakabe, *infra* note 128.

[134] National University of Educational Planning and Administration (NUEPA), *Elementary Education in India: Progress towards UEE, Flash Statistics DISE 2008–09* (New Delhi: NUEPA, 2010) at 2–3, 14, online: www.dise.in/Downloads/Publications/Publications%202008-09/Flash%20Statistics%202008-09.pdf

[135] Tooley & Dixon, *supra* note 123; Härmä, *supra* note 123 at 152; Kingdon, *supra* note 124 at 22.

education was forbidden in India and prohibition was fully enforced, these schools would not be an example of an institutional bypass. However, legislation is not fully enforced. The Right to Education Act prohibits unrecognized schools,[136] and some states have closed down such schools, but in many states their continuing operation (and proliferation) is *de facto* tolerated or acquiesced by state authorities.[137] On the other hand, critics emphasize that many private schools currently fail to meet governmental standards, particularly with regard to teacher compensation and qualifications. While salaries vary across states and schools, teachers in public schools earn two-and-a-half to more than ten times the compensation paid to private school teachers;[138] teachers in private schools also tend to have less experience and are less likely to have received formal training in education than their public school counterparts.[139] Similarly to private security services, it is the lack of compliance with stringent but often unenforced regulations that makes the system accessible to the lowest echelons of the Indian society.

Despite the lower salaries and weaker credentials of private school teachers, on average, students in private schools outperform their public school peers in cognitive assessments.[140] Moreover, evidence suggests that many of the students who have switched to private schools are receiving a better education.[141] Rather than reflecting the high quality of instruction in private institutions, however, the significant and increasing performance gap between students in public and private schools may be attributable to declines in the already-low performance of government schools.[142] Whatever the reason, these outcomes suggest that the government standards imposed on government schools, including those relating to teacher compensation

[136] *Right to Education Act*, s 18, available at Right to Education.in, "Centre: Acts, Rules & Notifications," online: http://righttoeducation.in/resources/centre

[137] India Institute, "Unrecognized Schools: The Story of the Daily Wrong," online: http://indiai .org/unrecognized-schools/; The CSR Journal, "Right To Education Act in India: Undermining Its Own Objectives" (Sep 22, 2015), online: http://thecsrjournal.in/rte-right-to-education-act-in-india-undermining-its-own-objectives/; Autar Nehru, Aruna Ravikumar, & Nadia Lewis, "SOS: Save 300,000 Budget Private Schools" (2014) *Centre for Civil Society*, online: http://ccs.in/ sos-save-300000-budget-private-schools

[138] Tooley, "Educating Amaretch," *supra* note 82; Tooley, *Beautiful Tree*, *supra* note 82; Härmä, *supra* note 123.

[139] National University of Educational Planning and Administration (NUEPA), *Elementary Education in India: Progress towards UEE, Flash Statistics DISE 2012–2013* (New Delhi: NUEPA, 2013), online: www.dise.in/Downloads/Publications/Documents/Flash%20Statistics%202012-13.pdf; Santosh Mehrotra, "Reforming Elementary Education in India: A Menu of Options" (2006) 26 *Int'l J of Educational Dev* 261; Karthik Muralidharan & Michael Kremer, "Public and Private Schools in Rural India" in Paul E. Peterson & Rajashri Chakrabarti, eds., *School Choice International: Exploring Public-Private Partnerships* (Cambridge, MA: MIT Press, 2008), 91.

[140] Robert French & Geeta Kingdon, "The Relative Effectiveness of Private and Government Schools in Rural India: Evidence from ASER data" (2010) University College London Department of Quantitative Social Science Working Paper No. 10-03; Pratham *supra* note 89.

[141] Karthik Muralidharan & Venkatesh Sundararaman, "The Aggregate Effect of School Choice: Evidence from a Two-Stage Experiment in India" (2015) 130:3 *QJ Econ* 1011.

[142] Pratham *supra* note 89.

and qualifications, are not contributing to the ultimate goal of providing accessible and high-quality education to children in India.

While growing enrollments in private schools may provide some students with access to higher-quality education than they would receive in public schools, equity issues remain highly salient. About two-thirds of Indian children continue to attend public schools, with all their infirmities. Hence, children from very poor and socially marginalized families still face significant financial barriers to attending private schools, even low-cost ones. The proliferation of low-fee private schools has extended private educational opportunities to some children from lower-income groups, but the most destitute and those traditionally marginalized in society (members of the scheduled classes, scheduled tribes, and other backward classes and Muslims) are still largely unable to afford private schools, leaving them over-represented in government schools.[143] Thus, the exodus of students from the public education system, which has recently accelerated with children from lower-middle-class families moving to low-cost private schools, may aggravate existing caste and socio-economic stratifications by leaving only the most vulnerable children in government schools.[144] However, a Supreme Court of India ruling in 2012 requiring recognized private schools to reserve a quarter of all primary and upper primary school placements for students from families making less than 100,000 rupees (US$1,900),[145] has at least the potential to ameliorate this concern. The government has agreed, in principle, to underwrite it.[146]

5.3.3. *The Conundrum: State Recognition of Private Schools*

While creating new private schools in India does not explicitly violate the legal requirements of the legal system, not all private schools can be classified as a bypass. Only those that are perceived to offer an alternative to the dominant system (public, private, or both) can be classified as such. While the previous section argued that the organic proliferation of low-cost private schools throughout the country, but especially in rural areas, can be considered a spontaneous institutional bypass, this claim raises an important conceptual challenge. How can a new private school offer

---

[143] Härmä, *supra* note 138; Santosh Mehrotra & Parthasarthi R. Panchamukhi, "Universalising Elementary Education in India: Is the Private Sector the Answer?" in Prachi Srivastava & Geoffrey Walford, eds., *Private Schooling in Less Economically Developed Countries: Asian and African Perspectives* (Didcot, UK: Symposium Books, 2007) 129; Geetha B. Nambissan, "The Global Economic Crisis, Poverty, and Education: A Perspective from India" (2010) 25 *J of Educ Pol'y* 729.

[144] Nadan Nilekani, *Imagining India: The Idea of a Renewed Nation* (New York: Penguin Books, 2008) at 180.

[145] *Society for Un-aided Private Schools of Rajasthan v. Union of India & Another* (2012) SCC 1 (India). See also Gayatri Rangachari Shah, "India Opens a Door to Private Education" (Aug 19, 2012) *New York Times*, online: www.nytimes.com/2012/08/20/world/asia/india-opens-a-door-to-private-education .html

[146] See e.g., Laura Day Ashley, "The Shifting Politics of the Private in Education: Debates & Developments in Researching Private School Outreach in India" (2012) 1 *Comp Educ* 14.

an alternative to the dominant system if the dysfunctionalities of such a system are largely caused by the sectoral regulations imposed by the state (that is, the state in its role as regulator, rather than provider)?

On the one hand, if a new private school complies with all governmental regulations, it will most certainly fail to provide an alternative pathway to the system, and thus fail to offer students and their parents an option that aims at addressing perceived dysfunctionalities in the dominant system. On the other hand, if this new private school fails to comply with governmental regulations, it may provide an alternative pathway to the dominant system, but it can only be classified as a bypass because the legal requirements of the system are not actually or effectively enforced. In other words, they are tolerated *de facto* but are not strictly speaking compliant with the *de jure* requirements imposed by the state.

Despite not complying with governmental requirements, these schools have produced positive results overall, as observed by the superior performance of their students in comparison to their counterparts in public schools. However, the long-term effects of these low-cost schools on the Indian educational system are unclear. One possibility is that they will signal to the government that existing regulations are preventing, rather than securing, access to better-quality education. If governmental requirements for the operation of private schools change, these low-cost schools could potentially become the prevailing educational institution model in India. In this case, they would cease to be considered bypasses and simply become part of the dominant system.

Another possible effect of the proliferation of low-cost private schools is the prospect that government schools will respond to competition by "shaping up." However, this requires a system of incentives and/or credible threats and often will demand strategies to overcome the strong system of path dependence that may create obstacles to change. At this point, it is not clear that Indian public schools have any incentive to shape up, even if students exit the system. Schools may indeed face diminished incentives to do so if quality and voice-conscious families are the ones most likely to exit. To address this concern, the government could create incentives or requirements for private schools to be more accessible to low-income families (such as those created in response to the 2012 Supreme Court decision).

5.4. CHOOSING DISPUTE RESOLUTION
MECHANISMS: *LOK ADALATS* IN INDIA

The UNDP reports that the co-existence of informal and formal legal systems is found in approximately seventy-three developing countries. The *Lok Adalats* in India, the *Shalish* in Bangladesh, and the *Gacaca* in Rwanda are amongst the more prominent examples.[147] Such alternatives have existed for decades, and in

---

[147] Ewa Wojkowska, "Doing Justice: How Informal Justice Systems Can Contribute" (2006) United Nations Development Programme Oslo Governance Centre at 15, online: http://siteresources .worldbank.org/INTLAWJUSTINST/Resources/EwaWojkowska.pdf

many cases, centuries. In particular, the colonial pasts of many developing countries ultimately led to the co-existence of informal (also referred to as "non-state," "traditional," "indigenous," and/or "customary") legal systems and formal (also referred to as "state") legal systems, or the phenomenon of legal pluralism.

Despite resolving 80 to 90 percent of disputes in a country,[148] these informal arrangements are often not considered central features of its legal system.[149] The fact that they continue to thrive highlights the resilience and ultimate importance of these arrangements to their communities.[150] Informal legal systems are most widely used by individuals in rural and/or poor areas, particularly where access to the formal system is limited, if not impossible, or is otherwise culturally uncongenial. The option of an informal legal system can be particularly beneficial where the formal system is perceived to be corrupt, inefficient, physically inaccessible, culturally alienating, costly, and/or protracted.[151]

In this section, we briefly explore one informal dispute settlement mechanism in India that has been recognized by the government, *Lok Adalats*, and the issues raised by the co-existence of formal court dispute settlement mechanisms and this traditional form of dispute resolution.

5.4.1. *The Problem: A Dysfunctional Lower Court System*

Formal courts in many developing countries often exhibit low levels of independence from the executive and legislative arms of government; reflect minimal levels of legal expertise and competence; are often afflicted with pervasive forms of corruption and patronage in judicial appointments and subsequent decision-making; are often burdened by extremely long backlogs of undisposed cases, especially civil cases; and are often ineffective in ensuring that their judgments are enforced. Efforts over the last two decades or so to reform weak courts in many developing countries, often sponsored by external donor agencies, have exhibited a mixed to weak record of success in redressing these problems.[152] Given this record, both policymakers and private parties have increasingly explored alternative adjudicative mechanisms to the mainstream formal court system in many developing countries. India is no exception. Despite the Indian Constitution's stated governance over all Indians regardless of race, religion, caste, gender, and birthplace, the formal legal system has

---

[148] Ibid. at 5.

[149] Ronald Daniels, Michael J. Trebilcock, & Lindsey Carson, "The Legacy of Empire: The Common Law Inheritance and Commitments to Legality in Former British Colonies" (2011) 59 *Am J Comp L* 11.

[150] Caroline Sage & Michael Woolcock, "Introduction" in Brian Z. Tamanaha, Carolina Sage, & Michael Woolcock, eds., *Legal Pluralism and Development: Scholars and Practitioners in Dialogue* (Cambridge, UK: Cambridge University Press, 2012) 1 at 1–2.

[151] Ibid. at 3.

[152] See Trebilcock & Daniels, *supra* note 19 at ch. 2.

remained inaccessible to most of the rural population.[153] And even in cases where courts are accessible, in addition to traditional problems of backlogs and delays, the public, which has little faith in the system's ability to grant meaningful redress, protections, and vindication, generally views the lower courts, the law, and lawyers with disdain.[154]

These problems with the Indian courts are not post-colonial phenomena, but were also observed during British colonization.[155] During that period, and particularly with respect to personal laws (including family matters), it became increasingly clear that British laws and judicial processes were not congenial to the local population.[156] In light of concerns by British administrators that the imposed Western legal institutions were a mismatch with Indian notions of justice, they incorporated *panchayats*, a kind of indigenous tribunal that existed prior to British colonization.[157] These *panchayats* differed to some degree from their pre-colonial origins, but nonetheless serve as an early example of the co-existence of informal and formal legal systems, and would eventually set the stage for the current *Lok Adalats*.

Following India's independence in 1947, social activists sought to replace modern courts and restore the indigenous legal system. By the late 1950s, *nyaya panchayats* were established for dealing with minor civil and criminal cases, despite being quite different from their original, indigenous predecessor. For example, rather than indigenous norms, the *nyaya panchayats* applied statutory law, their membership was not caste-based but determined through popular election, and their decisions were reached through majority rule rather than unanimity.[158] These *nyaya panchayats* encountered the same problems that plagued the more traditional *panchayats*, including an inability to establish independence, enforcement problems, and delays, and ultimately attracted very little local support.[159] Considered an "unappetizing combination of the formality of official law with the political malleability of village tribunals,"[160] the *nyaya panchayats* fell into disuse within a decade.

By the 1980s, with the rise of public interest litigation and the creation of legal aid programs in India, reform discourse re-emerged under the themes of informality, conciliation, and alternative dispute resolution.[161] This "new informalism"[162] was

---

[153] Werner Menski, *Comparative Law in a Global Context: The Legal Systems of Asia and Africa* (New York: Cambridge University Press, 2006) at 266.
[154] Marc Galanter & Jayanth K. Krishnan, "Debased Informalism: *Lok Adalats* and Legal Rights in Modern India" in Erik G. Jensen & Thomas C. Heller, eds., *Beyond Common Knowledge: Empirical Approaches to the Rule of Law* (Redwood City, CA: Stanford University Press, 2003) 96 at 100.
[155] Ibid. at 103.
[156] Menski, *supra* note 153 at 240.
[157] Galanter & Krishnan, "Debased Informalism," *supra* note 154 at 104.
[158] Ibid.
[159] Ibid.
[160] Ibid. at 105.
[161] Ibid. at 106.
[162] Ibid.

most notably exemplified through the creation of *Lok Adalats*, which its proponents viewed as representative of indigenous and traditional law in India.[163]

5.4.2. *The Response*: Lok Adalats

The *Lok Adalats* of India, literally meaning "the people's courts," are widely viewed as an alternative dispute resolution system in India based on indigenous, traditional forms of justice, rather than the formal British system. *Lok Adalats* hear a variety of cases, although many pertain to motor vehicle accident victims, and they do not typically deal with large sums of money or high-stakes civil litigation.[164] *Lok Adalats* are also divided into general and specific *Lok Adalats*, where general bodies handle everyday civil disputes, and specific bodies are dedicated to areas such as electricity matters, government pensions, and women's issues.[165] Furthermore, retired judges and senior advocates typically mediate the hearings.[166]

Since the first *Lok Adalat* was created in 1982, they ultimately earned statutory authority through the enactment of the *National Legal Services Authorities Act* in 1987, allowing states to organize *Lok Adalats* as they saw fit (although most of the provisions did not come into force until 1995).[167] The statute also gave *Lok Adalats* the jurisdiction to both determine and reach compromises and settlements over any matters before them, allowed pending cases in formal courts to be transferred to them, and rendered the awards of *Lok Adalats* enforceable in court.[168] Subsequent amendments further legitimized *Lok Adalats*, making them permanent fixtures in the Indian legal system. For example, a 1999 amendment to Section 89 of the Code of Civil Procedure granted courts the power to refer cases to alternative dispute resolution mechanisms, including *Lok Adalats*,[169] and a 2002 amendment to the Legal Services Authority Act permanently established specific forms of *Lok Adalats* (such as the public utilities *Lok Adalat* noted earlier). The growth of *Lok Adalats* ultimately created avenues for citizens outside the formal court system.[170]

---

[163] Ibid.

[164] Marc Galanter & Jayanth Krishnan, "'Bread for the Poor': Access to Justice and the Rights of the Needy in India" (2003–4) 55 Hastings L J 789 at 800.

[165] Ibid. at 810.

[166] Ibid. at 799.

[167] All provisions of the "Legal Services Authorities Act, 1987" (except Chapter III) came into force only from Nov 9 1995, as specified in footnote 1 of the Act, online: http://lawmin.nic.in/ld/P-ACT/1987/The%20Legal%20Service%20Authorities%20Act,%201987.pdf. For a brief history of the Act, see Anjali Singh, "Efficacy of the Legal Services Authorities Act, 1987" ch. VII at 203–5, online: Shodhganga: Indian Electronic Thesis & Dissertations, http://shodhganga.inflibnet.ac.in/bitstream/10603/12650/11/11_chapter%207.pdf

[168] Tameem Zainulbhai, "Justice for All: Improving the *Lok Adalat* System in India" (2011–12) 35 *Fordham Int'l L J* 248 at 259–60.

[169] The Code of Civil Procedure (Amendment) Act, 1999.

[170] Ibid. at 261.

The increasing integration of *Lok Adalats* into the formal court system and increasing formalization of these bodies has led to growing concerns similar in nature to those afflicting formal legal institutions. In many ways, the current state of *Lok Adalats* is criticized for being a mere extension of the formal courts.[171] To this end, some argue that the system has become a hybrid between central control and indigenization, which has ultimately cost them popular support.[172] Furthermore, *Lok Adalats* suffer from a lack of resources, inhibiting their effective administration.[173]

Some commentators believe that *Lok Adalats* possess crucial potential to transform the country's legal system by way of bringing social justice to millions, in an indigenized manner, that would render resolutions more salient to the local population.[174] Other commentators, however, are more skeptical. For example, Galanter and Krishnan argue that while *Lok Adalats* may have been created to provide a better (but not necessarily ideal) dispute resolution system than the formal court system, they simply represent an avoidance of problems plaguing the formal system, including delays, costs, and ineffective remedies and enforcement mechanisms.[175] As a result, they argue that insufficient focus has been placed on assessing the quality of justice meted out by *Lok Adalats*, which to them is a crucial consideration in determining whether the expenditures and commitment to this system, over other alternatives, is in fact justified.[176] Further, considering *Lok Adalats* as an alternative to a robust formal dispute resolution system is, according to the authors, a "romantic illusion."[177] Informalism in dispute resolution is useful when combined with reform of formal legal institutions, rather than what the authors consider a "resigned surrender to the inalterability of their defects."[178] Therefore, according to these authors, the informal *Lok Adalats* serve not as a bypass that delivers justice in a better way than formal courts, but rather a system delivering a "diluted version"[179] of what strong formal institutions should offer.

Other scholars share similar concerns. For example, Whitson argues that the popularity of the *Lok Adalats* system ultimately "pacifies and dulls"[180] the otherwise urgent need for reform of the formal legal institutions, muting pressure on government.[181] Thus, *Lok Adalats* according to Whitson merely perpetuate defects

[171] Ibid. at 263.
[172] Sarah Leah Whitson, "'Neither Fish, Nor Flesh, Nor Good Red Herring' *Lok Adalats*: An Experiment in Informal Dispute Resolution in India" (1991–2) 15 *Hastings Int'l & Comp L Rev* 391 at 391.
[173] Zainulbhai, *supra* note 168 at 263.
[174] Ibid. at 273.
[175] Galanter & Krishnan, "Bread for the Poor," *supra* note 164 at 809.
[176] Galanter & Krishnan, "Debased Informalism," *supra* note 154 at 115.
[177] Ibid. at 120.
[178] Ibid.
[179] Ibid.
[180] Whitson, *supra* note 172 at 444.
[181] Ibid.

of the formal system, leaving open the question as to whether resources are better expended correcting these deficiencies rather than seeking alternatives.[182]

5.4.3. *The Conundrum: Incorporating Informal Mechanisms into Formal Adjudication Systems*

Post-independence India has been characterized by its "remarkable plurality of laws,"[183] being composed of traditional personal laws (the majority governed through Hindu law), but also including Muslim, Christian, Parsi, and Jewish laws, as well as an optional secular family law.[184] This plurality of systems and the relationship between informal and formal legal systems raises important questions about the role of the state in managing their co-existence. Indeed, the degree of institutionalization of these sorts of informal legal systems varies by country, and has been widely discussed in scholarly literature on legal pluralism.[185]

A common concern over legitimizing informal legal systems is that in some contexts, customary or traditional legal systems undermine respect for basic human rights, gender, racial and religious equality, and due process. However, incorporation of these informal systems into the formal legal system can also yield poor outcomes, as the case of *Lok Adalats* suggests. For example, the system can become plagued by the same problems facing formal legal institutions such as backlogs, delays, and in some instances political manipulation and corruption. Furthermore, increasing divergence from indigenous processes can cause popular support to decline. More generally, reconciliation of the roles of formal and informal adjudicative systems appears to have important implications for contemporary broadly shared commitments to the rule of law.[186]

Thus, there seems to be a tension between state-imposed restrictions designed to ensure that some fundamental principles (such as the rule of law) are respected, and the adoption of requirements that allow for more flexibility, which can potentially make the provision of these services more accessible and attractive to users. Navigating this tension is a common theme in spontaneous institutional bypasses, as their transformative potential seems to be directly related to how far they diverge from the dominant system and its legal requirements. As discussed in the previous two sections, the cases of private security and education raise similar issues.

---

[182] Ibid.
[183] Ibid. at 249.
[184] Ibid. at 250.
[185] See Michael Barry Hooker, *Legal Pluralism: An Introduction to Colonial and Neo-Colonial Laws* (Oxford, UK: Clarendon Press, 1975); Menski, *supra* note 153, ch. 2 at 82–128; Sally Engle Merry, "Legal Pluralism" (1988) 22 *L & Soc Rev* 869; John Griffiths, "What Is Legal Pluralism?" (1986) 24 *J Legal Pluralism* 1; Daniels, Trebilcock, & Carson, *supra* note 149.
[186] See Daniels, Trebilcock, & Carson, *supra* note 149.

5.5. CONCLUSIONS

This chapter has traversed a broad domain of choices that at first sight may seem to share little in common beyond exemplifying the richness and complexity of governmental services and functions, and various solutions to shortcomings in the delivery of such services or performance of such functions in a contemporary development context. However, some common threads run through these various case studies.

First, the state, at least in principle, controls the extent to which alternative pathways are permitted to emerge or persist and on what terms. Unlike emails, for example, which have offered electronic alternatives to postal service monopolies, the state retains a substantial ability to control the terms of use or organizational choice between options in security services, education, and adjudication. This involves not only control over the possibility of alternatives being offered but also determining the terms of interaction between the pre-existing system and its alternatives, if these are authorized. The state could, for instance, allow alternatives to be offered but prevent them from functioning as substitutes for the dominant system. Therefore, despite not being spearheaded or promoted by the state, the potential for spontaneous institutional bypasses is intrinsically dependent on the government's openness to them. The examples discussed in this chapter have included both formal openness, as manifested by *de jure* legality of some of these initiatives, and practical openness, as manifested by *de facto* tolerance, that is, the lack of enforcement of legal provisions that would otherwise prevent these bypasses from operating.

Second, there is a tension between state regulations and restrictions and the usefulness or attractiveness of some of these alternatives. While the concept of an institutional bypass requires that a bypass not violate the legal requirements of the system in which it operates, regulation can sometimes be the primary source of the dysfunctions that the bypass is attempting to circumvent. Therefore, in order to be open to the transformative potential of spontaneous bypasses, flexible regulations are required. The main challenge lies in distinguishing between regulations and restrictions that are unwarranted and dysfunctional and those that are legitimate and justified. This is not an easy task. Some important considerations and concerns include the impact of spontaneous bypasses on the welfare of citizens who utilize the bypass and those that remain within the dominant system, including distributional impacts on vulnerable groups, especially the poor, women, and racial and religious minorities; the fact that some government functions exhibit natural monopoly or strong public goods characteristics that are antithetical to competitive provision; and the benefits of improving the delivery of social services at the expense of broader public interest goals, as encapsulated in health and safety and environmental regulations or due process and justice. Thus, states are left with the difficult decision of navigating the potential trade-offs and not insignificant risks of these regulatory choices.

Third, there are important questions about the potential for these spontaneous institutional bypasses to promote change in the dominant system. To the extent that they are substitutes, these alternative pathways may reduce the probability that users and constituencies will demand sustained attention to deficiencies and reform of the dominant systems. This problem may be especially acute in developing countries where influential constituencies may be the ones benefiting from the alternative pathway. Spontaneous institutional bypasses may also create no obvious incentives for the dominant, pre-existing system to "shape up" when there are no clear consequences attached to its failure to do so.

In sum, it is not clear if and when states should curtail or promote these spontaneous institutional bypasses.[187] Indeed, our three examples of spontaneous bypasses yield a mixed balance sheet. Private security services in Latin America that function as a substitute for public security services for firms, organizations, and wealthier families could be, on balance, welfare reducing, in that they might induce the migration of crime to poorer communities and attenuate public support for more strenuous efforts to reform the often woefully ineffectual public security services. School choice, at least in the case of India, yields a more complicated picture, given the growth of low-fee schools that cater to families of modest means but that are still not accessible to the poorest families (although proposed government-financed quotas for children from the poorest families may ameliorate this concern). The lack of any clear consequences for public schools when students move to private schools has tended to reinforce the status quo. Finally, formal and informal (traditional) forms of dispute resolution often co-exist in an uneasy and ambiguous tension. Again, there is little evidence of formal courts in many developing countries responding positively to these competitive threats to their jurisdiction by improving their performance, given the lack of sanctions for failure and/or rewards for success.

---

[187] See George Priest, "The Ambiguous Moral Foundations of the Underground Economy" (1994) 103 *Yale L. J.* 2259.

6

Conclusion

Institutional Bypasses and Their Potential Impact on Future Development Efforts

The institutional dimension of development moved to centre stage in the development agenda during the early 1990s with the emergence of the so-called "New Institutional Economics." Much learning has accumulated since that time as to the role that different classes of institutions play in promoting development and the feasibility of institutional change. Thus, while there is a consensus that institutions matter for development, scholars and policy makers are still struggling to find ways of actualizing this insight in order to successfully reform dysfunctional institutions.[1]

Over roughly the same period, universalistic prescriptions of either the ends or the means of development have attracted increasing skepticism, yielding a belated sense of modesty, even humility, on the part of development scholars from different disciplines and external development agencies. It is now widely recognized that what is both desirable and feasible is largely a function of the particularities of a given country's history, geography, culture, politics, natural endowments, ethnic and religious makeup, etc. (and the path dependencies that these particularities have created). As a result, emerging approaches take better account of the complexity and dynamism of the relationships between law, institutions, and development. They acknowledge that legal, political, and bureaucratic systems are composed of many interdependent parts that interact in complex ways in an endless process of adaptation.[2] The concept of an institutional bypass is an exemplar of this new trend.

While moving the development agenda and literature in a fruitful direction, these conclusions have also brought challenges. Approaches that acknowledge these

---

[1] Michael J. Trebilcock & Mariana Mota Prado, *Advanced Introduction to Law and Development* (Cheltenham, UK: Edward Elgar, 2014); see also Matt Andrews, Lant Pritchett, & Michael Woolcock, *Building State Capability: Evidence, Analysis, Action* (Oxford, UK: Oxford University Press, 2017); World Bank, *World Development Report 2017: Governance and the Law* (Washington, DC: World Bank Group, 2017).

[2] See David Trubek, "Law and Development: Forty Years after 'Scholars in Self-Estrangement'" (2016) 66:3 *UTLJ – Focus Feature: The Future of Law and Development* 301.

complexities struggle to identify empirical regularities in the relationship between specific legal institutions and development outcomes. Often the particularities of legal, political, and bureaucratic systems in developing countries are fleshed out through careful case studies, but these resist generalizations. Recent developments in the literature have responded to these challenges in two ways.[3] First, although case studies may not be amenable to generalizations, regularities in processes of institutional change may be generalizable. Second, firmly held beliefs about causal relationships between legal institutions and development outcomes have been abandoned in favour of experimentalism. Experimentalists start from the premise that we know very little about such relationships, and they value using experiments to untangle them. As a consequence, most development reforms should be based on hypotheses that need to be tested empirically. Rather than searching for a general theory of law and development, experimentalism promises a theory about a process for generating successful reforms and achieving desirable outcomes. The concept of institutional bypass fits well with these recent trends in the literature.

In this concluding chapter, we will indicate how the concept offers a significant contribution to the development literature, as it addresses some of the most pressing methodological concerns that confront the field today. We will also sketch the kind of research and academic investigations that could be developed based on the concept of an institutional bypass and how such analyses may help us identify and advance effective strategies in promoting appropriate conceptions of development in developing countries.

6.1. INSTITUTIONAL BYPASSES, GENERAL PRECEPTS, AND SPECIFIC STRATEGIES FOR INSTITUTIONAL REFORMS[4]

Some contemporary scholars focus on processes through which interdependent institutions adapt to changing circumstances. Focusing on processes of adaptation allows scholars to be sensitive to the complexity of interactions between legal systems and societies and points away from the idea that institutional designs are or should be static.

An example of this kind of analysis is the work of Milhaupt and Pistor.[5] Drawing on the literature on varieties of capitalism,[6] they argue that understanding how

---

[3] Kevin Davis & Mariana Mota Prado, "Law, Regulation, and Development" in Bruce Currie-Alder, Ravi Kanbur, David M. Malone, & Rohinton Medhora, eds., *International Development: Ideas, Experience, and Prospects* (Oxford, UK: Oxford University Press, 2014).

[4] This section is partially based on Davis & Prado, *supra* note 3, used by permission of Oxford University Press. https://global.oup.com/academic/rights/permissions/autperm/?cc=gb&lang=en

[5] Curtis J. Milhaupt & Katharina Pistor, *Law & Capitalism: What Corporate Crises Reveal about Legal Systems and Economic Development Around the World* (Chicago: The University of Chicago Press, 2008).

[6] Peter A. Hall & David Soskice, *Varieties of Capitalism: The Institutional Foundations of Comparative Advantage* (New York: Oxford University Press, 2001).

legal systems adapt to change is more important than a static analysis of the law. Using case studies of legal responses to corporate governance crises in six developed and middle-income countries, they trace different methods of legal adaptation. Similarly, Douglass North and his collaborators argue that institutional change is a path-dependent process. Institutions, like technological development, can be locked into a suboptimal equilibrium that is hard to change. Obstacles to change include institutional interdependences and culture.[7]

These approaches are attractive because, in contrast to case studies, regularities in processes of institutional change may be generalizable. However, these approaches threaten to mute dialogue between academics and policy makers by suggesting that such processes are too complex to permit intentional manipulation. For instance, the increasing recognition that path dependence casts a large shadow on both the present and future development trajectory of many developing countries suggests that many proposals for institutional and policy changes may be neither desirable nor, in any event, feasible. Assuming that processes of institutional adaptation are not amenable to intentional manipulation, however, would undermine an aspiration that has characterized law and development scholarship since its inception, namely, of providing guidance for action.

The literature has responded to this dilemma by searching for general precepts to guide reforms. While the contextual, case-by-case analysis cautions against the widespread invocation of particular institutional arrangements, it is possible to conceive of generalizable principles that may guide the strategy to promote change. For instance, based on the findings of path dependence, some scholars have attached a premium to reform strategies that are incremental, trial-and-error, and reversible in nature.[8] While avoiding proposing a particular institutional design (e.g., tenure for civil servants) or principles for reforms (e.g., bureaucratic autonomy), this kind of analysis proposes general strategies (e.g., incremental reforms) that are transferable across multiple sectors; diverse institutions; and a variety of social, political, and economic contexts.

While general precepts provide guiding principles for action, they cannot provide reformers with specific recommendations on how to implement such guidance. Any attempt to design an institutional formula that could capture these precepts would face the risk of failing to adapt to the particular circumstances of each case. Yet guidance for action is one of the aspirations of the law and development literature. By offering a distinctive reform strategy, the idea of institutional bypass bridges this gap. An institutional bypass proposes an institutional arrangement that is general enough

---

[7] Douglass C. North, *Understanding the Process of Economic Change* (Princeton, NJ: Princeton University Press, 2005).

[8] See Michael J. Trebilcock, "Between Universalism and Relativism: Reflections on the Evolution of Law and Development Studies" (2016) 66:3 *UTLJ – Focus Feature: The Future of Law and Development* 330.

to be transportable across a diverse set of contexts, while encapsulating some of the general precepts currently embraced by the academic and policy literature.

While the institutional bypass proposes a structure to promote institutional reforms, it does not present such a structure as an end in itself. Rather, institutional bypasses are transitory arrangements, used as a means to achieve institutional change in scenarios where it would otherwise be difficult to implement reforms. There is, however, a great deal of uncertainty regarding the outcomes produced by institutional bypasses. In Chapter 1, we provided a list of potential outcomes generated by the interaction between institutional bypasses and dysfunctional (dominant) institutions. After a period of coexistence, an institutional bypass may become the sole provider of services if the dysfunctional institution fades away. Alternatively, the dysfunctional institution may shape up or boycott the bypass, which then may cease to exist. There is also a series of arrangements in between, where both may continue to co-exist, while either dividing their functions or merging into a single institution. As a temporary solution that can generate a multitude of different outcomes, the bypass is a dynamic strategy. Its focus is to promote change, rather than provide a permanent institutional arrangement that guarantees functionality or enhanced social welfare.

In addition to being transferable across sectors and contexts, the institutional bypass describes attempts to promote reforms by a variety of agents. Indeed, the concept of intentional institutional bypasses illustrates how conscious, centralized, and innovative interventions may be spearheaded either by the state (e.g., central or local governments) or by specific members of civil society (e.g., leaders of social movements and other private actors).[9] The former is illustrated by three Brazilian cases: a bureaucratic reform in São Paulo (*Poupatempo*), a police reform in Rio de Janeiro (Police Pacifying Units or *Unidades de Polícia Pacificadora*), and a health care reform that started in Rio de Janeiro and was later replicated in all Brazilian states (emergency care units or *Unidades de Pronto Atendimento*). In these three cases, alternative social or public service delivery mechanisms were successfully implemented, initially on a pilot or experimental basis, by the state. Notably, in all three cases, the original pilot programs were initiated at a sub-national (i.e., state) level by political leaders or entrepreneurs who saw an opportunity to address widespread public dissatisfaction with the existing quality of public services and tap into at least latent demand for alternative service modalities. In turn, civil society innovations are exemplified by another Brazilian case study: the creation of the Workers' Central Union (*Central Única dos Trabalhadores*) by a labour movement, as an attempt to bypass corporatist trade unions in Brazil in the late 1970s, during the military dictatorship.

These intentional bypasses are distinct from spontaneous bypasses, in which the agents of change are dispersed and often are not consciously trying to promote

---

[9] See Chapter 4.

structural changes or large-scale institutional reforms.[10] In such cases, the institutional bypass as a strategy provides a descriptive tool to analyze complex dynamics in which a collection of small, independent, and uncoordinated efforts end up promoting significant changes, despite not being initially designed or intended to do so. This book illustrates the idea of spontaneous institutional bypasses by analyzing three case studies: private security services in Latin America, low-cost private schools in India, and alternative dispute resolution mechanisms (*Lok Adalats*), also in India. These case studies illustrate how the individual decisions of isolated agents, collectively, can transform the set of options available to users and may end up amounting to what one could consider an institutional bypass.

One might wrongly assume that in contrast to intentional institutional bypasses, which may serve as a prescriptive tool, guiding actions of reformers and policy makers, spontaneous bypasses can only be conceived as a descriptive tool. To argue otherwise requires one to assume that an actor could potentially manipulate the complex dynamics of a series of independent agents acting in an isolated and uncoordinated fashion to produce large-scale institutional change. Any intervention in this otherwise spontaneous process would more closely resemble an intentional rather than a spontaneous institutional bypass. As such, spontaneous bypasses would be confined to the task of helping scholars and reformers analyze dynamics that unexpectedly assume bigger proportions than those envisioned by each of the individual agents that decided to opt for an alternative pathway to the dominant system.

Such a limited view of the possible functions of spontaneous bypasses, however, ignores the important role that the state plays in this dynamic and decentralized process. As the case studies for spontaneous bypasses show, there can be more or less room for innovation and creativity depending on the stringency of state regulation and enforcement efforts. While the *Lok Adalat* case study shows spontaneous bypasses that are not only authorized but also supported by the Indian government, many of the low-cost private schools in India do not meet governmental requirements and thus operate outside the official regulatory framework, treading the very fine line between permissible and forbidden initiatives. The contrast does not suggest one single course of action. On the one hand, *Lok Adalats* are criticized for leaving room for serious violations of basic substantive and procedural rights, operating therefore in tension with the rule of law system. On the other hand, *Lok Adalats* may be perceived as a welcome alternative to dysfunctional or inaccessible courts. Similarly, requirements imposed on private schools may be perceived as unjustifiable bureaucratic limits that simply create obstacles for adequate delivery of education services throughout the country. These trade-offs should be confronted by state actors and policy makers in cases of spontaneous bypasses, as they raise important normative questions that are relevant in determining the role of the state

---

[10] See Chapter 5.

in opening more or less space for such spontaneous innovations through regulation and enforcement.

6.2. INSTITUTIONAL BYPASSES AND THE EXPERIMENTATION PROCESS[11]

This book begins and ends with the idea that an institutional bypass is intrinsically linked with a strand of academic literature that advocates experimentation. Some may be tempted to argue that these two are clearly distinct and dissociated from each other. While experimentation relates to the process of reform, the institutional bypass relates to its structure. Indeed, as a general strategy the bypass offers a structural arrangement that may embody certain broad precepts, such as experimentation, but there is no guarantee that all bypasses will be experimental.

While there is no intrinsic connection between the structure of reforms and the experimentation process, some structures are more conducive to experimentation than others. In contrast to top-down reforms that simply replace existing institutions with pre-existing blueprints, an institutional bypass opens up room for experimentation in at least two ways. First, by keeping the pre-existing institution in place, a bypass allows reformers to assess whether the reforms will produce the expected results and whether these are superior to those achieved by the existing institution, before making it a permanent feature of the institutional landscape. Therefore, even if the reforms are based on blueprints, the bypass allows one to test the results and reverse course to the status quo more easily than would be possible if the reform had replaced the pre-existing institution.

Consider the case of a police reform in Rio de Janeiro known as *Grupo de Policiamento de Areas Especiais* – Special Area Policing Unit (GPAE), which was a community policing effort concentrated in low-income neighbourhoods (*favelas*), similar to the *Unidade de Polícia Pacificadora* (UPP) discussed in Chapter 4. Both started with pilot projects. Based on the same idea of community policing, this internally initiated reform was initially successful, but the project lacked political support and its police were not specially trained for the distinct challenges of day-to-day interaction with distrustful *favela* residents.[12] Within the first year, 70 percent of GPAE police were transferred to other battalions for inappropriate conduct (*desvio de conduta*). Also, colleagues often ostracized the officers working on the project. Under a different political administration and with little political support, the GPAE became a high-profile public disaster that was eventually abandoned. In other words, while the project itself may be conceived as an experiment, the process

---

[11] This section is based on Graham Denyer Willis & Mariana Mota Prado, "Process and Pattern in Institutional Reforms: The Police Pacifying Units in Brazil as an Institutional Bypass" (2014) 64 *World Dev* 232. https://doi.org/10.1016/j.worlddev.2014.06.006

[12] Graziella Da Silva & Ignacio Cano, "Between Damage Reduction and Community Policing: The Case of Pavão-Pavãozinho-Cantagalo in Rio de Janeiro's Favelas" in Tom R. Tyler, ed., *Legitimacy and Criminal Justice: International Perspectives* (New York: Russell Sage Foundation, 2007).

that informed its day-to-day operation was not based on experimentation. This is evidenced by the fact that there do not seem to have been serious attempts to modify key features of the project when problems began to surface.

The second way in which a bypass creates room for experimentation is by allowing for constant and recurring change, in a constant adaptation to circumstances that ideally generates a positive feedback loop. This is illustrated by the most recent community policing effort concentrated in low-income neighbourhoods in Rio de Janeiro, the UPPs. Although traditional police officers served as UPP commanders, most shared a willingness to incorporate new ideas and welcomed the opportunity to create something of their *own* while simultaneously embracing a shift to experimentation. This happened because in the early days many of these police officers found common ground for the UPP project in circles of the police service that had voluntarily undertaken community police training with the Federal Secretary of Public Security (SENASP). Initially, important roles in the UPP project were filled by police officers who shared similar experiences and outlooks gained from this training.

The UPP units' lower ranks, by contrast with the GPAE, were staffed with officers who had undergone a different form of training and were sympathetic to changes. These officers were invited to contribute and actively participate in the reform process, as opposed to being dictated a model of reform defined technocratically and imposed from the top down. Moreover, the UPP officers received higher salaries than the traditional police officers, used different uniforms, and adopted more preventive strategies to reduce crimes. This and other innovations were only possible because the process of reform was conceived as experimental from the beginning. The reformers' success in further expanding the UPPs can at least partially be ascribed to the structure of reform adopted, which did not rely on existing institutions. But the contrast with previous attempts to implement community policing in Rio de Janeiro illustrates that this structure gained a great deal of strength due to the experimental process adopted.

The case of the UPPs underscores that while the structure of reforms is important, the process is also key. Thus, reformers should focus not entirely on *what* is implemented but *how* it is implemented. As a result of a number of lessons learned about where to garner resources, how not to implement the policy, what the demands of users are, how to respond to crises, and how to expand on successes, reformers were able to adapt and modify the UPPs, addressing unintended consequences and shortcomings that only became visible during the implementation phase.

The institutional bypasses that allow for an experimentation process to take place while the reform is unfolding may require us to rethink how certain institutional reforms should be evaluated. Current modes of assessment of most institutional reforms rely on external examiners focusing on concrete policy outcomes. In the case of police reform, for instance, these outcomes would include crime rates, police abuse, and community participation and approval. The success of the UPPs may be better measured by assessing how the project may have changed, however slowly, the way that citizens in marginalized areas perceive, establish trust in, and connect with the police force. These may have been positively reinforced with a reduction in crime rates and effective prevention, but the change in perception may occur independently of such indicators. Moreover, the project should be measured by the effects it may have had on the traditional police force over time. Regardless of the fact that UPPs have recently collapsed due to a variety of factors, including a fiscal crisis in the state of Rio de Janeiro, there is much to be learned from this project.[13] However, evaluating these broader institutional implications is admittedly a challenging new analytic terrain, as we discuss in the next section.

6.3. IMPLICATIONS FOR FUTURE RESEARCH

Our focus in this book has been on the provision of a wide range of social services in developing countries, and particularly on those services typically provided primarily by government. As a result of this focus, our analysis directly engages with Hirschman's classic book, *Exit, Voice, and Loyalty: Responses to Decline in Firms, Organizations and States*, which has exerted an enduring influence on thinking in many areas of public policy in both developed and developing countries. Hirschman brilliantly illuminated the symbiotic relationship between voice and exit as mechanisms for disciplining decline in firms, organizations, and states: excessive ease of exit may attenuate the voice of those citizens that remain captives of the dysfunctional institution, while voice without even the threat of exit may, in many contexts, simply fall on deaf ears. Hirschman's book was originally published in 1970, a development context that is quite different from our own, as we noted earlier in this conclusion.[14] While the conceptual framework provided by Hirschman's work is still useful today, it is amenable to refinements, which are exemplified in the concept of an institutional bypass.

While Hirschman framed exit as opting for the private delivery of services, in our three state-led bypasses, the *Poupatempo*, the Police Pacifying Units (UPPs), and the Emergency Care Units (UPAs), the exit option is offered by the state itself. Most importantly, these projects were not developed in a vacuum but rather were created in a way that gave users an opportunity directly or indirectly to voice their concerns, and such feedback was directly incorporated in the ongoing institutional design, adaptation and evolution of these initiatives. These examples show how exit can be used as an opportunity to create voice. Alternatively, these could be conceived as examples of *exit as voice*: once demonstrated to be successful, these initiatives quickly generated the political constituency required for a rapid expansion of the

[13] Stephanie Nolen, "How Brazil's Big Policing Experiment Failed to Make Rio Safer for the Olympics" (Aug 2, 2016 updated on Nov 12, 2017) *The Globe and Mail*, online: www.theglobeandmail.com/news/world/how-brazils-big-policing-experiment-failed-to-make-rio-safer-for-theolympics/article31222945
[14] See also Chapter 1.

alternative service modality. In either case, these examples seem to offer possible combinations of exit and voice that were not fully explored by Hirschman and that seem to deserve more serious attention.

In part because of the quite recent genesis of these initiatives, we acknowledge that our case studies shed very little light on the long-run institutional equilibrium that is likely to emerge from competition between the institutional bypass and the pre-existing institutions providing the same or similar services. Whether poorly performing pre-existing institutions would regenerate or degenerate or simply perpetuate some form of the status quo (stasis) in the face of new institutional competition is a topic that we have not explored in detail in this book. Some of our case studies have failed to produce change or have collapsed before generating much evidence of any significant response by pre-existing institutions to competition from the bypass. In some cases, this is not surprising, as in the early stages of the implementation of the bypass strategy, no consequences were attached to loss of patronage by pre-existing institutions, for example, reduction in budgets, personnel, wages and compensation, etc. Yet the topic is a rich field for potential future research, as a map of these processes of adaption (or lack of it) may provide insights into when and how an institutional bypass may promote broader, longer-lasting change. Further research is also warranted on variants of an institutional bypass strategy that also rely on choice, competition, and experimentation. One example includes the strategies that have been critical to launching China's remarkable growth, including creation of Special Economic Zones, exposing state-owned monopolies (SOEs) to competition, and decentralizing economic functions to local governments that then compete with each other in promoting new enterprises.[15]

The idea of institutional bypass also suggests a more optimistic, although speculative, view of the likely impact of institutional competition, whether public or private. While Hirschman's analysis focused on the impact of this competition on the performance of pre-existing institutions, we have instead suggested that such competition has a great deal of potential in promoting change, especially in situations where it would be otherwise difficult to alter the status quo. Our focus places less weight on the importance of attaching consequences to the loss of patronage by pre-existing institutions and more weight on the long-run impact on public perceptions and political dynamics associated with the demonstration effects of superior alternatives to the status quo.

Here, we are much influenced by a later book by Albert Hirschman, *The Rhetoric of Reaction: Perversity, Futility, Jeopardy*,[16] published in 1991, more than twenty years after *Exit, Voice, and Loyalty*. In this later book, Hirschman canvasses, from a

---

[15] Yingyi Qian, "How Reform Worked in China" in Dani Rodrik, ed., *In Search of Prosperity: Analytic Narratives on Economic Growth* (Princeton, NJ: Princeton University Press, 2003); Justin Lin, *Demystifying the Chinese Economy* (Cambridge, UK: Cambridge University Press, 2011).

[16] Albert O. Hirschman, *Rhetoric of Reaction: Perversity, Futility, Jeopardy* (Cambridge, MA: Harvard University Press, 1991).

historical perspective, rhetorical arguments commonly adduced by defenders of the status quo and opponents of institutional or policy change:

a. Perversity, where the proposed reform will actually make things worse relative to its ostensible objective;
b. Futility, where the proposed reform will have no significant impact on the ostensible objective of the reform; and
c. Jeopardy, where the proposed reform may actually jeopardize other, often highly valued pre-existing values or institutions that are not a direct focus of the reforms.

Hirschman describes in his book a wide range of historical contexts in which these arguments have been invoked, for example, with respect to recognition of civil rights, democracy, and the welfare state, where subsequent experiences revealed these concerns as groundless or at least grossly over-blown.[17]

In the context of our case studies, even if there are no direct or immediate consequences for pre-existing institutions in losing patronage to the new institutional alternatives, over time their public and political credibility in resisting reforms to their own structures and *modus operandi* could be attenuated by the living proof of demonstrated superior alternatives in their midst. We believe that this observation on the political economy of institutional reform, while speculative, provides a "bias for hope" (to borrow the title of another book by Hirschman)[18] in evaluating the long-run implications of many (but not all) institutional bypasses as a development strategy.

---

[17] Ibid. at 7.
[18] Albert O. Hirschman, *Bias for Hope: Essays on Development and Latin America* (New Haven, CT: Yale University Press, 1971).

Index